Praise for *The Hidden Face of God*

"This is a book that confronts momentous issues. It is especially appealing in being both frankly personal and boldly speculative. Richard Elliott Friedman, building out from his commanding knowledge of the biblical texts, proposes a striking evolution in the Western consciousness of God from the early iron age to the era of astrophysics."—Robert Alter

"Stimulating, provocative . . . conveyed with a dazzling display of learning, a graceful literary style and a leavening of wit. It will stimulate you immensely, whether you are believer, agnostic or religiously indifferent."—*The Plain Dealer*

"Friedman's biblical analysis is brilliant. An elegant and learned reflection on one of the central mysteries of the Bible and of modern life."—*Bible Review*

"Friedman writes with clarity and charm. He captures and holds one's interest, pours out fresh ideas in a torrent, and thoroughly intrigues. This is an unusual book—moving from the Bible to Nietzsche to Kabbalah and the Big Bang—and should command a wide readership of those interested in religion or in science, or in the relation between religion and science."—Frank Moore Cross

"Friedman has outdone himself as well as others in our field and beyond it. As always in the past, his analysis is acute, his observations pertinent and germane, in his inimitable style, combining élan and éclat so as to attract the undivided attention of neophyte as well as scholar. *The Hidden Face of God* is a stunning work, nothing less than the masterpiece for this year and years to come."—David Noel Freedman

"Insightful . . . a terrific book. The disappearance of God and the coming of age of the human race are threshold themes for the third millennium. What better way to raise them to the intellectual heights than to exhibit them at work in the Bible, in Nietzsche and Dostoevsky, and in astrophysics linked with the mysticism of the Kabbalah! These themes are so deftly laid out on page after page and traced through more than three millennia." —Robert Funk

"An enchanting and utterly fresh work of theological argument and religious reflection by a Bible scholar who writes with the pen of an angel. Friedman explores deep mysteries of Scripture, philosophy, theology, history, and science in quest of religious sensibility of this age of renewed encounter with the living God."—Jacob Neusner

"*The Hidden Face of God* is well written, well researched, provocative, and engrossing." —The Right Reverend John Shelby Spong, Bishop of Newark

"With a dazzling display of deep learning lightly presented, Friedman draws together the reflections of some of the most profound thinkers of the biblical, medieval, and modern periods with insights of current scientific debate about the history of the universe. Friedman addresses the fundamental moral and religious issues which confront the present malaise and future survival of our species. If we listen, there is hope." —H. G. M. Williamson, Regius Professor of Hebrew, University of Oxford

THE

HIDDEN FACE

OF GOD

THE
HIDDEN FACE
OF GOD

Originally published as
The Disappearance of God

Richard Elliott Friedman

HarperSanFrancisco
An Imprint of HarperCollins*Publishers*

The author is grateful for permission to include the following previously copyrighted material:

Excerpts from *Letters and Papers from Prison*, revised, enlarged edition, by Dietrich Bonhoeffer, translated by Reginald Fuller, et al. Copyright 1953, 1967, 1971 by SCM Press, Ltd. By permission of Simon & Schuster, Inc.

Excerpts from *Nietzsche: A Self-Portrait from His Letters*, edited and translated by Peter Fuss and Henry Shapiro. Copyright © 1971 by the President and Fellows of Harvard College. By permission of Harvard University Press.

Excerpts from *The Portable Nietzsche*, edited and translated by Walter Kaufman. Translation copyright 1954 by The Viking Press, renewed © 1982 by Viking Penguin, Inc. By permission of Viking Penguin, a division of Penguin Books, USA Inc.

Excerpts from *Selected Letters of Friedrich Nietzsche*, edited and translated by Christopher Middleton. Copyright © 1969 by The University of Chicago Press. By permission of The University of Chicago Press.

HarperCollins Web Site: http://www.harpercollins.com

HarperCollins®, ▦®, HarperSanFrancisco™, and A TREE CLAUSE BOOK® are trademarks of HarperCollins Publishers Inc.

FIRST HarperCollins PAPERBACK EDITION PUBLISHED IN 1997

Originally published by Little, Brown and Company as *The Disappearance of God*

Library of Congress Cataloging-in-Publication Data
Friedman, Richard Elliott.
  The hidden face of God / Richard Elliott Friedman.
  Includes bibliographical references and index.
  ISBN 0–316–29434–9 (cloth)
  ISBN 0–06–062258–X (pbk.)
  1. Hidden God—Biblical teaching. 2. Bible. O.T.—Theology. 3. Nietzsche, Friedrich Wilhelm, 1844–1900—Religion. 4. Big bang theory. 5. Creation. 6. Cabala. I. Title.
BS1192.6.F75   1996
231—dc20

98 97   RRD-H   4 5 6 7 8 9 10

This book is dedicated to my wife, Randy Linda, with love

CONTENTS

AUTHOR'S NOTE

Though I have written and lectured about aspects of these investigations before, this is not just a simplified version of material that I have already published in academic books and journals. It is new work, which addresses a wider audience than just my colleagues in the field of Bible and in the other fields that are covered in this book. I have therefore tried to present it in a form that is accessible to laypersons. I have aimed to keep notes and technical jargon to a minimum while trying to do research that is responsible from a scholarly point of view and of interest to non-specialists as well as to my colleagues.

Quotations from the Bible are my translations. For quotations from works other than the Bible, I have frequently indicated in notes where I have relied on others for translations.

There is much attention in contemporary religion to avoiding the use of terms that identify the deity as male or female. As will be very obvious in the last portion of this book, I too regard it as inappropriate to use these terms when speaking of God in the context of current conceptions, and I make a practice of avoiding them. But when one is dealing with the Bible and the world that produced it, this becomes more complicated because the authors of the Bible did picture the deity as male.[1] On this matter, therefore, I have followed the development in human conceptions and usage. In discussing the biblical period I use masculine terms because I am referring to the biblical world's concept of God and not my own or anyone else's. But when referring to God in present understanding and belief I avoid gender terms.

Citations of chapter and verse from the Hebrew Bible (also known as the Old Testament or *tanak*) refer to the Masoretic Text. In some English translations there are occasionally differences of a verse or two, or even several verses, in their numbering. For example, Ps 88:15 in the Hebrew text is Ps 88:14 in many translations. I have tried to point these variations out in several cases, but readers whose practice is to look up cited passages when reading books about the Bible are hereby advised to take this into account.

As is becoming common in academic and popular writing, instead of the initials A.D. I use C.E. (which stands for "Common Era" or "Christian Era"), and instead of B.C. I use B.C.E. ("Before the Common Era" or "Before the Christian Era").

I have tried to provide all the information necessary to enable people to read this book even if they have little or no background in Bible. Still, when people read about the Bible they almost invariably become curious about this or that point and have new thoughts and further questions to ask. The responses to my past books included letters from laypersons asking questions about an array of areas of biblical study, from details in the text to points of history and archaeology to matters of interpretation and history of scholarship. It was impossible to respond to the letters on so many points. Since that time a new tool has appeared in the six-volume, encyclopedic work *The Anchor Bible Dictionary*, edited by my distinguished colleague David Noel Freedman. The entries are written by hundreds of scholars (including myself), who come from a variety of religious backgrounds. Though some entries may not be as helpful as others, the overall quality is high, so that they provide a picture of the current state of scholarship, and they include bibliography for those who disagree or wish to pursue matters further. I therefore refer to the "ABD" a number of times in the notes in this book on specific points on which I believe the lay reader would find it helpful. And I hereby refer readers to this new aid generally if questions of detail arise in their reading of this book.

I have been critical of people in other disciplines who have tried to write about the Bible when they lack the expertise necessary to take on that rich and difficult book. Since this book covers a range of subjects and historical periods, I do not want to be guilty of the same thing. In dealing with these fields, first, I have consulted with colleagues who are specialists in those areas and asked them to read my work and criticize it. Second, I do not go into other people's fields with a bulldozer, trying to show the experts that I know more than they do. Rather, I speak from my perspective as someone from another field and hope that they will find it interesting and useful to them. I suppose that it comes down to finding the right mixture of trying to see and say something new while presenting it as an associate seeking response rather than as an interloper out to bypass the work of the specialists.

Three Mysteries

This book is about three mysteries. All three concern the presence or absence of God. Each had individually fascinated me for some time, and then I found them to be related to one another in intriguing ways. I can no longer even remember all of the circumstances that brought me to each of them — other than the love of the subjects and the attraction to mysteries. They involve elements of literature and history, religion and science, and philosophy. The first mystery is separated from the second and third by two thousand years. You may therefore wonder what they are all doing together, and you may find the movement from each one to the next a bit abrupt. I trust that the relationship of the three will be clear by the end of the book and that you will find, as I did, that they are linked more integrally than one would expect initially. And you may find that the last mystery contains the solution to the problems raised in the first two.

This book is about the Bible. It is also about Nietzsche, Dostoevsky, the mystical system known as Kabbalah, and the model of the universe that is known in physics as the Big Bang. The first half concentrates on the mystery of the disappearance of God in the Bible. The second half addresses mysteries that reflect the present form of this phenomenon.

You may choose to approach these mysteries as one would a detective story. The research of scholars does resemble detective work in a variety of ways — clues, deduction, false starts, breakthroughs, patience, unexpected twists — presumably because so much of life is, after all, a mystery. Still, this is not a work of fiction. And, though the pursuit of mysteries is fascinating and pleasurable in itself, this book is not intended merely to be an entertainment or an intellectual exercise. Mysteries are metaphors for broader phenomena, but it would be an evasion to say that the purpose of presenting these puzzles is only metaphorical. The problems are real and substantial in themselves, and a great deal is at stake. These mysteries concern ways in which we humans have portrayed and perceived the presence or absence of God, and they involve the moral consequences of our perceptions.

FIRST MYSTERY

THE DISAPPEARANCE
OF GOD IN THE BIBLE

Chapter I

THE HIDDEN FACE
OF GOD

"I SHALL HIDE MY FACE FROM THEM.
I SHALL SEE WHAT THEIR END WILL BE"

God disappears in the Bible. Both religious and nonreligious readers should find this impressive and intriguing, each for his or her own reasons. Speaking for myself, I find it astounding. The Bible begins, as nearly everybody knows, with a world in which God is actively and visibly involved, but it does not end that way. Gradually through the course of the Hebrew Bible (also known as the Old Testament, Holy Scriptures, or *tanak*), the deity appears less and less to humans, speaks less and less. Miracles, angels, and all other signs of divine presence become rarer and finally cease. In the last portions of the Hebrew Bible, God is not present in the well-known apparent ways of the earlier books. Among God's last words to Moses, the deity says, "I shall hide my face from them. I shall see what their end will be." (Deut 31:17, 18; 32:20). By the end of the story God does just that. The consequences and development of this phenomenon in the New Testament and in post-biblical Judaism are extraordinary as well.

Individual points within this development have been observed by other scholars and writers before me. To my knowledge, though, no one has ever observed the whole process in all of its stages before. On occasions when I have described this phenomenon to fellow scholars, to students, and to laypersons, there has frequently been surprise that this has not been pointed out before.

Here is the phenomenon:

In the first few chapters of the Bible God is utterly involved in the affairs of the first humans. The text pictures God and humans in a state of intimacy that is unmatched in subsequent biblical narrative. God personally breathes life into the first man, personally forms the first woman, personally plants the garden of Eden and fashions the animals (Gen 2:7–8, 19–23). God personally walks in the garden, and the humans hear the sound (3:8). And God speaks familiarly to the humans in conversation (3:9–19).

In the flood story that follows, there is not the same degree of intimacy as in the story of the garden of Eden, where both God and humans walk. Still, the deity, Yahweh, speaks to Noah and personally brings the flood: not just rain, as it is often pictured, but a cosmic crisis in which windows in the sky are opened and the waters above the firmament and the waters beneath gush into the secure, habitable world (Gen 7:12; 8:2). God also personally closes the ark (7:16). The creator's activity in the universe thus is depicted as being observable to the inhabitants of earth at both the cosmic and the personal level. Afterward God enters into a covenant with all creatures (9:8–17). The covenant is a contract composed according to the form and technical terminology of known legal documents of the ancient Near East.[1] That is, God is pictured in Genesis as binding Himself to all humans in the same concrete way that humans actually bound themselves legally to one another in their earthly affairs in the ancient world. In the subsequent story of the tower of "Babel" (*bābel* in the original, which is Hebrew for Babylon), likewise, the creator is manifestly present and involved in the affairs of the entire human population of the world. Yahweh personally "goes down" to see the city and tower (11:5). In these stories of the primeval history, the creator of the universe is pictured as being involved in life on this planet in ways that are visible and audible to the humans.

As the human population grows, the divine presence is never again made visible to all of humankind. The deity rather makes a second covenant with an individual man, Abraham, with the explicit aim that this relationship should ultimately benefit every family on the earth (12:3; 18:18; 28:14). God speaks to Abraham, as to Adam and Noah. Also a new expression to convey visible divine presence is added as God now, for the first time, is said to "appear" to Abraham. The word for "appear" is a Hebrew passive (Niphal) form of the root *r'h;* literally: the deity "was seen." In the account of the covenant, the divine appearance is via fire (15:17). It is unclear in the wording of the text whether this fire is an expression, a symbol, or a herald of God's presence — or even the actual form that the theophany itself takes, i.e., that God's appearance looks to Abraham like a flame of fire; (more on fire below). In other cases, the form of the divine appearance is left unspecified (12:7; 17:1). In a few dramatic cases, the appearances involve the introduction of angels into the Bible's story. As it turns out, the biblical depiction of angels is related to the matter of God's appearances to humans in a more direct way than one might suspect.

"HE FOUGHT WITH GOD . . . HE FOUGHT WITH AN ANGEL"

Most readers' concepts of angels are influenced by Renaissance art: wings, halos, tranquil faces. To know what is pictured in the biblical texts themselves, we have to scrutinize the specific stories in which angels appear. The first explicit mention of an angel in the Bible is in the story of Abraham's runaway concubine, Hagar (Genesis 16). Hagar is pregnant and alone, in flight from Abraham's wife, Sarah. "And the angel of Yahweh found her at the water well in the wilderness." The text does not say whether the angel is visible to Hagar or what it looks like. The angel only speaks, but what it says is strange: "I shall multiply your seed, that it will not be counted because of its multitude" (16:10). What is strange is that these sound more like the words of God than of some angel; they are a promise to make Hagar's descendants, the Ishmaelites, uncountable at some future time. Such huge controls of national destinies over many generations are not ascribed to angels elsewhere in the Bible but rather are solely within the power of the deity. To confuse things further, in the next verse the angel says, "for Yahweh has listened to your affliction." So the angel seems to be speaking God's words in the earlier verse and speaking its own words, referring to God in third person, in this latter verse. To confuse things still further, the text next reports that Hagar "called the name of Yahweh who was speaking to her. . . ." So the narrator who thus far identified the angel as doing the speaking now informs us that it was in fact Yahweh who was speaking to Hagar.

The curious thing is that several of the biblical stories involving angels contain confusions such as this, that is, confusions between when it is the deity and when it is the angel who is speaking or doing something. The two best known stories that display this are the story of the three visitors to Abraham and the story of Jacob's struggle with God. The story of Abraham and the visitors begins with the announcement, "And Yahweh appeared to him by the trees of Mamre" (18:1), thus informing us explicitly that this is to be a story of a divine appearance to Abraham. The form that the appearance takes is narrated beginning with the next verse:

> And he lifted his eyes and saw, and here were three people [Hebrew: *'ănāšîm*] * standing over him. And he saw and ran toward them from the tent entrance and prostrated himself on the ground and said, "My Lord, if I have found favor in thine [singular] eyes do not pass thy [singular] servant by."

Three people are in front of Abraham, but he speaks in the singular, that is, to one person, and he says "My Lord" (Hebrew: *'ădōnāy*), which elsewhere in the Bible refers only to God. One suggested reading of this story, therefore, outlandish as it may seem, has been that the three visitors should be understood to be God and two angels. This is supported by two more points in the story. First, the dialogue that follows between Abraham and the visitors fluctuates. Initially all three visitors are pictured as speaking (18:9). In the next verse, just an unnamed one of the three speaks (18:10). And then, a few verses later, Yahweh Himself speaks, and the words that He says identify Him with the unnamed one who spoke before (18:14). So God seems to be interchangeable with one of the three visitors. Second, the story reports further on that "the people turned from there and went to Sodom, and Abraham was still standing before Yahweh" (18:22). This would seem to contradict the idea that the three visitors were God and two angels, because the visitors have left for

---

* Transcriptions of Hebrew in this book follow the current conventions in the field of biblical studies.

Sodom while Abraham is still standing with God. But the first verse of the next chapter, which tells the famous story of Sodom and Gomorrah, begins: "And the *two* angels came to Sodom." Only two of the three visitors travel to Sodom — and Abraham is still standing with God! On the basis of this set of evidence from the text it has been argued that the third visitor is God. This understanding of the text is troubling, of course, to many Jews and Christians; and there are numerous other suggested explanations of this text. I used to be persuaded that this view was correct myself, but I now reject it. Before we try to reach any conclusions, though, we should look at the other story in which there is a confusion concerning divine and angelic identity, the story of Abraham's grandson Jacob and his night struggle with a mysterious figure.

In the middle of the story of Jacob and his relations with his twin brother, Esau, there occurs an incident that seems almost unrelated to the rest of the story. On the night before Jacob is to confront his brother Esau, whom he wronged twenty years earlier and has not seen since, Jacob separates from his wives and children and spends the night by himself. There follows this enigmatic episode:

> And Jacob was left alone. And a man struggled with him until the breaking of the day. And he saw that he could not prevail against him, and he struck him in the hollow of his thigh, and the hollow of Jacob's thigh was thrown out in his struggle with him. And he said, "Let me go, for the day is breaking."
>
> And he [Jacob] said, "I will not let you go unless you bless me."
>
> And he said to him, "What is your name?"
>
> And he said, "Jacob."
>
> And he said, "Your name will not be called 'Jacob' any more but rather 'Israel' [Hebrew: *yiśrā-'ēl*, understood here to mean 'fight with God'] for you have fought with God and with people, and you have prevailed."
>
> And Jacob asked and said, "Tell your name."
>
> And he said, "Why is this that you ask my name?" And he blessed him there. And Jacob called the name of the place "Peniel" [literal meaning: "face of God"] "because I have seen God face to face, and my life is preserved."

(Gen 32:25–31)

Now, on the face of it, this story appears to recount another appearance of God in human form. There is no mention of the word "angel." The being, called a "man," with whom Jacob has wrestled names Jacob "*yiśrā-'ēl*," namely, one who fights with *God*. This being says explicitly that this is because Jacob has "fought with *God*" as well as with humans. And Jacob names the place "*p^enî-'ēl*," i.e., face of *God*, and he, too, says that this is because he has seen *God* face to face. Also, the being refuses to give his name in response to Jacob's request, and this is consistent with the tradition developed elsewhere in the Bible that God did not reveal His name to any human this early, but only did so later, in the generation of Moses (Exod 3:13–15; 6:2–3). The text would thus seem to indicate that it is God whom Jacob has encountered. Still, there is some uncertainty about who it is that Jacob fights. Even in another book of the Bible this being was understood to be an angel. In the book of Hosea, the prophet Hosea refers back to the story of Jacob, and he mentions this specific scene, and the prophet describes it like this:

> And with his strength he fought with God
> And he fought with an angel and prevailed
> (Hos 12:4–5)

Here, in the second line, using the same specific term as in the Genesis story — he "prevailed" — the prophet perceives it to be an angel against whom Jacob prevailed. To confuse things further, the prophet still refers to Jacob's having fought with *God* in the first line. In a fairly well-known phenomenon of biblical Hebrew poetry, the two lines here are not separate but parallel. That is, they do not refer to two separate fights but rather create a poetic image of a single event through the two parallel lines of a bicolon. But how can this be? How can the poet say, literally in the same breath, that Jacob's fight was with God and with an angel?[2]

Obviously there is a confusion that is common to all of these biblical passages, a confusion concerning a seeming overlap between the deity and angels. But it is confusing only so long as we imagine angels as beings who are independent or separate from God. These texts indicate that angels are rather conceived of here as expressions of God's presence. The consistent biblical conception of God is that God cannot possibly be seen by a human ("A human will not see me and live." — Exod 33:20) and cannot possibly be contained in any known space ("The heavens . . . will not contain you." — 1 Kgs 8:27). God, in this conception, can nonetheless make Himself known to humans by a sort of emanation from the Godhead that is visible to human eyes. It is a hypostasis, a concrete expression of the divine presence, which is otherwise unexpressible to human beings. What the human sees when such a hypostasis is in front of him or her looks like "people," like a "man."[3] And the word for such a thing is "angel." Thus Jacob can encounter an angel and still say, "I have seen God face to face." And Abraham can face three angels and address "my Lord." And an angel can speak God's words in first person or can speak *about* God in third person. And Hosea can say in poetic parallel: "He fought with God . . . he fought with an angel." All this is so because in some ways an angel is an identifiable thing itself, and in some ways it is merely a representation of divine presence in human affairs.[4] An analogy might be listening to an orchestra on electronic equipment in one's home. One cannot house the entire orchestra in one's den, but one can hear this thing that derives from the real orchestra, emanating from it via a radio signal, a tape, or a disc; and after listening to it one can say that he or she "heard the orchestra." If it is on television one can even say that he or she "saw the orchestra" — which, in a sense, is true and, in another sense, is false. What one saw and heard was not the orchestra but waves of sound and light that derived from the orchestra. Thus biblical persons see and hear angels and say afterward that they have seen and heard their God.[5]

For the same reason, it is unclear what the nature of the fire that appears in the Abrahamic covenant story is. It may be another type of visible expression of the deity's otherwise invisible presence, or it may simply be a sign or symbol.

"YOU WILL KNOW THAT I, YAHWEH, AM IN THE MIDST OF THE EARTH"

These apparent markers of divine presence on earth continue in the book of Exodus, which recounts the development of Abraham's and Jacob's descendants, the Israelites, into a free people. The first revelation to Moses in Exodus, his famous encounter at a bush in the wilderness of

Horeb, combines an angel and a miraculous fire: "And an angel of Yahweh appeared to him in a flame of fire from inside a bush, and . . . the bush was burning with fire, and the bush was not consumed" (Exod 3:2). Yahweh then makes Himself known in the world through a well-known series of miraculous events which result in the liberation of the Israelites from slavery in Egypt. A stick turns into a snake in front of the Egyptian court. Ten plagues devastate the agriculture, livestock, property, and human lives of Egypt. The Red Sea divides to provide an escape route for the Israelites and then closes and drowns the pursuing Egyptian military force. The great burst of miracles that fills the first half of Exodus is depicted explicitly as "signs," evidences of Yahweh's involvement in the world; Yahweh declares that He causes a plague to happen in a particular way "in order that you will know that I, Yahweh, am in the midst of the earth" (Exod 8:18; cf. 7:17; 8:6; 9:14, 29). In the last of the ten plagues, the deity is said to pass personally through Egypt, striking the Egyptian firstborn mortally. Not Moses, not an "angel of death" as later tradition claimed, but God Himself goes through Egypt on that night (11:4; 12: 12, 13, 23, 29). (There is no such thing as an "angel of death" in the Hebrew Bible.) The miracles are witnessed by entire nations (at least Egypt and Israel) and are heard of by other peoples as well (15:14–15; 18:11).

This is a world of upheavals of nature, of immediate proofs of divine presence. It is not a world of belief in God but of *knowledge* of God. Indeed there is no word for "to believe" in biblical Hebrew. The word that is frequently translated as "to believe" means, in the original, something more like "to trust"; that is, it means that one can rely on this God to do what He has said He will do (Hebrew: *h'myn*; e.g., Exod 14:31). It does not mean "to believe" in the sense of belief that God exists. God's existence is understood in these texts to be a matter of empirical knowledge, demonstrated by divine appearances and miraculous demonstrations. This, by the way, is what makes the stories of human rebellion in the Hebrew Bible so remarkable. It is not that the humans doubt the deity's existence. The impressive thing is rather that, *knowing* that this God exists, they consciously rebel against His authority.

For the generation of the exodus, more than any other in the Bible, this is so: the divine presence is depicted as a known, manifest fact. This generation of the Israelites is presented as having continuous miraculous evidence of the divine presence in full view at all times for forty years. A column of cloud stands in front of them by day, and it turns to a column of fire by night. It moves in front of them, leading them on their journey to a promised land. Also they are fed daily by the miraculous precipitation of food, "manna," on the ground each morning (Exod 16:2–35) as well as provision of birds, which miraculously fly over the camp and drop on the ground to be eaten (Num 11:31–32); and, in several instances, miraculous provision of water in the wilderness (Exod 15:23–25; 17:1–7; Num 20:2–13).[6] More powerful experiences of the divine presence occur when something that is identified only as the "glory of Yahweh" appears. The narrative never identifies what the "glory" is, only that it is visible to human eyes and that it generally is not seen directly but is veiled within a cloud (Exod 16:7, 10; 24:16, 17; 40:34, 35; Lev 9:6, 23; Num 14:10; 16:19; 17:7). Whatever it is, the glory involves something that emanates from the deity and is associated with cases of immediate intervention in specific human situations. Overall, then, the generation of Israelites who journey through the wilderness for forty years is one that experiences direct divine closeness as a daily fact of life for that entire period.

This culminates in what is presumably the ultimate experience of God by a large mass of people in the entire Bible, the revelation at Mount Sinai. Yahweh personally "comes down," descending on the mountain in fire (Exod 19:11, 18, 20), and speaks out loud from the sky over the mountain to the thousands of Israelites below (19:19; 20:1, 22). They see the divine fire and hear the divine voice, which terrifies them. The words that they hear Yahweh pronounce are the ten commandments, which are the text of the third of the divine covenants with humans (Exod 20:1–17).

This is followed by an account of an exceptional experience of God by a smaller group, as seventy-four Israelites are privileged to have a shared vision of the deity and to partake of a sacred meal in the divine presence. It is described thus:

> And Moses and Aaron, Nadab and Abihu, and seventy of the elders of Israel went up, and they saw the God of Israel, and under

His feet it was like a brickwork of sapphire and like the essence
of the sky for clearness. . . . And they envisioned God, and they
ate and drank.

(Exod 24:9–11)

This in turn is followed by the account of the ultimate, exceptional
experience of God by an individual in the Bible, Moses' seeing the actual
form of God on Mount Sinai (Exodus 34). It is arguably the culminating
moment of human history since Adam and Eve in this narrative, and it is
as mysterious as anything in the Bible. Moses sees God from behind. The
sight that he is privileged to behold is not described, just as the vision of
the seventy-four and the voice that the thousands hear are not described.
These things are understood to belong solely to those who experienced
them, and they are not to be repeated in any subsequent generation.

"LET GOD NOT SPEAK WITH US, LEST WE DIE"

Thus, in the experiences of an individual, a group, and a community,
the apparent presence of God reaches a high point here in the middle of
the second book of the Bible. God speaks from the sky, descends into the
earth in fire, is seen in a vision by a group, and is seen in His actual form
by a man. But after this things change. After this the apparent presence
of God in the Bible starts to diminish. Miracles continue to occur, but no
other man or woman sees the form of God as Moses has. No other group
has a vision of the sapphire-like, sky-like throne-dais beneath God's
"feet" (!). No other generation of Israelites or any other people on earth
ever hear the voice of God aloud from the sky. The period of visible,
audible encounters with the divine gradually passes, and not subtly, but
rather expressly in the text. The people's hearing of the divine voice is
not to be repeated — and this is depicted as being the stated request of
the people who experienced it themselves. Terrified, they tell Moses:

"You, speak with us, and we will listen; but let God not speak with
us, lest we die."

(Exod 20:19)

In that moment prophecy as a defined institution is born. By prophecy here I mean mediated communication between the deity and human communities. After this scene in the Bible, Yahweh never again speaks directly to an entire community Himself. All communication from the deity is directed only to individuals, prophets, who then deliver the message to whomever they are told. Prophecy is mentioned in passing in the book of Genesis (20:7), but prophecy in this formal sense of divine messages mediated through individuals begins here in Exodus at Sinai.[7]

Moses' personal experience is never to be repeated either, and this, too, is declared categorically in the text. In the curious story of Moses' Cushite wife and "snow-white" Miriam (Numbers 12), the priest Aaron and his sister Miriam criticize or challenge Moses with the argument: "Has Yahweh spoken only just through Moses? Has he not also spoken through us?" Yahweh "comes down" in a column of cloud and reprimands Aaron and Miriam for this presumption, declaring that Moses' experience of the divine is indeed superior to that of any other prophet. He identifies the distinction like this:

> If there will be a prophet among you,
> I, Yahweh, shall make myself known to him in a vision;
> in a dream I shall speak through him.
> Not so my servant Moses,
> most faithful in all my house.
> Mouth to mouth I shall speak through him, and vision
> and not in enigmas,
> and he will see the form of Yahweh.
> And why did you not fear to speak against my servant Moses?
> (Num 12:6–8)

All subsequent prophecy in the Bible, in the light of this declaration, must be understood as being experiences through dreams and visions, explicitly inferior to that of Moses. All of the fifteen books of the Bible that bear the names of prophets (Isaiah through Malachi) either identify the form of those prophets' experiences as visions or else leave the form of the experience undescribed. They never ascribe to any of the prophets a revelation comparable to that of Moses (which I shall discuss more specifically in Chapter 3). Some people might say that a revelation that comes by way of a dream or a vision is no less valid than one that comes by empirical experience. Somehow though, I think, no matter how impressed any of us would be at having a dream or vision in which the deity spoke to him or her, we would be a good deal more impressed if the door of our room opened and God "Himself" stepped in.

The period in which the Israelites live in the wilderness, which takes up the remainder of the book of Exodus and all of the books of Leviticus, Numbers, and Deuteronomy, thus has a curious quality to it. It is a period of incubation, nurturing, and unusual closeness to the divine, and at the same time a period of developing divine hiddenness and mystery. There are still stories of miracles, and Yahweh is still involved in human affairs, but not in the direct ways of the immediately preceding accounts. The omnipresent column of cloud and fire conveys God's presence, but at the same time a cloud "masks" the divine: the deity's glory can only be seen through that surrounding haze. Moses, the man who has seen God, moves among the people, but he is depicted as wearing a veil over his face for the rest of his life (except in moments of revelation); for some reason which remains unclear in the difficult wording of the text, Moses' face has been transformed so that he is now too fearful for the people to approach him (Exod 34:29–35).[8] Yahweh (or Moses; 34:1, 27–28) has inscribed the text of the ten commandments on stone tablets, and these sacred objects are kept among the people in the wilderness, but these tangible markers of the covenant between Yahweh and the people are housed within a series of layers: first one enters a courtyard; from there one enters the Tabernacle; inside the Tabernacle there is first an outer room called "the Holy"; then there is an inner room called the "Holy of Holies" which is enclosed in a fabric pavilion; in the inner room is a box (the "ark"); and inside the box are the tablets. The Tabernacle itself, the place where God communicates through Moses, is a tent composed of another series of layers: a framework of wooden trellises, which is covered by an embroidered linen fabric, which is itself covered by a woolen fabric, which is then covered by a red leather outer covering. Only priests can enter the Tabernacle. Laypersons can go only as far as the courtyard. That is, there is a sequence of zones, which are less and less directly accessible.[9]

This quality of hiddenness becomes explicit when Yahweh finally tells Moses, "I shall hide my face from them. I shall see what their end will be." This is followed by the account of Moses' death (Deuteronomy 34). The death of the one man who has seen the deity may be understood as yet a further step of distancing between the deity and the human world. And adding yet another shade of hiddenness and separation, the text there notes that "no man has known his gravesite to this day" (34:6). The narrative of the first five books of the Bible (known as the Five Books of Moses, the Torah, or the Pentateuch) thus has flowed from an era of creation, cosmic crisis, and extraordinary divine intervention in human affairs to a time in which the deity has begun to be hidden — and to a promise of increasing hiddenness in the future.

"IF YAHWEH IS WITH US, THEN WHERE ARE ALL HIS MIRACLES?"

As the people settle in their promised land, which is narrated in the next two books of the Bible (Joshua and Judges), the remaining signs of divine presence and communication begin to diminish gradually. In the book of Joshua, the column of cloud and fire is no longer present, the glory of Yahweh no longer appears, and the text notes that the manna ceases on the day after the people first eat naturally grown food in the land (Josh 5:12). The disappearance of the signs of divine presence is gradual; some still remain at this stage of the story. In the book of Joshua there is an appearance by a mysterious being who is identified as the "captain of Yahweh's army" and who is perhaps comparable to an angel (5:14). There are also still major miracles. The Jordan River splits for Joshua and the people to enter the land, and the text notes, "*That day* Yahweh magnified Joshua in the people's eyes" (4:14); that is, the miracle is taken to be the confirmation that Yahweh is "with" Joshua (3:7). And two of the most famous miracles of the Bible occur in this era: the walls of Jericho miraculously fall so that the Israelites can capture the city (Joshua 6), and the sun stands still in the heavens to provide enough daylight for the Israelites to defeat a confederation of kings who oppose them (Joshua 10). In the next chapter, though, we shall see that the miracles of Joshua include an element which participates in the transition that is developing in the text.

The following book, Judges, includes an occasional miracle or angel as well. A line in Judges is arguably the clearest expression of the idea that miracles are conceived of as signs of the deity's presence. The judge Gideon says (to someone who turns out to be an angel), "If Yahweh is with us, then . . . where are all His miracles that our fathers told us about . . . ?" (Judg 6:13). This period is pictured as an age of fewer miraculous signs, and here a major figure in the story takes this absence of miracles as reason to be uncertain of the presence and involvement of God. Gideon in fact gets his miracle (*fire* comes from a rock; 6:21), but miracles are fewer and farther between after this. The one large group in Judges after this is in the stories of Samson, but in the next chapter we shall see how these miracles, too, participate in the transition toward divine hiddenness. There are then some miracles at the beginning of the book of 1 Samuel — a statue of the Philistine god Dagon falls, seemingly bowing, before Israel's ark, and the Philistines suffer plagues (specifically, hemorrhoids) until they return the ark, which they had captured from Israel (1 Samuel 5–6) — but for most of 1 Samuel there are few miracles, and in 2 Samuel there are almost none at all.

The diminishing apparent presence of God continues and even accelerates from this point. The last person to whom God is said to have been "revealed" is Samuel (1 Sam 3:21). The last person to whom God is said to have "appeared" is Solomon; this occurs early in the next biblical book, the book of 1 Kings (3:5; 9:2; 11:9). From the beginning of the Bible to this point in the narrative, the deity has been said to have appeared to Abraham, Isaac, Jacob (Exod 6:3), Moses, Joshua (Deut 31:15), Aaron (Lev 16:2), Israel (Lev 9:4; Num 14:14), Samuel (1 Sam 3:21), David (2 Chr 3:1), and Solomon. But now, with about five centuries of the story still to be told in the Hebrew Bible, the deity has appeared to a human being for the last time. Yahweh speaks to David and to Solomon, who are Israel's second and third kings respectively; but the words "And Yahweh said to X," are never applied to any of the thirty-eight kings who come after them. (It is the less direct expression "And the word of Yahweh was to X" that serves all across the chronology of the biblical books.) The sole possible exception is a statement, concerning the Judean king Manasseh, that "Yahweh spoke to Manasseh and all his people" (2 Chr 33:10). But this verse is hardly meant literally. There is no suggestion that the deity somehow speaks out of the sky over the entire country for everyone to hear. And, in any case, most strikingly, the text notes at the end of that verse: "And they did not pay attention"!

The last appearance of the cloud and glory, meanwhile, also occurs at the time of Solomon, on the day of the dedication of the Temple (1 Kgs 8:10–11; 2 Chr 5:14; 7:1–3). The coalescence of the two — the inauguration of the Temple and the last appearance of the cloud and glory — is notable itself. The glory, the supernatural sign of divine presence which has hitherto been associated with divine communications to humans, is now replaced by a natural, man-made structure which is associated with human communications to the divine. Solomon explains in his Temple dedication prayer that a building, of course, cannot contain God; but he asks Yahweh to "cause your name to dwell" in the Temple — so that Israelites may then direct prayers toward the Temple, invoking the name Yahweh, and the deity will hear (1 Kings 8). The Temple thus houses both the material signs of God's presence (the ark, tablets, Tabernacle, and other sacred objects) and the more abstract entity, the divine name, by virtue of which the Temple becomes the established channel to the deity.[10]

Other episodes involving miracles further mark the Temple as the divinely sanctioned channel. When the Israelite king Jeroboam I builds an alternative center of worship at Beth-El, a prophet denounces it, King Jeroboam's arm withers, and the Beth-El altar cracks (1 Kings 13). The Temple's status thus is initially confirmed by divine word, glory, and miracle. And after that, as these divine signs recede, the Temple itself gradually will become the only visible channel to God.

The last public miracle in the Hebrew Bible comes just a few chapters after the Beth-El events. By "public" miracle I mean one that is witnessed by all of the people of Israel — or at least a substantial portion of the people — and which participates in some significant way in the history that is being narrated. I mean this as opposed to smaller, "personal" miracles, in which an individual is able to use supernatural powers for his or her own purpose or in service of a relatively small group. The plagues in Egypt would be examples of public miracles, witnessed by the Israelite and Egyptian populations and manifestly participating in the destiny of Israel. Many of the feats of strength in the Samson story would be examples of personal miracles, used by the hero as a result of his own experiences. Now, the last public miracle is in the story of the prophet

Elijah at Mount Carmel (1 Kings 18). It takes place around a hundred years after Solomon's dedication of the Temple, in the reign of King Ahab and his Phoenician queen, Jezebel.

Ahab and Jezebel have sanctioned the worship of the god Baal in Israel, and Elijah challenges the prophets of Baal to a test of divine presence. They meet at Mount Carmel (the site of present-day Haifa) in front of the King and "all of Israel" (18:19, 20, 21, 30, 39). They set two sacrifices on two altars, one for Yahweh and one for Baal. The catch is that neither Elijah nor the prophets of Baal may use fire to ignite the sacrifice. Rather, the deity who really *is* God must provide his own fire. Since Baal is the god of wind and storm in the Phoenician and Canaanite pantheon, a bolt of lightning should be no problem for him; but no fire from Baal is forthcoming. Elijah openly ridicules the prophets of Baal ("Call out louder! For he's a god! And he could be having a chat or a pursuit, or he's indisposed. Maybe he's sleeping, and he'll wake up!" — 18:27). And then, "the fire of Yahweh fell and consumed the offering and the wood and the stones and the soil. And all the people saw and fell on their faces. And they said, 'Yahweh, he is God! Yahweh, he is God!'" (18:38–39). The miracle thus involves fire once again, and it is presented as a resounding visible demonstration of the presence of God.[11] And that is the end of public miracles in the Hebrew Bible's narrative.

"WHAT ARE YOU DOING HERE?"

One of the most remarkable juxtapositions in the Bible is in the arrangement of the story of Elijah at Mount Carmel (1 Kings 18), for it is immediately followed by the story of Elijah at Mount Horeb (1 Kings 19). Despite Elijah's great victory at Carmel, he is forced to flee Israel because of Jezebel's fury at him. He runs (for forty days and nights!) to Mount Horeb. Horeb is another name for Sinai. Mount Sinai has not figured in the Bible's story at all since Moses and the Israelites were there several centuries earlier. Now, suddenly, we have an episode of a prophet on the mountain, alone, in communication with his God, a scene which cannot but recall to our minds the picture of Moses, the prophet, alone, who had the greatest revelation of all time on that site. But the similarity ends there. God's first words to Elijah are: "What are you doing here?" (Hebrew: *mah l'kā pô;* meaning literally "What do you have here?" in the sense of "What business do you have here?"). Elijah responds by expressing his frustration and asks to die. The deity "passes," accompanied by three extraordinary phenomena: a crag-shattering wind, then an earthquake, and then a fire. Each of these phenomena has been associated with divine activity in other biblical episodes. God is associated with wind in the creation account (Gen 1:2; 2:7); with an earthquake in the story of the rebellion of Dathan and Abiram against Moses (Num 16:28–34); and with fire numerous times, as we have seen. But in the story of Elijah at Horeb the report of each of these phenomena is followed in the text by the notation: "Yahweh was not in it." Then all are followed by what has usually been translated as "a still small voice" (1 Kgs 19:12). That is a somewhat misleading translation. Grammatically, it should more properly be rendered as something like: "a sound of thin hush." [12] That is, it is the sound of silence. Moses had seen the form of God (Exod 33:23; Num 12:8) and had heard God reveal a formula describing the divine character (Exod 34:6), but Elijah sees phenomena in which God is not present, and he hears nothing. The scene of the last great public miraculous confirmation of the divine presence at Mount Carmel has been followed by the scene of the divine refusal to appear at Mount Horeb/Sinai.

I am not the first scholar to identify this scene at Mount Horeb/Sinai as a pivotal moment in the manifestation of the presence of God in the Bible. My teacher, Frank Moore Cross, wrote:

> The abrupt refusal of Yahweh to appear as in the traditional theophany at Sinai marked the beginning of a new era in his mode of self-disclosure. [13]

And Samuel Terrien wrote about this scene:

> The threefold repetition, "And Yahweh was not in the wind," "And Yahweh was not in the earthquake," "And Yahweh was not in the fire," constitutes a repudiation not only of the mode of divine intervention on Mt. Carmel but also of the possibility that the Mosaic theophany on Mt. Horeb could occur again in later history. The era of theophany is now closed. . . . [14]

What I want to emphasize here is that this scene is even more significant when we see it in the context that we are now encountering. It is just one dramatic stage in a series of stages, spanning the entire Hebrew Bible, through which God step-by-step removes the visible markers of His presence.

Following the sound of thin hush, the deity does speak again to Elijah. He says, "What are you doing here?" that is, the exact same thing He said before. Apparently the wind, earthquake, fire, and hush were supposed to make a point, but apparently the point is lost on Elijah, who in turn repeats his own words from before: he expresses his frustration and asks to die. God, seemingly dropping the matter of divine appearances, turns to other matters. Yahweh tells Elijah to appoint two new kings and a prophetic successor for himself, the prophet Elisha (19:15–16).

And that is the last time in the Hebrew Bible's narrative that the text says "And Yahweh said" anything to anyone.

The Elijah story also includes the last appearance of an angel in the Hebrew Bible (2 Kgs 1:3,15). In the few accounts of angels after this, the angels are not said to appear, and the stories do not suggest that they are seen by anyone (2 Kgs 1:3, 15; 19:35).

What we then see develop in the Elijah episodes and especially in the episodes of his successor Elisha is a transition in the depiction of miracles, with personal miracles replacing the great public miracles of the earlier stories. These personal miracles of Elijah and Elisha are witnessed by fewer people, and they serve fewer people's interest. For example, in a story in which an Israelite king sends a troop of fifty soldiers to fetch Elijah, Elijah says to the officer of the troop, "If I am a man of God, let fire come down from the sky and consume you and your fifty." And it does. The same thing happens to a second troop of fifty. (2 Kgs 1:9–15). No witnesses are mentioned, and there is no suggestion that these fires from the sky serve a purpose in the destiny of the world or of Israel comparable to the role of the fire in which God descended on Sinai or the fire that consumed the offering on Mount Carmel. The account of Elijah's ascent in a whirlwind is a similar case. It involves a wondrous scene: Elijah and Elisha walk together, a chariot and horses made of fire come between them, and Elijah goes up to the heavens in a whirlwind. Some take this to mean that Elijah never dies; alternatively this may in fact be the story of his death. Either way, there is only one witness in the story, and the event does not, on the face of it, serve a direct role in the destiny of humankind or of the people of Israel. (Later religious traditions, taking this to mean that Elijah never died, identified Elijah as the person who would one day return to announce the coming of a messiah; but this idea is not developed in the text of the Hebrew Bible itself.)

Eventually, personal miracles cease as well. In a story of the prophet Isaiah, which takes place about a century later, the Judean king Hezekiah asks for a sign to confirm that a prophecy of Isaiah's will come true (2 Kgs 20:8–11). Isaiah gives the king the choice of whether a shadow on the steps is to move forward or backward.[15] Hezekiah asks for the unusual: let it back up. It does. And that is the last miracle in the narrative. All miracles in the books of Kings cease after the prophet Isaiah.

The account of the days of Isaiah and Hezekiah also includes the last report in the Hebrew Bible of an angel acting on earth — unseen, as I said above. The angel strikes the camp of the Assyrian army secretly by night as they beseige Jerusalem (2 Kgs 19:35; Isa 37:36; 2 Chr 32:21). The only angels to be mentioned after this will occur in dreams or visions.

The Hezekiah section also includes an episode in which another old sign of divine tending exits from the story. Back in the book of Numbers there is a brief story in which poisonous snakes bite and kill great numbers of the Israelites on their journey in the wilderness. At Yahweh's instruction, Moses makes a bronze snake and sets it on a pole. Then, whenever someone is bitten by a snake, if the victim looks at the bronze snake, he or she is miraculously cured (Num 21:4–9). The account of King Hezekiah reports that in that king's day, the people are burning incense before this bronze snake, which is called Nehushtan. Hezekiah smashes Nehushtan, and it is never mentioned again (2 Kgs 18:4).

With over two hundred years still left to the story, there are no more fires from the sky, no more miracles, public or personal, no more angels, seen or unseen, no more cloud and glory, no more "and Yahweh said to X." The only remaining visible channel to God is the Temple, housing the ark in Jerusalem, and it is destroyed by the Babylonians, in fire, at the end of the books of Kings and Chronicles (2 Kgs 25:9; 2 Chr 36:19). It is interesting and ironic that the last reference to fire should be the burning of the last visible marker of the presence of the deity on earth. The text, further, expresses the destruction of the kingdoms of Israel and Judah with the words: "Yahweh turned them out from before His face" (2 Kgs 17:23; 23:27). The prediction in the deity's last words to Moses has come true.

"WHO KNOWS?"

The book of Daniel comes as something of a surprise in this development, because it includes a few miracles, which we would not expect at this late date in the story. The book involves some events in the years following the destruction of Jerusalem, when the nation is exiled in the Babylonian and then the Persian empires. The miracles of the book of Daniel are of the smaller, personal type; they certainly are not witnessed by the people of Judah. It is in fact not clear if they are witnessed by large numbers of people at all. They do not affect the destiny of Israel or of the world. Daniel survives a night in a den of lions (Daniel 6), and his three friends survive a stay in a burning furnace (along with a mysterious fourth figure; Daniel 3). (Daniel himself refers to an angel's having shut the lions' mouths, but it is unclear whether this is meant literally or figuratively; and the narrator's voice does not comment on the nature of Daniel's survival in the den.) The famous story of the appearance of fingers writing a message of doom for the Babylonians on a wall is not clear as to whether anyone other than the Babylonian king sees the mysterious hand, and that king dies later that night (Dan 5:5). The strange book of Daniel, written in Aramaic rather than Hebrew, containing chapters of curious visions, is therefore something of an enigma. Perhaps it serves to convey the notion that a few miracles are called for in this age in which the Jews, recently exiled from their land, are encountering life in foreign lands. The miracles may thus function as indicators that their God's presence extends beyond the borders of their land and pervades the entire world, still relating ultimately to all the families of the earth.

The remaining books of biblical narrative, which tell the last chapters in the story, have a decidedly different feeling to them. The books of Ezra and Nehemiah contain the story of the return of the Jews to rebuild their country, their capital city, and their Temple after decades of domination by the Babylonians. The Persians have conquered the Babylonians and have allowed the Jews to rebuild their homeland. The story in these two books contains no miracles, no angels, no divine appearances. God is never said to have spoken to anyone. The Temple is rebuilt, but this second Temple contains no Tabernacle, no ark, no tablets, no Nehushtan. No glory or cloud appears on its dedication day.

The book of Esther also pictures the fate of the people in this period of Persian sovereignty. And in the book of Esther, *God is not mentioned.*

The closest we come to even a veiled reference to the deity in Esther is in an enigmatic remark by the book's hero, Mordecai, to its heroine, Esther. Esther, a Jew, is the wife of the Persian emperor, and Mordecai tells her that she must go to her husband to implore him to save her people in a time of a threat of annihilation. Esther fears to step forward on her people's behalf, but Mordecai tells her:

> If you keep silent at this time, relief and deliverance will arise for the Jews from another place, and you and your father's house will perish; and who knows whether you have attained royalty for just such a time as this?

> (Esth 4:14)[16]

"Who knows"? "From another place"?! This ambiguity and uncertainty are a far cry from the world of the earlier biblical narratives. Compare the story of Joseph back in Genesis, in which the Israelite Joseph has, like Esther, risen to high station in the monarchy, of Egypt in his case. Joseph's brothers, who wronged him years earlier, now fear the power that he has attained since then. But Joseph assures them that their wrong was part of a divine plan to enable him to be in a position one day to save them all. So different from Mordecai's ambiguous words, Joseph's response is:

> Do not fear, for am I in the place of God? You meant evil against me; God meant it for good, in order to accomplish as it is this day, to keep many people alive.

> (Gen 50:19–20)

In the Genesis story there have been miraculous signs (accurate predictive interpretations of dreams) that participated in Joseph's rise, and so he speaks with certainty of divine involvement. Esther has risen to the palace by rather more worldly means. Specifically: after Esther and women from all over the empire have each spent a night with the emperor, Esther is the one he loves most (Esth 2 : 1 – 17). The narrator does not suggest that this is a divine plan, and Mordecai's words convey that Mordecai is depicted as truly not knowing for sure.

These last books not only lack actual depictions of appearances, revelations, and miracles. They lack any of the kind of language that conveys divine presence in the earlier books: "the spirit of God," "God appeared," "God said," etc. It is not that these terms have been replaced by others of equal force. It is not a matter of terminology or metaphor or style. These latter books are simply different. They feel different. They do not convey the sense of awe, of wonder, of power, and of mystery that the earlier books of the Bible do. Leon Wieseltier, in a remarkably insightful essay, refers to the scene of the book of Esther as "a postrevelation world." [17] The initial biblical depiction of a world in which the deity is intimately involved has gradually transformed into a picture of a reality not so different from the one we know at the time that I am writing this. In the latter books of the story, no snakes talk, no seas split, no one wrestles with the creator — not literally, anyway. The presence of God that is apparent, that is a matter of knowledge, at the beginning, has become, at the end, a hidden thing, a matter of belief, or of hope. The text never says that the deity ceases to exist, to care, or to affect the world. It only conveys that these things are no longer *publicly visible* at the end of the story in the way that they are at the beginning. One might still conceive of the deity as being present and involved in undetected ways. One might speak of the natural wonders of nature as conveying, for some people, the divine presence. But regarding the *apparent, manifest* presence of God, as conveyed in the particular terms and descriptions of the earlier biblical episodes: that ceases by this point in the story.

The books of the Bible that I have mentioned so far were composed by a great many authors, according to both traditional religious views and modern critical scholarship. The phenomenon of the diminishing apparent presence of God across so many stories, through so many books, by so many authors, spread over so many centuries, is consistent enough to be striking, impressive, and ultimately mysterious.

But the hiding of the divine face is only half of the story. There is another development, also extending across the course of the entire narrative of the Hebrew Bible, which we must see before we can appreciate the full force of this phenomenon, and before we can pose a solution to the mystery of how this happened.

Chapter 2

THE DIVINE-HUMAN BALANCE

For many readers it will have come as a surprise that we were able to follow a development through the entire course of the biblical narrative. Most people learn the Bible in very small units: a story in Sunday school, a verse in a sermon. Even courses in universities and seminaries or in Bible study groups usually cover just a single biblical book or a group of books. People rarely think of the Bible as housing a continuous story — but it does. In the Hebrew Bible, or Old Testament, this story is an account of the relations of the deity, Yahweh, with the human community, with particular focus on the record of these relations as they work through the people of Israel.[1] In my view, two crucial developments take place in these relations. The first is the diminishing of the apparent presence of the divine among humans, the hiding of the face of God, which I traced in Chapter 1. The second, and presumably related, development is a shift in the balance of control of human destiny. This development is at least as remarkable as the disappearance of God. Gradually from Genesis to Ezra and Esther, there is a transition from divine to human responsibility for life on earth. The story begins in Genesis with God in complete control of the creation, but by the end humans have arrived at a stage at which, in all apparent ways, they have responsibility for the fate of their world. So we have to go back to Genesis and go through the story again. While the apparent presence of God was diminishing, something else was happening as well.

"WILL THE JUDGE OF ALL THE EARTH NOT DO JUSTICE?"

In the early stories of Genesis, God is the primary actor and controller. For most of the first chapter of the Bible, God is alone, creating the universe according to His will. When Yahweh creates the humans on the sixth day of the creation, He declares that they are to have dominion over the earth (Gen 1:26, 28), but their dominion is a limited one, to say the least. It is God who determines what their role in the world is to be. The primary way in which God communicates with humans is through *commands*. He commands them to multiply until they fill the earth. He commands them regarding what they may or may not eat. When they rebel in the garden of Eden, He pronounces sentence upon them. The first two humans, Adam and Eve, take little responsibility themselves. They do not design or build anything. When they are embarrassed over their nudity they do not make clothes; they cover themselves with leaves. It is God who makes their first clothing for them (3:7, 21). Little character or personality is ascribed to them in the text. It is difficult to get a feeling for them as individual persons. If we were making a film of the story, we could cast just about anyone for the parts. Perhaps that is as it should be, that the parents of all humankind should be nondescript, "everyman" and "everywoman." Nonetheless, the effect of this is also that they appear as weak, childlike creatures. At their most independent, these "parents" are more like naughty children, eating fruit that was forbidden, than like noble beings proudly proclaiming their independence by a defiant act of civil disobedience.

Adam's and Eve's descendant of the tenth generation, Noah, is pictured differently. God still controls the cosmos, causing the flood, determining its timing precisely, deciding who will be spared and what the vehicle of their survival will be: a giant box (not a boat!), the "ark." Nevertheless, more responsibility is expected of Noah than of his ancestors Adam and Eve. The deity determines the exact dimensions of the ark and instructs Noah precisely, but Noah must execute the instructions, assembling the gigantic structure himself. We might say as a symbolic formula: the deity makes Adam's and Eve's clothes, but Noah has to build his own ark. By the end of the story, Noah acts even more independently.

In the last portion of the story he plants grapes, makes wine, and gets drunk (9:20–28). No one commanded him to do that. By no means a fully developed personality, Noah is not an "everyman" either. Broadly speaking, he reflects a step beyond Adam and Eve in human character and responsibility.

Noah's descendant ten more generations later, Abraham, reflects a further step in the growing up of the species. The deity requires substantially more responsibility of Abraham than of his ancestor Noah. God's first words to Abraham are still a command: "Go from your land" (12: 1), and the commands continue; but the particular things that Yahweh commands Abraham to do involve a level of initiative that exceeds that of Noah, as Noah's exceeds that of Adam. The commands to Noah are factual ("Build the ark . . . make it so-many cubits . . . take pairs of animals . . .") without any reference to Noah's own ties to the people who are about to be destroyed. The commands to Abraham, on the other hand, emphasize the personal burdens that these acts imply. Yahweh's first command to him is not simply, "Go on a journey." It is, "Go from your *land*, from your *birthplace*, and from your *father's house* to the land that I show you" (12:1). Later, in one of the most famous stories of the Bible, God makes the ultimate demand of Abraham: to sacrifice Abraham's (and his wife Sarah's!) child, Isaac; and the text there contains a similar emphasis on what is at stake for Abraham personally, drawing out the description of his bond with the boy whose life he must take. It does not simply say, "Take Isaac," but rather:

> "Take your *son*, your *only* one, whom you *love*, *Isaac*!"
> (22:2)

The stakes of human responsibility are explicitly being raised.

Beyond the accounts of divine commands that Abraham carries out, the narrative also includes a variety of stories in which Abraham acts on his own initiative. He divides land with his nephew Lot; he battles kings; he takes concubines; he argues with his wife Sarah; on two occasions he tells kings that Sarah is his sister out of fear that they will kill him to get his wife; he arranges his son's marriage. In the place of the single story of Noah's drunkenness, there are in the case of Abraham the stories of a man's life. The Abraham section thus develops the personality and character of a man to a new degree in biblical narrative while picturing in him a new degree of responsibility.

The change from Noah to Abraham, though, ultimately goes much further than character development or emphasis on Abraham's responsibility in the events of his own life. Abraham extends the boundary of human behavior vis-à-vis God. In the episode of the destruction of Sodom and Gomorrah, Abraham dares to challenge a divine decision. Earlier, when God tells Noah, "I am bringing the flood . . . to destroy all flesh" (6:17), Noah does not argue or even question. Indeed, not one word of dialogue is attributed to Noah in the entire flood story. Through three and a half chapters, Noah does not speak. But when God makes known to Abraham that "the cry of Sodom and Gomorrah is great" (18:20) Abraham opens his mouth and enters upon one of the most remarkable confrontations between a human and God in the Bible. He actually dares to question the creator of the universe on the divine intentions regarding the fate of these cities:

> "Will you also destroy the righteous with the wicked?"
> (18:23)

He dares to argue that it would not be right for God to perform such an act:

> "Far be it from you to do a thing like this."
> (18:25)

He questions whether God can act inconsistently with His own standards:

> "Will the judge of all the earth not do justice?"
> (18:25)

This is not what most people think of as the way to talk to God.

Abraham proceeds to pursue a negotiation over how many righteous people in Sodom and Gomorrah would be enough for God to spare the cities from destruction, with the negotiation starting at fifty and arriving at ten (which still turns out to be more good people than can be found in these cities anyway). Abraham's arguments are phrased exceedingly humbly ("I am dust and dirt. . . . Let my Lord not be angry . . . let me speak

just once more . . ."), but the fact remains that the substance of the dialogue is nothing less than a human challenge regarding a divine action.
One might imagine that the presence of such an element in the Abraham
story but not in the Noah story may serve simply to depict Abraham as a
more compassionate individual than Noah. But, as we shall see, that is
not a sufficient explanation, for these two stories are just a small part of a
larger phenomenon that runs across the whole of biblical narrative. It is
not just that Abraham is kinder, gentler, more intrepid, more ethical, or
a better debater than his ancestor Noah. Rather, both the Noah and the
Abraham stories are pieces of a development of an increasingly stronger
stance of humans relative to the deity. Before the story is over, humans
will become a good deal stronger and bolder than Abraham.

"I CANNOT DO A THING UNTIL YOU GET THERE"

Soon after this come episodes that involve further steps in the process of
humans' increasing participation in the realm of divine prerogatives. In
the account of what happens at Sodom and Gomorrah, which comes in
the next chapter after Abraham's negotiation, there is a curious exchange
between a man and Yahweh. The man is Lot, Abraham's nephew, who
lives in Sodom. The two angels who arrive at Sodom lead Lot and his
wife and daughters out of the city to save them from the coming destruction of Sodom and the other cities of that region. Most people remember
the story for the part in which Lot's wife becomes seasoning because she
disobeys the divine instruction not to look back at the destruction of
Sodom. But Lot himself seeks a change in the divine instructions as well,
and he gets it. The difference perhaps is that he has the sense to ask first.
The angels direct Lot to flee to a mountain, but Lot protests. He insists,
contrary to what the angels have told him, that he cannot flee to the
mountain in time, and he proposes an alternative to what Yahweh has
commanded him through the angels. (As in the stories we considered in
Chapter 1, Lot speaks to the angels who stand before him but addresses
"My Lord" — *'ădōnāy* — 19:18.) He asks to be allowed to flee to a
nearby city instead. Yahweh agrees to Lot's amendment, which is impressive in itself, but what Yahweh says next is even more impressive: "Flee

there quickly, because *I cannot do a thing until you get there*" (19:22). It is hard not to feel that the narrative has come some distance from the creation story in which "God said 'Let there be light' and there was light," through the Eden story in which God says not to eat from the tree, the humans eat anyway, and God chastises them for it, to the present story in which God says to do one thing, a man says that it will not work and asks to be allowed to do something else instead, and God agrees but says to do it quickly because "I cannot do a thing" until then. Humans are not independent of God here, to be sure, but, let us say, the human voice in the story is certainly growing louder.

Another human's voice reflects this a few chapters after the story of Lot, in the account of the search for a wife for Abraham's son, Isaac. In this episode, even one of Abraham's servants involves himself in the divine activity in the world. Abraham directs his servant to travel to Abraham's homeland to find the appropriate spouse. Arriving at Abraham's brother's town, the servant asks his master's God for a sign:

> He said, "Yahweh, God of my lord Abraham, cause something to happen before me today, and practice fidelity with my lord Abraham. Here I am standing by the water spring, and the daughters of the people of the city are coming out to draw water. And let it be that the girl to whom I shall say, 'Lower your jar, and I shall drink,' and she will say, 'Drink, and I shall also water your camels,' she will be the one whom you have appointed for your servant Isaac, and thereby I shall know that you have practiced fidelity with my lord."
>
> (Gen 24:12–14)

And it happens that way, of course. The servant asks a girl for a drink; she says, "Drink"; and she voluntarily waters his camels. Moreover, the girl, Rebekah, turns out to be none other than the granddaughter of Abraham's brother, a not-too-close and not-too-distant relative. The story is interesting in a number of ways, but my main point for now is that the servant himself decides to seek the sign from God and personally determines what the sign should be. One could argue that the deity, theoretically, is free to choose not to provide the sign, or to provide a sign other than the one the servant determines. And, theoretically, that is true; but factually that is not what happens. What happens is that the deity provides what the servant chooses. The only caveat, interestingly, is that the servant and Rebekah do not exchange the *exact* words that the servant mentions in his request. This has the effect of leaving us (and the servant?) in some doubt as to whether the deity has followed the servant's program or not. At minimum we can say: (1) a human being has asked for a personal act of God, (2) the human has himself named the form that he wants this act to take, and (3) the act has immediately taken place, albeit with a slight change of wording. In a sense, even the doubt that this story leaves has a role in the shifting balance of control from divine to human hands. Future stories in the Bible will contain further cases of humans determining signs that the deity then provides, and in those stories the divine actions will correspond more precisely to the human determination, as we shall see. Thus the element of uncertainty in human control will itself diminish, and humans will more clearly and specifically determine the form of divine actions.

"YOU FOUGHT WITH GOD . . . AND PREVAILED"

Abraham has taken his giant step in human status relative to God. His nephew and his servant have taken steps, as well, which suggests that the reader should not picture Abraham's act as an isolated instance but rather as part of a new stage in human possibilities. And all of these steps are outdone in turn two generations later by Abraham's grandson Jacob, the man whose very name is changed by God Himself to Israel, "one who fights with God." One can see this transition in Jacob by comparing two episodes in the narrative of the patriarchal succession. For the first episode we return to the point at which God tells Abraham that he and Sarah will have a son and that this son, Isaac, is to be Abraham's primary heir. Abraham and Sarah are childless and *very* elderly at this point in the story, and so he finds it difficult to believe that this could happen:

> And Abraham fell on his face and laughed, and he said in his heart, "Will a child be born to a hundred-year-old man? And Sarah, will a ninety-year-old woman give birth?!"
>
> (17:17)

Like Lot, even though Abraham has received a communication from the creator of the universe, he questions whether it is correct. And, like Lot, he proposes an alternative. Abraham already has a son, Ishmael, the child of Hagar, and Abraham asks God to accept Ishmael as the covenantal heir (17:18). But the deity refuses Abraham's wish. God promises great things for Ishmael but declares that the succession is to be through Isaac. In the end, the decision on the succession is God's, not Abraham's.

In the second episode, this situation arises again a generation later (Genesis 27). Now it is Isaac who is the old man who must pass the mantle. Of his twin sons, Esau and Jacob, he chooses his favorite: Esau (25:28). But Isaac's wife, Rebekah, has other plans. Her favorite is Jacob, whom she directs to pose as his brother Esau and thus deceive his father into giving him the blessing meant for Esau. The deception works, and Jacob is blessed with the preeminence, as Isaac declares: "Be lord over your brothers" (27:29). In the next chapter, Yahweh speaks to Jacob for the first time and declares fidelity to him. The deity continues speaking to Jacob a number of times after this but never speaks to Esau. What has happened here is that the succession has been determined through the dynamic of intra-family relations, including conflicting parental preferences, sibling rivalry, and human manipulation that is morally questionable at best, and *the creator of the universe has accepted the outcome*. Who chooses Isaac? God. But who chooses Jacob? Jacob! (And Rebekah!) The human role in the covenantal succession has manifestly increased.

Twenty years later, this man Jacob struggles with God (32:25–33). In Chapter 1, we considered this scene in terms of the closeness it pictures between God and a man. My concern there was the close physical contact between the man and a being — perhaps an angel — who is in some way a concrete expression of the divine presence, and the place of this story in the gradually diminishing apparent presence of God. Now we must consider this strange story anew, this time for its place in the shift in the divine-human balance. After all, it is not just a story of a man having contact with divinity. It is a story of a man having a *fight* with divinity.

The fight comes seemingly out of nowhere. We are never told why they are struggling. What we are told, remarkably, is that this struggling divine being "saw that he was not prevailing against him." The divine being then tells Jacob to let him go, but Jacob says, "I will not let you go unless you bless me" (a strange thing to say to someone whom one has been fighting all night in any case). And the divine being then changes Jacob's name to Israel, explaining: "For you have fought with God and with people and have prevailed" (32:26–29). Every angle of this story is extraordinary: that God in some form fights with a human, that the human prevails, that the human *demands* to be blessed, that the deity acquiesces. Indeed, it seems to me that, if someone were not already familiar with this story, we would have a hard time persuading him or her that it really is in the Bible. But my point here is precisely that this story is consistent with a continuing progression in the Bible's narrative, and it is a stunning, dramatic, and symbolic element of that progression: Adam disobeys God. Abraham questions God. Jacob fights God. Humans are confronting their creator, and they are increasing their participation in the arena of divine prerogatives.

"NOT I. GOD"

The remainder of the book of Genesis concerns Jacob's twelve sons, concentrating especially on his favorite son, Joseph. This portion of the story is difficult to approach because it is a narrative of many colors, and the colors are not expressly theological. It deals with politics and especially monarchy, introducing the first major king in the book, the Pharaoh.[2] It continues the matter of sibling rivalry and succession to the place of the father. It involves quite explicit scenes of sexual relations, jealousies, and betrayals. It develops the notion of justice and recompense in human affairs: Jacob had deceived his father Isaac so as to displace his brother Esau, and now Jacob's own sons deceive *him* in order to displace their brother Joseph; Joseph's brothers sell him as a slave, and later he rises to power in the Egyptian court and they kneel before him and offer to be *his* slaves. It is a tale of intra-human relations, with no one directly rebelling against, questioning, or fighting with God.

On one level, the concentration of the story now in the human realm itself participates in the matter of the shifting divine-human balance, for the narrative has moved from the creation account, which was focused on God and the cosmos, to the Joseph account, which is focused on these earthly scenes of relations of men and women. In this sense, the book of Genesis is a sort of microcosm of and introduction to the entire biblical narrative, which will develop this movement more completely, as we shall see.

On another level, the manner in which the deity's actions are conceived in the Joseph story adds still another stage to the ascending human stance relative to God. Joseph does not have the audacity to question a divine decision or propose his own alternative to a divine command, much less wrestle with God. Yet in a way — in an important way — Joseph exceeds Abraham and Jacob in participation in the realm of the divine. Joseph is endowed, presumably by God, with a superhuman power, the power to read the future in dreams. No man or woman prior to Joseph has been pictured wielding any such ability. Until now God has controlled all the exceptional events, while the humans' actions have been, well, human.[3] But now Joseph comes and listens to people's dreams and then accurately informs them of their fates.

First Joseph hears the dreams of the Pharaoh's cupbearer and his baker, whose respective fortunes then follow Joseph's predictions. Later, Joseph accurately interprets the Pharaoh's dreams and rises thereby to high station in the court. Joseph is so much in control of powers that have belonged to the divine realm until now that, significantly, he must continuously insist to people that it is not he but God who is making these things possible. When Joseph is able to interpret the dreams of the royal cupbearer and baker, he says, "Do interpretations not belong to God?" (40:8). Nonetheless, when the cupbearer later commends Joseph to the Pharaoh, the cupbearer speaks only of Joseph himself and says, "*He* interpreted our dreams for us" (41:12, 13). The Pharaoh then says to Joseph, "I have heard it said about you that when you hear a dream you can interpret it" (41:15), to which Joseph insists once again, "Not I. *God* will answer regarding Pharaoh's wellbeing" (41:16; cf. 41:25, 28, 32). Thus Genesis arrives at a point at which God is working behind the scenes (39:2–3, 21, 23; 45:5–9) while a man controls a divine power enough that he must persist in informing people that the power is really God's and not the man's.

Character development also continues to increase through the course of Genesis. As Abraham was more an identifiable personality than Adam or Eve or Noah, so Jacob and Joseph are far more developed personalities than Abraham. The fact is that Abraham's character does not undergo substantial change from the first story about him to the last. There may be subtle developments, worth unearthing and analyzing, but Abraham is to a very large extent the same man in Genesis 24 that he was in Genesis 12. Much more obvious and striking is the character development of Jacob and Joseph. Jacob, the active deceiver in his younger years, is by the end of his life a relatively passive man, himself alternately deceived and cared for by his sons. And we first meet Joseph as a naive seventeen-year-old, who does not appear to comprehend the meaning of his own grandiose dreams of dominion over his brothers and who draws his brothers' hostility by reporting his dreams to them; but later in his life he is a wise and sensitive man, who administers the Egyptian economy and who forgives his brothers for all their injury to him.

The increased character development of Jacob and Joseph is partly related to the fact that there are more and lengthier stories about them than about Noah or Abraham or Rebekah, and it is partly because of the nature of the stories themselves. The effect of this growth is that, through the course of the first book of the Bible, the humans become more human, more identifiable as individuals, as they encounter the deity, grow in their position relative to the deity, and become more in control of their destiny.

"I HAVE MADE YOU A GOD TO PHARAOH"

And then comes Moses. Every aspect of this development becomes still more intense in the person of Moses in the next four books of the Bible (Exodus, Leviticus, Numbers, Deuteronomy). There is substantially more character development in Moses than in Jacob or Joseph, based on both Moses' strengths and his weaknesses, conveying his growth and change as a man. Though these books, especially Exodus, depict Yahweh's making Himself known on the stage of world events, Moses' own character plays such a powerful role that in some ways the story is more focused through him than through God. In the biblical presentation of this story, it is God who ultimately causes all the great miraculous events, but Moses is so much in control of the timing, the execution, and the drama of the miracles that, even more than Joseph, he has to remind his people repeatedly that it is God and not he who is doing these things. When the Israelites first escape from Egypt, they complain about the hardships of the wilderness, and Moses has to say, "Your complaints are not against us [Moses and Aaron] but against Yahweh" (Exod 16:7, 8). And later, when there is a rebellion in the wilderness to challenge his leadership, Moses declares again that "Yahweh sent me to do all these things; it is not from my [own] heart" (Num 16:28).

It is understandable that the Israelites (and probably most readers) are so focused on Moses. From the beginning, Moses' own part in the execution of the miracles is emphasized. The narrative identifies some of the plagues in Egypt as being initiated by God (Exod 9:15, 18), but more often it pictures Moses controlling their presentation and timing (8:27; 9:22, 33; 10:12, 18, 21, 22). Even though God selects and directs Moses, God nonetheless gives sufficient authority and power to Moses himself that at the outset God actually tells him, "See, I have made you a *god* to Pharaoh" (7:1; cf. 4:16). These words are remarkable by any reckoning, but they are particularly impressive in the context of the shift in the divine-human balance. Joseph was the first human to have a single divine power, dream interpretation, seemingly placed in his possession. Now Moses comes to wield a whole host of divine powers, and the deity confirms that to manage such powers is to be godlike in the eyes of other humans.

The comparison to a god is even more poignant in this context of the growing human position when we recall the way in which the whole process started back in the garden of Eden. The words that the snake says to the woman in the garden to get the humans to eat from the tree of knowledge of good and bad are: when you eat it "you will be like God" (Gen 3:5). And the deity confirms this after they have eaten it, saying: "Here the human has become like one of us . . ." (3:22). Both in Eden and now in the case of Moses, humans' acquisition of powers from the divine realm is explicitly marked as rendering the humans godlike.

What happens in a man who is as close to the deity as Moses is and who wields such powers? Moses' own character and experience convey a leap in the trend of increasing human status relative to God in the Bible. At first Moses appears to be timid about the role Yahweh has assigned to him. Moses is a shepherd in Midian, having fled there from Egypt after killing an Egyptian slavemaster to aid an Israelite slave. Now suddenly his ancestral God appears to him in a miraculous burning bush and tells him to return to Egypt to liberate the Israelites. Moses does not jump at the opportunity. He tries in five different ways to get out of the assignment.[4] And when God gives him his first miraculous ability — Moses' staff becomes a snake — Moses' response upon seeing the transformed staff is to run away from it (4:2–3). Also before his first meeting with the Pharaoh Moses protests twice to God that he thinks that the Pharaoh will not listen to him (6:12, 30). By his last meeting with the Pharaoh, however, after having performed Yahweh's wonders, the timid Moses is gone. Instead, we find a Moses who, in his anger, actually redirects the Egyptian court's attention from God to himself. Here is the text of Moses' last, furious speech to the Pharaoh, in which he announces the tenth plague. Note that Moses starts out quoting God's words to the Pharaoh, but somewhere in the course of the speech Moses ceases to be quoting God and turns out to be talking about himself:

> And Moses said, "Thus said Yahweh: About midnight *I* am going out through Egypt, and all firstborn in the land of Egypt will die, from the firstborn of the Pharaoh who sits on his throne to the firstborn of the maidservant who is behind the mill and all the firstborn of the beasts. And there will be a great cry in all the land of Egypt, such as there has never been, and such as will never be again. But not a dog will move its tongue against any of the children of Israel, from man to beast, so that you will know that Yahweh is distinguishing between Egypt and Israel. And all these servants of yours will come down to *me*, and they will bow to *me*, saying: 'Go, you and all the people who follow you.' And, after that, *I* will go." And he went out from Pharaoh in burning anger.
>
> (Exod 11:4–8)

The word "I" refers to God in the first line but to Moses in the last few lines. Moses is not confusing himself with God, but he has made a grammatical (and more than grammatical) jump, so that it is difficult to know where in the text he stops quoting the deity and starts speaking about himself. He has indeed become like a god to Pharaoh; and, it seems, he has begun to become more comfortable with his personal role in the exercising of divine power.

Moses' role as the intermediary who has one foot in the human realm and one in the divine realm advances still further at Sinai. In Chapter 1, I discussed the birth of prophecy in the Sinai account as a stage in the decreasing appearances of God. In that context, the arrival of prophets meant that God was one step further removed from the larger community. Now, in the context of the shift in the divine-human balance, prophecy also means that individual human beings affect — in an essential way — the conveying of the divine word in the world. The words that prophets speak are understood in the text to be determined by God. The selection of these humans who are to do the speaking is understood to be God's choice as well. But then the individual personalities of these prophets affect the impression that their speeches make. The same words can come out differently when spoken by a man who exudes boldness or one who exudes meekness. They may sound different coming from a rich man or from a poor man. Or an enthusiastic man or a reluctant man. Or a large man. Or a small man. Or a woman. My point is that prophecy, by its very nature, means increased human involvement in a realm that has been God's alone prior to this. Human mediation has become an essential part of divine communication. Symbolically significant: Yahweh Himself inscribes the words of the ten commandments on the tablets, but a man, Moses, carries them to the people.

How much power does that give to Moses? The proof is in the pudding. Moses smashes the tablets.

And the second set of tablets is not inscribed by God but by Moses (cf. Exod 34:1 and 27–28).

And, again, we cannot view these episodes about Moses in isolation from the rest of the story. Moses is not just one singular, unrelated character in a self-contained account. He is part of a series of stages in a shift in the position of humans relative to God. Abraham questioned God, but Abraham's debate did not alter the divine decision on Sodom and Gomorrah in the end. Moses, however, more than once *successfully* persuades God to relent and actually change a divine decree. First, in the matter of the golden calf at Mount Sinai, Yahweh tells Moses that He will destroy all of the people and start over with a new nation descended from Moses (Exod 32:10–11). Moses responds with two arguments. The first is: "Why should the Egyptians say, 'He brought them out for bad, to kill them.'" The second is: "Remember that you made a promise to Abraham, Isaac, and Israel." The result of Moses' arguments: "And Yahweh repented over the bad that He had said he would do to His people" (32: 12–14).

A similar divine relenting occurs later on, in the episode of the spies. The people have journeyed from Mount Sinai to the border of the promised land. Moses sends spies to scout the land, and they return with a mixed report: the land is good, "flowing with milk and honey," but the inhabitants are fierce. Hearing this, the people cannot be persuaded that they can trust in their God to enable them to face these fierce Canaanites, and they even propose to return to Egypt. God again tells Moses that He will eliminate them all and start a new nation descended from Moses (Num 14:12). Moses again has two arguments. The first is: "The nations that have heard about you will say, 'Because Yahweh was not *able* to bring this people to the land that He promised them He slaughtered them in the wilderness.'" The second is: the Lord's great strength is that He is so merciful and forbearing. The result: "And Yahweh said, 'I have forgiven according to what you said'" (14:15–20).

In both the golden calf and the spies episodes, the man argues a case, and God alters His stated plan.⁵ Moreover, Moses does not use the kind of exceedingly humble formulations that filled Abraham's appeal. Where Abraham is supplicating, Moses is forceful: What will the Egyptians say?! What will the nations say?! Remember your promise!

And even these two scenes are not the pinnacles of Moses' manner of addressing the creator. To me, the scene that most dramatizes the distance that the human stance has come, as expressed in the way a human speaks to God, is in an episode that falls between these two. It is an account of the first events after the people have left Mount Sinai and set out for the promised land. The people complain that they are fed up with manna, they miss the good food that they had in Egypt (!), and they want meat. (Which is better? To be a well-fed slave or to be hungry and free?) Moses seems finally to break under the weight of his task, and he speaks as no one before him has spoken to God in the Bible:

> Why have you injured your servant, and why have I not found
> favor in your eyes, to put the burden of this entire people on me?
> Did I conceive this entire people? Did I give birth to it, that you
> say to me, "Carry it in your bosom," the way a nurse carries a

suckling, to the land that you swore to its fathers? From where do I have meat to give to this entire people, that they cry to me, saying, "Give us meat, and let us eat"? I am not able, myself, to carry all of this people, for it is too heavy for me. And if this is how you treat me, then kill me, if I have found favor in your eyes, and let me not see my suffering.

(Num 11:11-15)

If it was extraordinary for Abraham to dare to say to his God, "Far be it from you to do a thing like this," then how shall we estimate Moses' saying, "If this is how you treat me, then kill me"?! Abraham spoke more audaciously than Adam. Now Moses speaks with God "the way a man speaks to another man" (Exod 33:11).

"SHALL *WE* BRING WATER FROM THIS ROCK?"

It is not just talk. Ultimately Moses crosses a boundary that no human before him has crossed. He alters a miracle. This occurs in the episode of water from a rock, possibly one of the most famous yet underappreciated stories in the Bible. It is the account of the great sin of Moses, the event that results in his death and in his never setting foot in the land of Israel.

The story: the people complain because, once again, they are without water in the wilderness. God instructs Moses to speak to a rock, and water will come out. Moses, with his brother Aaron, has his orders, but he changes them. Perhaps out of anger, he says to the people, "Listen, rebels, shall we bring water from this rock for you?" He strikes the rock with the staff, and the water comes out. God's response is to declare that Moses (and Aaron) have failed to sanctify God in the people's eyes, and their penalty is that they will not live to bring the people to the land. Aaron and Moses will die in the wilderness. In the touching last scene of the Five Books of Moses, Moses will come close enough to see the promised land, he will beg his God for a pardon, God will refuse, and Moses will die within sight of the land (Deuteronomy 34).

People have argued through the centuries over what exactly the sin of Moses is. Is it that he hits the rock instead of speaking to it? Is it that he says, "Shall *we* bring water out of this rock?" instead of "Shall *God* bring water out of this rock?" Really, both of these are related. By his actions (the striking) and by his words ("Shall *we*") he has boldly, publicly, and tragically stepped over the line. Until now, he has said, "It is God, not I, doing these things." But now he has done the opposite; he has directed the people's attention to himself instead of to their God.

Moses' stepping over the line is so remarkable, so dramatic, that one could miss a point in the episode that is in fact a turning point in the Bible's story: Even though Moses strikes the rock instead of speaking to it, *the miracle still works.* The water comes out. Admittedly, Moses suffers a horrible punishment for this. It is arguably the worst thing that could be done to Moses, as he now will never set foot in the promised land. But the severity of the punishment communicates how serious the thing is that he has done. Moses has changed a miracle. Is it that the deity has made the miracle work anyway so as not to humiliate Moses? Or has Moses really acquired this power himself? The text does not say. All we know is that a human's direction of miracle has reached a new height. And it will go higher.

"YAHWEH LISTENED TO THE VOICE OF A MAN"

In many ways Moses' life experience is exceptional, with nothing and no one comparable in the rest of the Bible. But, in this matter of human management of miracle, subsequent figures do exceed him. Moses alters a miracle in the matter of the water from the rock, but his successor Joshua does more than this. Joshua picks his own miracle. After he has fought the battles of Jericho and other Canaanite cities, Joshua faces an alliance of five Amorite kings (Joshua 10). Yahweh aids the Israelites in the battle by hurling giant hailstones on the Amorites. They retreat, and it appears that they will be able to escape under cover of darkness, but Joshua prevents their escape by stopping the sun from setting. He calls out for the sun and moon to pause in the sky — and God complies! In one of the great miracle stories of the Bible, the sun halts, and there is daylight until the Israelites have victory. Joshua has thought of a miracle himself — and not just any miracle, but one that affects the movements of the sun, earth, and moon — and he calls out for it, and the creator of the universe provides it for him. No one before him, not even Moses, has ever done that. The narration makes a special point of this, informing us:

> And there never was a day like that before it or after it that Yahweh listened to the voice of a man.
>
> (Josh 10:14)

The English translation "listened to" ("hearkened to" in the older translations) is a bit misleading. Obviously there are many other times in the Bible when God listens to humans, so it may seem strange to see the statement here that there was no other day like it that Yahweh listened to a man's voice. The particular grammatical form of the verb in this verse, however, carries the connotation of "listening" in the sense of "obeying."[6] The words for hearing and listening in English can carry this same connotation: "Listen to your mother!" "Do what I say, do you hear?!" It would be an overstatement to speak of the deity as "obeying" Joshua here, but in context the verse carries the meaning that Joshua calls for something, God listens to Joshua and provides it, and this kind of divine fulfillment of a human's design is something unique in history. It vastly exceeds the case of Yahweh's fulfilling Abraham's servant's request for a sign to indicate the right woman for Isaac. There the servant humbly requests a sign in a prayer directed to God. Here Joshua calls to the sun and moon publicly, and the deity makes it happen. In the Bible's own terms, Joshua has exceeded even Moses in tipping the divine-human balance.

And subsequent figures exceed Joshua. In the next book of the Bible, the book of Judges, more space is devoted to the hero Samson than to any other figure, and Samson has more personal, idiosyncratic control of power from the divine realm than anyone in the Bible before him. The story involves some interesting twists and ambiguities, so that the line between the deity's control of Samson's life and Samson's own control is blurred. Before Samson's birth, an angel declares to his mother that the fetus in her womb is a male and that he will have a special destiny, initiating Israel's freedom from the Philistines (Judges 13). Samson does indeed begin that liberation, but the text depicts his motivation as more of a personal vendetta than a devotion to God, mother, and country. Miraculous power is deposited, as it were, in him in the womb so that he is born with legendary physical might. Miraculous feats are thus at his disposal, to use according to his personal wishes. Samson is then drawn into conflict with the Philistines, not through religious or political zeal but via a series of relationships with women. First, he marries a Philistine woman, and then her family takes her back and gives her to another man. Samson expresses his rage by singlehandedly wreaking havoc on the Philistines (Judges 14–15). In another episode he spends a night with a prostitute in the Philistine city of Gaza, Philistines surround the city, and Samson shows off his invulnerability by carrying the city gates on his back out of the town for miles and depositing them on a hilltop (16: 1–3). In the most famous episode of the story, the woman Delilah betrays Samson to the Philistines. They pay her to uncover the secret of his strength, she "nags him to death" (16:16), he reveals to her that if his hair were cut "my strength would depart from me and I would be weak and be like any human" (16:17), she has a man cut his hair while he sleeps, and the Philistines capture and blind him. In the famous conclusion of the story, out of defeat comes Samson's greatest conquest, as his hair grows back and he is summoned to perform for the entertainment of thousands of Philistines in a great hall. Samson's strength returns, and his performance brings the house down, literally, killing the thousands of his enemies and himself (16:21–31).

Now, all of Samson's miracles are pictured as his own doing, performed at his own initiative, for his own motives. The text is ambiguous (deliberately, I think) as to the degree of divine control. The power and the terms under which it functions are determined by God before Samson is born. Thereafter the power is Samson's to use as he pleases; but there are hints, nonetheless, of divine involvement as well. Samson tells Delilah that if his hair were cut "my strength would depart," but after his hair is actually cut the narrator reports in successive verses both that "his *strength* departed from upon him" (16:19) and that "*Yahweh* departed from upon him" (16:20). Whatever the precise ratio of divine-to-human ingredients, though, Samson's personal participation in divine powers still surpasses that of any figure prior to him. From Abraham, who performed no miracles, to Joseph, who had a single power of dream interpretation, to Moses, who enacted a host of miracles and once altered a miracle, to Joshua, who called for a miracle himself, now to Samson, who has miraculous powers invested in him at his beck and call, the divine-human balance is evolving.

"YOU HAVE REJECTED YOUR GOD TODAY"

The balance shifts in the nonmiraculous realm of social and political authority as well. The next several centuries of the story — as told in the books of Samuel, Kings, and Chronicles — are largely the story of kings. From the start, the biblical narrative appears to be ambivalent toward the very existence of kings over Israel, so that it is difficult to say at times whether the Bible overall favors human rulers or is opposed to them. In the scholarship on the book of 1 Samuel, for example, a number of biblical scholars have concluded that the book is composed of two originally separate accounts, one of which is "pro-monarchic" and the other "anti-monarchic." Personally I would say that neither of the accounts in this hypothesis is pro- or anti-monarchy; rather, both are mixed on the subject of the throne. But my purpose for now is not to argue my side of this issue; my point is rather that the existence of this issue among scholars reflects just how mixed the Bible's signals are concerning the appropriateness of monarchy. After all, what does it mean to have a king? Does a people who believe they are ruled by the creator need a human ruler as well? Is having a human monarch inconsistent with the existence of the divine monarch? Is a human ruler an intermediary, a barrier, a challenge to the deity — or simply God's instrument?

The texts seem to indicate that having kings is permissible but that it nonetheless involves some movement away from God. The first text dealing with this is the "Law of the King," which appears in Deut 17:14–20. There the Mosaic law expressly allows Israel to have a king, and it sets up the terms, requirements, and limitations of his rule. These include that the king must be someone "whom Yahweh your God will choose" (17:15), which in ancient Israelite terms seems to mean prophetic designation. That is, one could not claim the throne in ancient Israel without the support of a prophet who would identify the claimant as the deity's choice. The Law of the King also includes the requirement that the king must personally make a copy of the law and read it all his life (17:18, 19). We do not know whether this meant that the king was to write a copy of the Law of the King itself or a copy of a larger law code in which it is embedded (all or part of Deuteronomy 12–26). Thus kingship is presented in the Bible as a divinely and constitutionally limited monarchy.[7]

Despite the fact that monarchy is understood to be permitted but limited, the stories of the first attempts to establish kings paint a rather negative picture of the institution. The first man to be offered the throne of Israel is Gideon (Judg 8:22–23), but he rejects the offer, saying:

> I shall not rule you, and my son will not rule you. Yahweh will
> rule you.

Gideon thus eschews both his own kingship and the establishment of a dynasty, insisting that God alone will reign. In the next book of the Bible, 1 Samuel, kingship is established, but it is clouded with doubts, warnings, and a reprimand. The people demand that the prophet-priest-judge Samuel give them a king. Samuel does not like the idea, but Yahweh tells Samuel,

> Listen [again in the sense of "obey"] to the people's voice, to all
> that they say to you, for they have not rejected *you*, but rather
> they have rejected *me* from ruling over them.
>
> (1 Sam 8:4–7)

Samuel follows Yahweh's instructions, but on the day of the selection and anointing of the king, he begins the ceremonies by saying to the people: "You have rejected your God today" (10:19), which presumably put something of a damper on the occasion. More to the point, the story, together with the Gideon story and the Law of the King, conveys that human kings are regarded as inherently a rejection of God, that monarchy involves humans' appropriation of some of the deity's dominion over them and giving that dominion to a fellow human instead; and it conveys that God, for reasons that are not stated in the text, allows this appropriation to take place.

Later, Yahweh even sanctions the monarchy with a covenant, promising the Israelite king David a dynasty that will last forever. The deity swears that David's descendants are to rule Jerusalem and Judah eternally, *even if they violate the law.* Yahweh declares that if a descendant of

David is guilty of wrongdoing he may be chastised, but Yahweh will still not halt His fidelity (Hebrew: *ḥesed*) to the covenant. Even if David's successors on his throne err:

> Your house and your rule will be secure before you forever;
> Your throne will be established forever.[8]

And indeed they err. No king of Israel or Judah gets a perfectly good rating from the biblical historians (with the possible exception of King Josiah), but David's descendants still keep the throne for centuries, with explicit notations in the narrative such as:

> He committed trespasses . . . and his heart was not whole with Yahweh his God like the heart of David his father. But for David's sake, Yahweh gave him a royal holding[9] in Jerusalem to establish his son after him and to establish Jerusalem.
> (1 Kings 15:3–4; cf. 11:34–36; 2 Kings 8:18–19)

The force of this Davidic covenant is remarkable and barely possible to overstate. The deity here has not only ceded to humans the right to have their own human rulers, but He has conveyed to one family of rulers even the power to violate His own law without losing the throne.

It is also significant that this promise is attached to David, because character development reaches a new pinnacle in him. The quantity and variety of material relating to him is comparable to that of Moses; he grows and changes over the course of the narrative with more complexity than Jacob, Joseph, or arguably even Moses; and the person of David figures in a pronounced way over the whole course of the following narrative of the kings of Judah. All of the kings are his direct descendants, and most are explicitly compared to him. Not only has character development increased in the narrative, but a particular man's character and life story have come to loom as an essential premise upon which all the future kings' powers and actions will be based.

"EXCEPT BY MY WORD"

The power of the kings comes into conflict with the power of prophets. It is a clash that provides a curious combination of the heightened powers of humans in the political realm and in the miraculous realm. This conflict reaches a crescendo in the stories of the prophets Elijah and Elisha: The Israelite king Ahab, together with his wife, the Phoenician princess Jezebel, supports the worship of the god Baal. This is conceivably the supreme expression of a human monarch's prerogatives, going so far as to violate the essential first commandment of Yahweh's covenant: "You shall have no other gods before me." In response to this king and his successors come Elijah and then Elisha, two men who bring personal control of miracle to a point that dwarfs anything that Samson ever did. The first verse of the Elijah stories sets the tone: Elijah swears by Yahweh that there will be no dew or rain for years "except by *my* word" (1 Kgs 17:1). In the context of the verse, the word *my* refers to Elijah himself, not to God. Now we might say that anything that a prophet says is understood to come from God (Deut 18:18 says as much), so that this verse does not necessarily mean that Elijah is claiming that he will personally control all precipitation. Nonetheless, even on this understanding, Elijah has come a long way from Moses' protestations that it is God and not he who controls miraculous power. This sounds more like the "Shall *we* bring water from this rock" that got Moses into trouble; but Elijah does not get into any trouble for it, and there is not a hint of criticism of him in the text.

One of the Elijah stories that I cited in Chapter 1 stands in particular contrast to one of the Moses stories in this respect. In both stories fire consumes a group of people who challenge the prophet's authority. In the earlier account, Korah (who is Moses' cousin), Dathan, Abiram, and two hundred fifty followers challenge Moses' position as leader of the Israelites. An earthquake swallows Korah, Dathan, and Abiram; and a fire consumes their followers. In this episode, Moses is careful to point out in advance that it is God making these things happen and that Moses is not doing things "from my own heart" (Num 16:28–30). In the Elijah story, which occurs about four hundred years later, a troop of fifty soldiers comes to fetch Elijah to the king. Elijah, apparently disapproving of the manner of their officer's summons, says, "If I am a man of God, let fire come down from the heavens and consume you and your fifty" (2 Kgs 1:10). And it does. The same thing happens to a second troop. Finally the officer of a third force of soldiers abjectly pleads for mercy, and Yahweh directs Elijah to go along with them. It is difficult to say what degree of divine involvement is implied in the account of the first two troops. In theory it could be the same as in the Moses story. Nonetheless the narrator does not expressly picture Yahweh as involved until the third troop comes, Elijah does not appeal to the deity as Moses does, and Elijah does not *credit* the deity as Moses does. Moreover, the miraculous fire that consumes the challengers in the Moses story is a public miracle. It is witnessed by the entire people (Num 16:19) and serves an essential purpose in the history being narrated: confirming Moses' leadership and Aaron's priesthood. The fires that Elijah calls for, in contrast, are more for his personal use. They are a demonstration of divine power, true, and they perhaps convey a lesson concerning the proper way to treat a prophet (though that lesson will soon be lost in any case). Nonetheless, Elijah's control of power here more closely resembles that of Samson than of Moses. It may ultimately serve a larger function in history, but its immediate purpose is to satisfy the personal wishes of the human who wields it.

The story of the prophetic succession from Elijah to Elisha, likewise, conveys the shift in the divine-human balance by its stark contrast to an earlier story, the story of the arrival of the Israelites in the land of Canaan in the book of Joshua. The Jordan River divides to let Joshua and the Israelites enter the promised land (Joshua 3), similar to the splitting of the Red Sea earlier for Moses and the Israelites when they fled Egypt. In Joshua, the miraculous splitting of the Jordan is the dramatic marker of the Israelites' return to the land of their ancestors. But the Jordan will split twice more in biblical narrative, and the circumstances will be very different. When the time comes for Elijah to pass the mantle (literally, as it turns out) to Elisha, the two men find it difficult to be alone because a group of prophets follows them to see what is going to happen. Elijah takes off his cloak, strikes the water of the Jordan River with it, and: the river divides, allowing Elijah and Elisha to cross on dry land, and then it closes again. Having thus achieved privacy, Elijah rides off into the sky in a whirlwind, and as he goes his cloak falls, and Elisha picks it up. On the return trip, Elisha once again comes to the Jordan. Will it work for him as well? He strikes the waters with the cloak, and, sure enough, the river divides (2 Kgs 2:1–15). Now, whatever the degree that we might imagine the divine hand playing in these acts of Elijah and Elisha, the fact remains that they are manifestly more personal than the great miracle of the parting of the Jordan for Joshua. One responds to these characters, Elijah and Elisha, differently from the way one responds to Moses or Joshua, I think. They are men of power. These and other stories about them focus on their particular, personal circumstances and motives for executing miraculous deeds. Thus:

When an impoverished woman who has nothing in her house but a little oil cries to Elisha for help, he directs her to borrow all the containers she can; and then the containers miraculously fill with oil, enough to pay her debt and save her family (2 Kgs 4:1–7).

When a man is swinging an ax, and the iron ax head comes loose and falls into a river, Elisha throws a stick into the water, and the ax head floats to the surface (6:4–7).

When a poisonous herb is cooked into a stew, rendering it deadly, Elisha directs people to pour flour into the stew, the stew becomes edible, and a mass of people is fed (4:38–41).

When a crowd of children throw stones at Elisha and mock him for being bald, he curses them in the name of God, and two bears come and tear up forty-two children (2:23–24).

Come again? Could that last story be in the Bible? Even if we assume that the deity is at work behind the scenes here, is it still His role to fulfill a curse that a prophet invoked because he was personally annoyed at some brats? And, indeed, the notation that Elisha curses them "in Yahweh's name" is the only mention of God in these last four Elisha stories that I have cited. The focus of these stories is on the man. There are other stories of the miracles of Elijah and Elisha which do refer to the deity (1 Kgs 17:4–6, 12–16; 18:46; 2 Kgs 2:21f.; 4:42–44), but I think that the effect of all of the miracle stories of the Elijah/Elisha cycle together is still to produce a picture of humans who are more in control of miraculous power than anyone preceding them.

Probably the supreme expression of Elijah's and Elisha's use of divine power is the resuscitation of the dead. No one in the Bible has brought the dead back to life before this (though a woman at En-Dor has communicated with a ghost or spirit of Samuel in 1 Sam 28:7–25). Now come three accounts of resuscitations. The first two are extremely similar stories, one about Elijah (1 Kgs 17:17–24) and one about Elisha (2 Kgs 4:18–37), in each of which the prophet knows a woman, her son dies, the prophet is left alone in a room with the dead boy, the prophet stretches out on the boy's body, and the boy comes back to life. Then comes an even more bizarre third story, which takes place after Elisha's own death: A burial is interrupted when the mourners spot a band of Moabites invading, so they hastily cast the dead body into Elisha's grave; and when the body touches the prophet's bones the dead man returns to life (2 Kgs 13:20–21).

Even the order of these three stories is intriguing. In the first, Elijah cries to God, asking for the return of the boy's life. The text reports the words of Elijah's prayer, and it notes that "Yahweh listened to Elijah's voice" (the same words that were used to describe the deity's response to Joshua in making the sun stand still). The story ends with the boy's mother recognizing the power of Elijah and the power of God:

> Now I know that you are a man of God,
> and the word of Yahweh in your mouth is truth.
> (1 Kgs 17:24)

In the second story, the focus and emphasis on the deity are much less. Instead of conveying the words of the prayer to God as the first story did, it only says, "and he prayed to Yahweh." And, instead of culminating with the woman's recognition of the power of God that works through the prophet, the second story ends with the woman acting out her awe and gratitude before the prophet himself, with no reminder of the deity's part:

> And she fell at his feet, and she bowed to the ground,
> and she lifted her son and went out.
> (2 Kgs 4:37)

And in the third story it appears that the mere contact with Elisha's bones results in the resuscitation of the corpse. The whole episode is reported in just two verses, and God is never mentioned. No matter what we might imagine the divine contribution to these events to be, the fact remains that, in the progression of the three resuscitations, the narrative increasingly places the human participants in the center of the action. And this progression just amplifies the already extraordinary fact of how far the divine-human balance has come when two humans play a role, *any* role, in the giving of life. Indeed, many readers of these stories of the prophets stretching out over the boys' bodies have made the association between them and the creation story in Genesis, in which Yahweh breathes life into the nostrils of the first human (Gen 2:7).

Elijah's and Elisha's special role in the taking and giving of life is also underscored in another episode of the Elisha cycle, the account of Naaman's leprosy (2 Kings 5). In this story Naaman, the commander of the army of the king of Aram, is leprous; and his king, having heard of the Israelite prophet's powers, writes to the king of Israel, asking him to arrange for Naaman to be cured. The king of Israel, distressed at such a request, says:

> Am I God, to take and give life . . . ?!

That is an ironic wording in context, for this story comes just a few verses after the story of Elisha and the resurrection of the dead boy. The king declares that the power to give life and death is God's, but this declaration is juxtaposed in the narrative precisely to the story in which a human has participated as never before in the bestowal of life itself.

FROM EVE TO ESTHER

The dynamic between human control of miraculous power and of political power reaches an intriguing denouement in the stories of Isaiah. In Chapter 1, I described the story of the last miracle in the narrative of the monarchy: When Isaiah tells the Judean king Hezekiah that Yahweh will cure the king of an illness, Hezekiah asks for a sign that this is true. Isaiah gives him a choice: shall a shadow on the steps go ten steps forward or ten steps back? Hezekiah answers that it is easy for a shadow to move forward, so let it reverse itself and go back. And it does (2 Kgs 20:8–11). We have watched human direction of miracle growing, and we have seen the rise of human power in the political realm, and we have seen the two come into conflict. Now, precisely in this story which recounts the last miracle in the narrative of the monarchy, this conflict arrives at a fascinating turning point as the prophet who deals with miraculous power offers the political leader the choice of how the miracle should operate. The king accepts the offer, the miracle occurs, and the rest of the narrative after this will concentrate on the realities of human relations in the political realm.

It is also interesting that this denouement in the dynamic between miraculous and political power occurs in the person of King Hezekiah. Recall from Chapter 1 (p. 25) that Hezekiah is the king who smashes the Nehushtan, the brass snake that Moses had made. It was an object associated with miraculous power, the power to cure fatal snakebites when the Israelites were in the wilderness. Here the political figure destroys the visible remnant of the miraculous power of Moses, the father of all the prophets. And this is the king who plays the pivotal role on the story of the final transition from miraculous to political power in the earth.

Some might say that when the text ceases to show humans performing miracles it is a step backward in the growing human role that we have been seeing, but I think that would be a mistake. By eliminating the miraculous from the story altogether, the biblical narrative has completed the jump into the human realm. It appears that the disappearance of miracles means not only the hiding of the face of God but also a concentration in the Bible's story now on the dynamic among the various sources of political authority. From here on, the Bible portrays a world of humans interacting with other humans, especially with powerful humans. The portions of the books of Kings and Chronicles that follow the account of Hezekiah's reign, and the remaining narrative books of the Bible (Daniel, Esther, Ezra, and Nehemiah), deal with the power of the Mesopotamian empires — first Babylonia and then Persia — over Judah. Notably, fire has been a frequent element of miracles, especially those of Moses, Elijah, and Elisha. But the last great fire, the fire that destroys the Temple in Jerusalem, is unmiraculous, set by human hands, and by order of a Babylonian commander (2 Kgs 25:9). There are a couple of miraculous events in the book of Daniel, but the degree of divine involvement in them is noticeably ambiguous. Daniel's three friends who survive being thrown into a furnace are joined in the fire by a fourth figure who is never identified and whose function is not stated. Daniel's survival in the lions' den remains a mystery with no first-hand witnesses. And the mysterious fingers that write a prophecy on the Babylonian palace wall belong to . . . whom? Though the images of the furnace, the lions' den, and the fingers writing on the wall are the most memorable to those who learned this book in Sunday school or through art, in a serious reading of the book one discovers that it is more centrally concerned with life under the Babylonian and Persian rulers. (It also involves some apocalyptic visions of the future, but more on that later.)

Likewise in the books of Ezra and Nehemiah, the two men for whom these books are named are governors over the Jews. There are no more Israelite or Judean kings on the throne. The kings have been replaced by these governors, who are appointed by the Persian king. That is, they are human authorities who derive their position not directly from God but from another human authority. Though they are empowered to enforce the law of God (the Torah), it is a mortal who so empowers them. Even if we think that the hand of God is understood to be invisibly causing all of this, still we can say at the very least that the chain of authority is growing more complex —and more human.

The chain takes a special turn in the book of Esther, the book in which God is not mentioned. It is an exceedingly human story, involving sex, violence, and political intrigue, and culminating in the Jews' narrow escape from genocide. They are saved by turning to a woman, Esther, who has become the Persian king's wife. It is an ironic finish in at least one sense: Because of the perceived role of Eve in the first story of the Bible, womankind has frequently been blamed for the initial estrangement from God. It is an ironically appropriate culmination of the shift in the divine-human balance that humans, at the end of the story, should turn to a woman, who is credited with effecting their salvation.

More broadly, from Adam to Ezra, and from Eve to Esther, we have observed a process in which humans have gradually come to acquire responsibility for their world. Though there is no suggestion that they are supposed to give up prayer and faith, the text unequivocally concentrates more on what they must do for themselves. The face of God has become hidden. The miracles of God have passed ever more into human direction and then have ceased. For better or worse, a shift in the divine-human balance has taken place, and humans are left in control of their destiny.

We should not forget that it is the *apparent* control that is shifting, just as the disappearance of God refers to the diminishing *visible* divine presence. One might conceive of the deity as still controlling every blink of every eye on earth from His dwelling on high in invisible ways. But the biblical narrative nonetheless leads us through a story in which *apparent* control of the affairs of humankind is progressively ceded to humankind.

God cedes (or transfers? or relinquishes?) more and more of the visible control of events to human beings themselves. Or do humans *take* it? Or is it neither of these; but rather, like children growing and separating from their parents, the biblical story too is about the growing, maturing, and natural separating of humans from their creator and parent?

Chapter 3

HISTORIANS AND
POETS

THE WORDS OF THE PROPHETS

The combination of the two phenomena — the hiding of the face of God and the shift of the divine-human balance — is extremely powerful. The longer the story goes on the more powerful this combined development becomes as it persists through so many texts, by so many authors, covering such a span of centuries. And that is only in the narrative books of the Bible, that is, the books that tell the Hebrew Bible's story, from creation to the time of the second Temple in Jerusalem. Other books of the Bible make this development more vivid and thus even more powerful. I have concentrated on the narrative books because this is a development that is bound to time. Traced chronologically through history, it is a property of the books that tell that history.

The other books of the Bible do not recount history. They are composed primarily in poetry, not in prose narrative. Still, in some important ways they reinforce this development. The great majority of these remaining books are the books of the prophets. Alongside the books that recount history, the prophets appear as witnesses, as voices out of this history. For example, we can read the accounts of the reigns of King Uzziah of Judah and King Jeroboam II of Israel in the books of Kings and Chronicles; and then we can open the book of the prophet Amos and see it introduced in the first verse as the words of a man who lived during those reigns:

> The words of Amos, who was among the herdmen of Tekoa, which he envisioned concerning Israel in the days of Uzziah, King of Judah, and in the days of Jeroboam son of Joash, King of Israel . . .

The text then proceeds to quote words that it attributes to Amos himself. It is thus complementary to the history. One work gives a narrator's account of what happened, and the other gives an individual's account of his own experiences in that era.

Like Amos, most of the books of the prophets begin with a notice identifying their moment in history:

> Hosea, Isaiah, Micah, Zephaniah, Jeremiah, Ezekiel, Haggai, Zechariah

Some of the prophets are mentioned by name in the narrative books:

> Isaiah in 2 Kgs 18–20 and 2 Chr 26:22; 32:20, 32; Jeremiah in 2 Chr 35:25; 36:12, 21–22; Jonah in 2 Kgs 14:25; Haggai and Zechariah in Ezra 5:1; 6:14

Some of the prophetic books even include chapters of history that are almost verbatim duplications of chapters in the narrative books:

> Isa 36:2–39:8 is nearly identical to 2 Kgs 18:17–20:19; and Jer 52:1–27 is nearly identical to 2 Kgs 24:18–25:21.

Sometimes the prophets refer to specific episodes in the narrative; for example, as I mentioned in Chapter 1, Hosea refers to the story of Jacob's struggle with God or an angel as told in Genesis. The prophets speak therefore in their own voices, often in first person, but they still relate to the history in the narrative books, and they shed light on it.

Every one of the prophets in the fifteen prophetic books comes late in the story. They are not contemporaries of Moses, or even of David, or even of Elijah. They all live after Elijah and Elisha. Elisha's ministry as a prophet lasts down to the reign of the Israelite king Joash (or Jehoash). The earliest of these prophets who have biblical books named after them (Hosea, Amos, Jonah, Isaiah) begin their ministries in the reign of Jeroboam II, who is the next king after Joash. And the latest of the prophets (presumably Haggai and Zechariah) come before Ezra and Nehemiah. All of the prophets thus come at a fairly late point in the development of divine hiddenness. By this point back in the narrative books, there are no more appearances of the deity to anyone; the last person to whom Yahweh is said to have appeared was Solomon a century and a half earlier. At this point prophetic experience is solely in the form of visions and dreams; the last person to have seen the actual form of the deity was Moses. At this point there are no more appearances of the cloud and "glory" of Yahweh, no more appearances of angels, no more public miracles, and few "personal" miracles; communication with God is mediated by prophets, and the prophets are frequently pictured in confrontation with kings. All of these conditions prevail in the prophetic books as well:

The words "And Yahweh appeared unto X" never occur in connection with any of the prophets in these books.

These prophets encounter the deity via visions. As I quoted in Chapter 1, God declares in the story of Moses' Cushite wife that all prophets after Moses will have only dreams and visions, never seeing the divine form (Num 12:6–8), and these fifteen prophetic books fulfill that declaration. They either identify those prophets' experiences as visions or else leave the form of the experience undescribed (Ezek 12:27; 40:2; Hos 12:11; Hab 2:2; Mic 3:6). Several of these books identify their contents explicitly as the prophet's vision in the first verse:

"The vision of Isaiah" (Isa 1:1; cf. 2 Chr 32:32)
"The vision of Obadiah" (Oba 1)
"The book of the vision of Nahum" (Nah 1:1)
"The words of Amos . . . which he envisioned[1]" (Amos 1:1)
"The word of Yahweh that came to Micah . . . which he envisioned" (Mic 1:1)
"The oracle[2] which Habakkuk the prophet envisioned" (Hab 1:1)

Ezekiel, too, begins with a report of visions of God, including a vision of the divine figure enthroned that resembles the vision that the seventy elders had in the Exodus narrative.

In the narrative books, the last time the divine cloud and "glory" were seen was at the dedication of the Temple of Solomon. Consistently in the prophetic books, which all come long after Solomon, there is no appearance of the divine cloud or glory to any of these prophets. Notably, Ezekiel sees the glory at the Temple in a *vision* (Ezek 1:28; 3:23; 10:4, 18, 19). That is especially interesting because the cloud and glory may constitute a sort of shield or mask that prevents humans from seeing the deity directly. As Ezekiel now sees the masking glory, and the glory itself is in a vision, the deity is, as it were, twice removed. Even more notably, in Ezekiel's vision of the divine glory at the Temple in Jerusalem, the glory *leaves* (11:23). Other references to the glory in the prophetic books use the term figuratively, not as an immediately visible entity (Isa 6:3; Zech 9:14); or they are predictions of a reappearance of the glory, figurative or actual, in some distant future (Isa 35:2; 40:5; 60:1–2; Ezek 43: 4–5; 44:4).

No angels are seen by any prophet. The prophet Zechariah has a vision in which there is an angel, which the prophet refers to as "the angel who speaks in me" (Zech 1:9, 14; 2:2, 7; 4:1, 4, 5; 5:5, 10; 6:4). Interestingly, Yahweh is heard speaking to the angel in Zechariah's vision, and then the angel speaks to Zechariah. This construction of the angel in a medial position between the deity and the prophet, plus the fact that the whole thing occurs in a vision, once again represents the deity as "twice removed." Indeed, since the prophet himself occupies a medial position between God and the human community, one might even conceive of the deity as thrice removed in these cases.

Ezekiel, too, sees a "man" in a vision, who seems to be an angel (Ezekiel 40; 41). Notably, in the narrative books Daniel has a vision in which he sees a "man," named Gabriel, who seems to be an angel as well (Dan 9:21). Since Ezekiel and Daniel are contemporaneous figures, this is another point of correspondence between the narrative and prophetic books in this regard.[3]

In the prophetic books there are no more grand public miracles and few personal miracles. In all fifteen books, there are only two classic miracle stories. The first is the story of the fish that swallows Jonah. It is a personal miracle; no one witnesses it except Jonah himself. In the story, Jonah tries to run away from delivering the prophetic message that God has assigned to him. Yahweh has sent him east from Israel to the Assyrian city of Nineveh (in what is now Iraq), but Jonah boards a boat heading west across the Mediterranean Sea to Tarshish (thought to be in what is now Spain[4]). He is sent to a site in Asia. He heads for Europe. Yahweh causes a storm to overtake the boat, the crew cast lots to see whose fault the storm is, the lot falls on Jonah (of course), the sailors cast him into the sea, and the storm subsides. Yahweh then arranges for Jonah to be swallowed by a fish, which carries Jonah back east and vomits him on the shore. There are therefore few witnesses to the storm portion of the miracle and no witnesses to the fish part except Jonah himself.

After Jonah, probably the other most striking miracle in the books of the prophets is the story of Isaiah and the shadow that turns back on the steps (Isa 38:7–8). This, too, is a personal miracle, with few witnesses; and, as we have seen already, this very story also appears (in slightly different form) in the narrative books (2 Kgs 20:9–11). Also, Isaiah and Jonah are two of the earliest of these prophets, coming in the generation after Elisha, so that the paucity of miracles in all the prophets who follow further contributes to the picture of the diminishing signs of the apparent presence of God.

Thus the rarity and character of miracles in the prophetic books is consistent with what we saw in the narrative books. In general, the age of the great visible miracles was past at this point in the narrative books; and, likewise in the books of the prophets, miracles simply are no longer what the books are about.

These prophets work more through symbolic acts. Hosea's marriage to a prostitute is perhaps the most famous example (Hos 1:2–3). To convey the message that Israel has been untrue to Yahweh by worshipping Baal, Hosea does not call down fire from the sky or turn a stick into a snake in front of the Israelite king. Rather, the man of God marries a prostitute. Meaning: God has "married" Israel by covenanting with it, but Israel has acted like a prostitute, sleeping with many others besides her husband, Yahweh. The symbolism is rendered doubly effective because it embodies a pun. The word "baal" in Hebrew also means "husband."

Also Hosea and Isaiah give their children names that are symbolic of their prophecies. Hosea prophesies that the deity's mercy will no longer hold back the fall of the kingdom of Israel, and he names his daughter Lo-ruhamah, meaning "No Mercy." He reports that the deity tells Israel that they will no longer be His people, and he names his son Lo-ammi, meaning "Not my people." He prophesies that God will avenge the blood that King Jehu spilled at Jezreel, and he names his son Jezreel (Hos

1:3–4, 6 ,8–9). Isaiah prophesies the despoiling of Samaria and Damascus by the Assyrians, and he names his son Maher-shalal-hash-baz, meaning "Fast spoil quick plunder" (Isa 8:3; cf. 7:3). Children of clergy have often had a hard time in many religions, but being a child of a biblical prophet was tough by any standard.

Other examples of prophetic symbolic acts: To prophesy the Assyrian defeat of Egypt and Ethiopia, Isaiah goes naked (Isa 20:2). To convey the divine message that Judah and its neighboring countries must submit to the Babylonian king Nebuchadnezzar, Jeremiah wears a yoke on his neck (Jeremiah 27). Ezekiel draws a model of Jerusalem on a brick and besieges it (Ezek 4:1–3).

And, most of all, these prophets work through words. More striking than what the prophets do is what the prophets say. Speaking for the most part in poetry, they frequently produce formulations whose artistic qualities are as impressive as the messages they convey. Complementing the narrative books, and more exquisitely than the narrative books, the prophetic works convey the development from the acts of God to the words of God.

"I SHALL NOT SPEAK IN HIS NAME ANYMORE"

Thus the prophetic books fit with the development of the hiding of the face of God in the narrative books. They fit with the shift in the divine-human balance as well. Certain episodes, particularly in the books of Jonah and Jeremiah, dramatize the extent of this transition. The entire story of Jonah, after all, revolves around a prophet's attempt *not* to deliver the message that God has commanded him to carry. In a sense this exceeds even Moses' and Elijah's requests to God that they be allowed to die rather than continue their heavy task. Arguably, Jonah brings the conflict between prophet and God to a new plateau as, instead of merely requesting, he actually tries to run away from carrying out his divinely appointed mission. Only in the end of the book, having tried but failed to resist, he finally asks the deity to take his life. But, as in the cases of Moses and Elijah, the deity refuses.

Later, the prophet Jeremiah also tries to resist his assigned mission.

He declares that he has tried to hold the divine word inside him and not deliver it:

> And I said: "I shall not mention it, and I shall not speak in
>   His name anymore,"
> but it was in my heart like a fire burning, bound up in my bones,
> and I grew weak with holding back, and I did not prevail.
>   (Jer 20:9)

On one hand, Jeremiah has not prevailed as Jacob once did in a struggle with God. (It was like a *fire* that he could not contain. Note the recurrence of the image of a divine fire.) That might be seen as going against the flow of the shift in the divine-human balance. On the other hand, Jeremiah, unlike Jacob, is a prophet to a nation. His role is more comparable to that of Moses or Elijah or Jonah than to Jacob's. As *mediator* in the relationship between God and humans, the prophet cannot prevail in escaping from his essential position. Nonetheless, as a *human*, he is still pictured as contending with the God he serves. Moses and Elijah *ask* God to release them. Jonah tries to escape by running away. Jeremiah tries to contain the divine word with his own physical and spiritual force. Even though none of these men can actually defeat the creator of the universe, still, in ever stronger terms, some of the divinely selected human mediators are struggling with their God.

"GOD HAS NOT SENT YOU"

This aspect of the heroes of the prophetic books, that they are *mediators* between God and humans, above all, expresses both the hiding of the face of God and the shift in the divine-human balance. Like the prophets in the narrative books, their very existence and role is the replacement of the kind of direct communication between God and humans that occurs at Sinai. For all their lack of experiencing direct appearances, glory, angels, and miracles, these prophets are understood to be the humans who are experiencing the *most* divinity of all humans. The boundaries on what they encounter should sharpen our sense of how much farther the rest of humankind is understood to be from the experience of the divine. In these biblical books the prophet is presented as a person who has had a revelation from God — and who cannot get through to people.

The role of the prophets as mediators, moreover, means a focus on *them*, on their *personalities*, as *individuals*. As in the narrative books, putting the divine words in the mouth of a human messenger involves setting the stamp of that human's own character on those words. Through the centuries readers have taken an interest in the prophets as individuals. Ezekiel is a priest, and Amos is a cow herder. Isaiah is eager, and Jonah is reticent. Jeremiah does not marry, Hosea marries a prostitute, Ezekiel's wife dies and he is not permitted to mourn. Isaiah is positive, and Jeremiah is depressive. Haggai pushes the people to rebuild the Temple by criticizing them, and his contemporary Zechariah pushes by encouraging them. Joel quotes and often reformulates words from the prophets who came before him. Perhaps the most significant expression of the shift in the divine-human balance in these books is the extent to which these messengers' own qualities come to the fore. To get a sense of what a difference it makes to have one personality or another recite the assigned words, one might consider the often-repeated bit of movie trivia that the role that Humphrey Bogart played in *Casablanca* was originally cast for Ronald Reagan. It would have made a difference. Now imagine a speech by any of the biblical prophets in another prophet's mouth. This point is not merely theoretical. After all, one of the most famous of all prophetic speeches is delivered by two different contemporary prophets:

> And they will beat their swords into plowshares
> and their spears into pruning-hooks.
> A nation will not raise a sword against a nation,
> and they will not learn war anymore.

This great prophecy of peace appears in both the book of Isaiah (2:4) and the book of Micah (4:3). The idea of those two different men saying these same words, each in his own manner and his own voice with his own emphases, is at least as striking as the difference between Bogart and President Reagan saying, "We'll always have Paris."

One thing that all fifteen of the prophetic books have in common is that they are all about the word of God in the mouths of men; and that means fifteen more expressions of a phenomenon that is developed in the Bible's historical narrative. The books of the prophets are constructed around these individual personalities, they picture them as profoundly in touch with the divine presence, and they picture the rest of humankind as profoundly out of touch with it. They do not picture all humans as immoral or irreligious, but simply as not in touch with the divine presence.

This unshared experience of deity is illustrated especially vividly by the matter of false prophecy. In both the narrative and the prophetic books it is understood that there are many persons out there who are claiming to be prophets of Yahweh. In the absence of a voice from the heavens or a confirming miracle, how is the king or the common person to know which prophet has really experienced the deity? The law code that Moses gives in Deuteronomy provides a criterion for distinguishing between the true prophet and the false: If the thing that the prophet said does not happen, then he was a false prophet (Deut 18:22). Well, that is fine for hindsight, but it still leaves the man and woman in the street unable to know whom to believe in the moment when they hear conflicting prophecies. This problem arises a number of times in the books of the prophets (Isa 9:14; Mic 3:5–12; Jer 14:13–14; 23:16, 26ff.; 28:15; Ezek 13:1–23). To me the quintessential case of this is in the book of Jeremiah. Jeremiah has prophesied a series of frightful events — the Babylonians will conquer Judah, Jerusalem will fall, the Temple will be destroyed, the king and priests and others will be exiled — but his words go unheeded, and people believe prophets who predict peace instead (6:13–14; 8:10–11). As Jeremiah's prophecies come true, the leaders of the people, terrified of the anger of the Babylonians, consider leading the people to Egypt. They now recognize that Jeremiah is the true prophet, they ask him to inquire of God what course they should take, and they swear that "we shall listen to [again in the sense of 'obey'] the voice of Yahweh our God to whom we send you" (Jer 42:6). Jeremiah goes away for ten days and returns with the word of Yahweh: "Don't go to Egypt." The leaders respond, "You are speaking a lie. Yahweh our God has not sent you" (43:1), and they take the entire people, including Jeremiah, to Egypt (Jer 43:5–7; cf. 2 Kgs 25:26).

People simply have no way of knowing if a prophecy really comes from the deity. Even a proven record of fulfilled prophecies does not guarantee that a prophet has really heard from God; perhaps he was simply an insightful man, or perhaps just lucky. The Deuteronomic criterion only *in-*

validates prophets whose prophecies did *not* come true; it does not say that prophets whose prophecies *did* come true are thus *validated.* And so Jeremiah, like prophets before him, is presented as a true prophet, who has really experienced God, but who is not believed.

All of these elements in the prophetic books contribute to the picture of the diminishing of the apparent presence of God that is developed in the Bible's narrative books. And if this does not make it vivid enough, some of the prophets simply refer to the hiding of the face explicitly.

"WHERE IS HE?"

I have referred to the gradually diminishing apparent presence of the deity in the Bible as the disappearance of God. I do not use that terminology merely for shock value but rather with the intent of being descriptive, to convey that the deity in fact dis-appears in the course of the narrative. In Genesis and Exodus you see Him; by Ezra and Esther you don't. The Hebrew Bible itself uses a more metaphorical phrase: God hides His face. The phrase occurs over thirty times in the Hebrew Bible.[5] Notably, the major prophets (Isaiah, Jeremiah, and Ezekiel) all use it. As I said at the beginning of this book, this phrase occurs among God's last words to Moses before summoning him to die. The deity predicts to Moses that the people will someday leave their God and break their covenant with Him:

> And my anger will burn at them in that day, and I shall leave
> them, and I shall hide my face from them . . . and they will say in
> that day, "Is it not because our God is not among us that these
> evils have found us?"
>
> (Deut 31:17)

Moses then gives the people a song to memorize through the generations as a token and witness of this prediction (31:19–22). The song (Deuteronomy 32) includes the line:

> I shall hide my face from them;
> I shall see what their end will be.
>
> (32:20)

The prediction is fulfilled in the end of the book of 2 Kings. The people have split into two countries, Israel in the north and Judah in the south. Both the Assyrian destruction of Israel and the Babylonian destruction of Judah are reported with a notice that God "removed them from before his face" (17:23; 23:27). The prophets use the same metaphors as those in the narrative books to describe these catastrophes. In the period preceding the Assyrian conquest of Israel, Isaiah says:

> I shall wait for Yahweh, who is hiding His face from
> the house of Jacob.
>
> (8:17)

And Isaiah's contemporary Micah gives a warning to his people's leaders who say that the deity is present and that therefore they have divine protection from harm ("Is not Yahweh among us? Evil will not come upon us." — 3:11). Micah warns that recompense is coming, and:

> Then they will cry to Yahweh, and He will not answer them,
> And He will hide His face from them at that time . . .
>
> (3:4)

And Jeremiah, the prophet who personally witnesses the fall of Jerusalem and the end of the kingdom of Judah, uses the same phrase that Isaiah and Micah used for the fall of the kingdom of Israel. During the Babylonian siege of Jerusalem, Yahweh tells Jeremiah, "I have hidden my face from this city" (Jer 33:5), and He says that He means "to remove it from before my face" (32:31; cf. 7:15; 52:3).

And in the book of Jeremiah's contemporary Ezekiel, the deity states and immediately repeats, "I hid my face from them" (Ezek 39:23, 24). The prophet later predicts a day when the divine face will no longer be hidden, but this, like Ezekiel's prediction of the return of the divine "glory," is understood to be at some unspecified time in the future (39:29). It is an eschatological vision of a renewed divine presence, as Terence E. Fretheim puts it, "on the far side of hiddenness."[6]

The latter part of the book of Isaiah (Chapters 40–66) relates to the years following the time of Jeremiah and Ezekiel, namely, the exilic and post-exilic periods.[7] There the prophet bemoans the apparent absence of the God of old, who used to move among the Israelites and do wonders like splitting the Red Sea:

Where is He who brought them up from the sea with the
    shepherd of His flock?
Where is He who put His holy spirit among them,
Who made His glorious arm go at Moses' right hand,
Dividing the water before them to make an everlasting
    name for Himself?

(Isa 63:11b-12)

"Where is He?" *Where is He?* A strange thing for a prophet to say.[8] This
prophet knows that things have changed since Moses' days as surely as
the narrators of this era in the books of Kings and Ezra know it. This
prophet longingly tells his God that he wishes God would make Himself
known through miracles as in those olden times:

Oh that you would rend the heavens,
that you would come down
— at your presence mountains would melt —
as when fire ignites brushwood, when fire makes water boil,
to make your name known to your adversaries
— at your presence nations would tremble —
as you do wonders we did not hope for,
that you would come down
— at your presence mountains would melt.

(63:19b–64:2)[9]

The prophet longs for splitting seas, melting mountains, and burning
fires; but he recognizes that he lives instead in a time of divine hiddenness. A few verses later, he says, like the prophets before him, "You have
hidden your face from us" (64:6).[10] The phrase occurs one other time in
the latter portion of Isaiah, this time in a beautiful, hopeful passage looking forward to a time when positive connections with the deity will be
reestablished:

For a small moment I left you,
but with great mercies I shall gather you.
In a little anger I hid my face for a moment from you,
but with everlasting faithfulness I shall have mercy on you.

(54:7–8)[11]

People have sometimes spoken of "the Old Testament God of wrath," but, as expressed poignantly in this passage, the Old Testament itself pictures the divine characteristic of mercy as vastly outweighing the characteristic of anger. And, more to the point of our present concern, it suggests, here and in Ezekiel, that the development of divine hiddenness is not permanent; it will end at some time in the future. We shall return to this point.

Not to overstate the case: the prophets may use the phrase "the hiding of the face" with a variety of shades of meaning and with more than one historical situation in mind. I do not mean to claim that every time it occurs in the prophets it refers to the progression that I described in Chapters 1 and 2. What the recurrence of the phrase indicates is that the diminishing apparent presence of God was not only a literary-historical development in biblical narrative, but rather it was felt, consciously, acutely, by sensitive persons in the biblical world. In every occurrence the phrase reflects a condition in which the deity is understood to exist but to be unavailable to humans, giving no visible signs of presence, leaving a human community to face their troubles on their own. The prophetic books do not so much add proof of the development; rather, they make it deeper, more vivid. They convey the human, emotional response to the disappearance of God.

"WHY DO YOU HIDE?"

Thus the prophetic books reinforce the phenomena of the hiding of the face of God and the shift in the divine-human balance. The remaining books of biblical poetry shed less light on these phenomena on the whole because they are so much less concerned with the flow of history. Even the book of Job, which is directly concerned with the nature of divine activity in the world, is not presented as belonging to a particular, known moment in human history. Most of the one hundred fifty songs that make up the book of Psalms, likewise, are not set in any particular moment in history. Though many of them begin with the notation "To David" or "A Psalm to David" (or: A Psalm of David), that phrase does not necessarily denote that the song is supposed to have been composed by King

David himself. The phrase can mean this, but it also can mean that the composition is dedicated to King David or attributed to him. In modern scholarship few psalms are thought to be David's own compositions, and dating most psalms is, in my opinion, one of the most difficult tasks in scholarship; but my point for now is simply that, as the psalms are presented in the biblical text, most of them are not set in historical time. Rather, they are general songs, some of praise, some of supplication, some of wisdom, some of trust, which might be relevant in most any era or region. Not tied to history, they do not connect directly to the phenomena of the hidden face of God or the shift in the divine-human balance. Nonetheless, like the prophetic books, the book of Psalms includes occurrences of the specific expression "God hides His face," which are worth noting. Psalm 10 begins:

> Why, Yahweh, do you stand far off?
> Why do you hide in times of trouble?

The psalm goes on to deplore the fact that the wicked man therefore assumes that he can get away with his offenses because the deity is not paying attention, and the psalmist concludes this thought about the corrupt man with a familiar phrase:

> He has said in his heart, "God has forgotten,
> He has hidden His face, not seeing, forever."
> (10:11)

The psalmist then pleads with God to arise and not to forget those who suffer. The psalm thus expresses a state of divine hiddenness, which some persons cynically enjoy and others pray will end. It seems that some humans are happier with the shift in the divine-human balance than others.

Other psalms, too, speak of the hiding of the divine face together with the notion of God's forgetting (which is a strange notion in any case):

> How long, Yahweh? Will you forget me forever?
> How long will you hide your face from me?
> (13:2;[12] cf. 89:47)

> Why do you hide your face?
> Why do you forget our affliction and our oppression?
> (44:25)[13]

These cries for help recur:

> Why, Yahweh, do you reject my soul?
> [Why do] you hide your face from me?
>
> $(88:15)^{14}$

> Don't hide your face from your servant, for I am in trouble;
> Soon, answer me.
>
> $(69:18)^{15}$

> Don't hide your face from me in the day when I am in trouble.
> Incline your ear to me in the day when I call.
> Soon, answer me.
>
> $(102:3)^{16}$

> Soon, answer me, Yahweh,
> My spirit fails.
> Don't hide your face from me.
>
> $(143:7)$

> You hide your face;
> They are terrified.
>
> $(104:29)$

> You hid your face;
> I was terrified.
>
> $(30:8)^{17}$

"MY GOD, MY GOD, WHY HAVE YOU LEFT ME?"

Probably the most poignant context in which the expression "the hid-ing of the face of God" occurs in the book of Psalms is in Psalm 22. In verse 2,[18] one of the most famous verses in the Bible, the psalmist cries: "My God, my God, why have you left me?" The most common English translation of this verse is "why have you forsaken me?" and it has also been rendered "why have you abandoned me?" These translations are accurate, but to my mind the simple verb "to leave" conveys the literal meaning best. It is the appropriate translation of the word (Hebrew: '*zb*) as it occurs in most other contexts in the Bible, and to me it particularly resonates with the feeling that the narrative books, the prophetic books, and the other psalms I have cited convey. The deity simply leaves humans on their own. This, after all, was what God predicted to Moses in the first occurrence of this phrase in the Bible, which I quoted above: "And my anger will burn at them in that day, *and I shall leave them*, and I shall hide my face from them . . . and they will say in that day, 'Is it not because our God is not among us that these evils have found us?'" (Deut 31:17). In Psalm 22, the poet looks back to past generations, when God would answer humans' cries (22:4–5); but in the poet's own time, "I cry by day, and you do not answer" (22:3). The psalmist urges those who fear Yahweh to keep the faith because God has helped in the past:

> For He has not despised and has not abhorred the
>   affliction of the afflicted,
> And He has not hidden His face from him,
> And when he cried to Him, He listened.
>
> (22:25)[19]

This time the hiding of the face of God occurs in the Psalms as a reference to past occasions, when the divine face was not hidden, and with an implication of hope (or confidence) that the deity's presence will once again be apparent in the future. At the same time, though, the psalm speaks from a current condition of divine hiddenness. Like some of the passages we saw in the prophets, the psalm declares that the deity was present, listening, and answering in the past, and it suggests that the deity will be so again in the future, but for the present God is hiding His face. Generalized human contact with the deity is understood to belong to the past and the future, not to now.

In sum, the prophets and some of the other biblical poets complement the development of the disappearance of God in the narrative books in a variety of ways. Above all, the narrative books depict the diminishing of the apparent divine presence step-by-step, and the poetic books depict the emotional responses of individual human beings to divine hiddenness. They convey the gamut of human feelings in reaction to that phenomenon: boldness to flaunt the law, piety to hold on to the law, wonder, confusion, anger, faith, uncertainty, terror. These books communicate that the disappearance of God is a more terrifying condition than divine punishment, in the way that children would be less afraid of their parents' punishing them than of their parents' leaving them. Frequently the psalms in which references to the hiding of the face occur set this thought in parallel with references to the deity's not seeing, not hearing, and, as we have seen, forgetting. It is one thing to cry out to one's God and hear the divine voice saying, "You've been bad." It is another to cry out and hear nothing but the sound of thin hush.

My point is that someone who has read the narrative books and observed the deity's diminishing presence in them would not then turn to the prophetic and other poetic books and be jolted by a contradiction or dramatic difference on this theme. Rather, in a variety of ways, these books can be felt to reflect and even enhance one's perception that the manifest presence of the deity in the early biblical periods gradually diminishes. I have not found a major conflict between the prose and the poetry of the Bible in this matter. The poetry rather reinforces the story and makes its picture more vivid. That picture is pervasive, and it is conveyed in a variety of ways. And that is why I say that it is so powerful. For those who believe the Bible's story literally, take *this* part literally. For those who see it as a myth, take this as part of the myth. But either way, come to terms with this: in the Bible God creates humans, becomes known to them, interacts with them, and then leaves.

Chapter 4

THE GOD OF HISTORY

A POWERFUL AND TROUBLING THOUGHT

The fact that the relationship between humans and God changes through the course of the Bible is not so extraordinary in itself. There is no reason, really, to expect it to remain the same at all times. There is no reason why consistency is theologically or aesthetically more attractive than variation in this regard. What I think is extraordinary is the particular course that this change takes, namely, toward fewer divine appearances, and ultimately none, and toward greater human responsibility. As miracles and all other signs of divine presence come to an end, humans are left on their own, apparently completely responsible for their world. If the deity is still present and affecting events, it is in ways that are not observable empirically. All that remains of divine acquaintance in the latter books of the Hebrew Bible is the text of laws that God reveals to Moses, the Torah. As Ezra reads that text publicly, the word of God takes the place of the acts of God. The Hebrew Bible thus tells the story of the development of God and humankind from a world of splitting seas and talking snakes and visible interaction with the divine to the world that we know, a world in which humans' relationship with the divine is a matter of personal belief. For those persons who believe they have experienced the divine, or even the miraculous, in their own lives, such occurrences remain just that: their own experiences, personal, not a public experience of deity in the manner of the sun's standing still or the revelation at Sinai.

If this is true, that God's presence diminishes and the human role grows, it seems to me to be among the most important facts of the Bible. It is at the very heart of the Bible's story. Yet, as I said at the beginning, it has not been observed before. It should at least be mentioned commonly in introductions to the Bible and in Bible courses, but it is not. Whenever I have taught it to knowledgeable laypersons and students they have been amazed that it is not commonly known. Certainly people knew that God is not mentioned in Esther, nor was I the first to see that the great, stunning miracles of Genesis and Exodus are not matched in subsequent books. But no one known to me has observed this whole intricate development through the course of the books of the Hebrew Bible. The German scholar Martin Noth noted the shift downward in miraculous activity at the point of the rise of King David. Professors Cross and Terrien, whom I quoted in Chapter 1, noted the significant juncture in the story in which the deity does not appear to Elijah at Mount Horeb. And many scholars have observed that things change after the Babylonian destruction of Jerusalem and the exile.* These observations are significant, but they are still just individual points on the line. Indeed, the concentration on the exile in particular has been, if anything, misleading in this matter, focusing on one moment as a watershed instead of revealing the whole development. The destruction of the Temple and the exile of the people of the covenant are terribly important, but they are part of only one stage of a long process, a progression in which God departs and humans are called upon to grow up. Two works known to me cover a larger number of the steps of the progression, one by a biblical scholar, Dale Patrick, and the other by the psychologist Erich Fromm. Patrick speaks of a change in the "mediatorial role" of prophets starting with Moses; and he notes that the "dramatic depiction" of the deity de-

---

*Most recently my friend Jack Miles has emphasized the shift that begins at this juncture in *God: A Biography* (New York: Knopf, 1995), especially pages 360f. Since my initial publication outlining this development in an article ("The Hiding of the Face," in *Judaic Perspectives on Ancient Israel*, ed. by Jacob Neusner, Baruch A. Levine, and Ernest S. Frerichs [Philadelphia: Fortress Press, 1987], pages 207–222), Miles has been the most receptive and encouraging among my colleagues and the first to include the idea in his own research.

creases in Samuel and Kings from what it had been in Genesis through Judges, that it passes from narrative to the prophetic word, and that it "dies out" soon after the exile. Fromm does not concentrate on the hiding of God's face, but he does observe the shift in the divine-human balance and sees the disobedience in Eden as initiating a chain in which "the whole further evolution of the concept of God diminishes God's role as man's owner." Fromm's work can be criticized for errors on individual points of history, but he deserves recognition for insights as well. He and Patrick have each dealt with the continuity in the Bible and have identified several of the transitions in its account of human relations with the deity.[1]

There are also scholarly theological discussions of divine immanence and transcendence. But, first, I am not sure that "immanence and transcendence" are the right categories. It does not appear to me to be so much a matter of God's "transcending" history as simply dis-appearing, becoming more and more hidden. And, second, such theological reflections still do not trace the step-by-step diminishing of God's apparent presence across the whole biblical narrative. That is more a literary and historical observation, though ultimately with theological implications. Indeed, I think that the disappearance of God in the Bible is an area where literary scholars, historians, and theologians can all meet in a particularly meaningful way, each offering useful contributions and exchange to the others. Perhaps this is also an area where the orthodox or fundamentalist reader and the critical reader can find mutual concern. Though they may see different reasons behind this development and implications of it, they can both appreciate and be struck by the fact of it.

The lack of treatment of this phenomenon is itself something of a mystery. One scholar, Samuel Balentine, did a book-length analysis of the expression "hide the face" in the Hebrew Bible, and he, too, commented on how strange it is that there has been so little attention to the entire matter of the hiddenness of God in the Bible. He wrote:

> The phrase "hide the face" is but one element from a large stock of language which gives expression to the motif of the hiddenness of God in the Old Testament. In terms of frequency alone this language suggests the importance of this theme and should guarantee it a prominent place in Old Testament studies. Yet sur-

prisingly little notice has been taken of this aspect of Israelite religion. . . .[2]

This may be partly because it does not occur to us to look for a "plot" in the Bible. Even books and courses on "the Bible as literature" rarely speak of plot. As I said earlier, most of us are accustomed to studying the small passage or single biblical book. After all, who would have guessed that a work with so many authors, spread out over so many years, would have so continuous a story? We would have expected an anthology of stories, arranged in roughly chronological order, but in fact we have a coherent history. (I must admit that my fundamentalist students give me a knowing wink at this point.)

The lack of treatment of this phenomenon may also be partly because the disappearance of God in the Bible is a powerful and troubling thought. I am not saying that scholars are afraid to address troublesome concepts. They are not. But the combination of the complexity of this development, running through so many texts, and the fact that it is not a readily attractive concept that an interpreter would be drawn to pursue may explain, at least in part, why it has not been worked out before. Toward the end of this book I shall say why I think it can be a less troubling thought in the present and future generations.

WHO WROTE THE BIBLE?

The enigma that I want to address, though, is not why this development has failed to be fully observed before, but how it happened in the first place. If we were dealing with a novel or a history book — in short, with a work that was written by one author — then this continuous development through the work would be interesting, and important, but not mysterious. But we are dealing with the Bible. The Bible was not written by one person. The books of the Bible that we have just reviewed were composed by a large number of authors and editors, over a hundred individuals, and these persons were dispersed over a millennium. The earliest lines of the Hebrew Bible were written some thousand years before the last lines. So each of the authors knew only a few, if any, of the other writers. Some were familiar with works that came before them. Some were not. Some wrote works that deliberately differed with works that came before them. And the editors of the Bible combined these works in ways that the authors never dreamed of. It is sometimes said that the Bible is the only book that was successfully written by a committee. But — and maybe this is the secret of the success — the committee never held a meeting.

For those who are new to the question of biblical authorship, let me provide some background. In the present state of critical biblical scholarship, nearly every book of the Hebrew Bible is thought to be composite. According to traditions that orthodox and fundamentalist readers follow, the first five books of the Bible (Genesis, Exodus, Leviticus, Numbers, and Deuteronomy) are supposed to have been written by Moses himself, but among contemporary critical biblical scholars there is hardly a scholar on earth who attributes those books to Moses, and there are no more than a few who would suggest that they are by any one person. The prevailing view for over a century has been that this work — called the Torah or Pentateuch — was originally four separate works, which were brilliantly combined by editors to form one continuous narrative. Similarly, the history that extends from Deuteronomy through the books of Joshua, Judges, 1 and 2 Samuel, and 1 and 2 Kings — called the Deuteronomistic history — is understood by most scholars to have been constructed by a historian who used a group of works by many persons as sources. The same applies to the history that runs through the books of 1 and 2 Chronicles, Ezra, and Nehemiah — called the Chronicler's history. We are now at a point at which we can separate these various source works in the narrative books of the Bible and identify, to a large extent, who wrote what. Our knowledge is incomplete. In most cases we still do not know the names of the authors. But we can frequently say when an author lived, from where the author came, whether the author was male or female, a priest or a layperson, to what group or party the author belonged, what the author's interests were, and frequently a good deal more. The dates and identities of the authors are controversial in some cases, and in other cases there is basic consensus among scholars. The story of how the Bible came to exist was the subject of my last book.[3] There I described the results of my own research and the research of my predecessors, teachers, and colleagues in biblical scholarship. It is an extraordinary, intriguing subject in itself, but my concern now is what this multiplicity of authors of the Bible means for the phenomenon of the disappearance of God. The question is: how is it possible that this phenomenon flows as consistently as it does through a work that was written by so many people?

THE ORDER OF THE STORIES AND THE ORDER OF THE AUTHORS

To demonstrate, here are some of the steps in the disappearance of God that I traced in Chapter 1, in the order in which they occur in the narrative:

1. Moses sees God at Sinai.
2. Moses, the one man who has seen God, wears a veil.
3. God tells Moses, "I shall hide my face from them."
4. The last time God is said to be "revealed" to a human: the prophet Samuel.
5. The last time God is said to have "appeared" to a human: King Solomon.
6. The last public miracle: divine fire for Elijah at Mount Carmel; followed by God's refusal to appear to Elijah at Horeb/Sinai.
7. The last personal miracle: the shadow reverses before Isaiah and Hezekiah.
8. God is not mentioned in Esther.

These are eight steps that contribute in a major way to the development of the diminishing apparent presence of God in the narrative. Now the reason why I chose these eight stories here is that they were written by eight different people. No two are by the same author. How does the hiding of the face of God progress as consistently as it does through so many works? We might hypothesize that it is the result of increasing sophistication by writers of successively later periods. The assumption would be that writers become more restrained about things such as talking animals, miracles, and angels as time goes on, and they gradually eschew them. Or we might surmise that the authors of the later stories were familiar with the early stories, observed some diminution of divine manifestations, and just chose to follow the direction of the narrative. But these are not possible explanations. First of all, it is not necessarily true that any of the later authors of the Bible were any more sophisticated than the earliest biblical prose authors of the ninth century B.C.E. In fact, the opposite is probably true. And, second, *these stories were not originally written in the order in which they now occur in the Bible.* Early and late texts are wound around each other in the Bible in such a way that the book is a brilliant, intricate combination of texts. Late chapters in the story may have been written by authors who lived centuries before the authors of early chapters. Bear with me while I fill in the information concerning when each story was written, and it will be obvious that the order in which the stories occur in the narrative does not correspond to the order in which the authors lived:

1. **Moses sees God at Sinai** (Exod 33:17–34:8; cf. Num 12:8).
   This story is a combination of two texts. One is known to scholars as the Yahwistic or Jehovistic source or, for short, is simply called J; and the other is known as the Elohistic source or, for short, E. I have argued that both were composed between circa 922 and 722 B.C.E.[4]

2. **Moses, the one man who has seen God, wears a veil** (Exod 34:29–35).
   This story is part of a text called the Priestly work; for short, P. I trace the composition of P to early in the reign of King Hezekiah, late in the eighth century B.C.E.[5] (Most scholars have dated P to a later period, the sixth or fifth century B.C.E.)

3. **God tells Moses, "I shall hide my face from them"** (Deut 31:17–18).
   I trace the composition of these lines to an editor who made a revised version of the Deuteronomistic history, known as Dtr[2], shortly after the destruction of Jerusalem by the Babylonians in 587 B.C.E.[6]

4. **The last time God is said to be "revealed" to a human: the prophet Samuel** (1 Sam 3:21).
   I attribute this to one of two major source texts that were combined to make what is now the book of 1 Samuel. This text is known in

scholarship as the Samuel B source. I date it to the same period as J and E (and I have recently argued that it may even be by the same author as J), between 848 and 722 B.C.E.[7]

5. **The last time God is said to have "appeared" to a human: King Solomon** (1 Kgs 9:2).
I trace this account to the original edition of the Deuteronomistic history, known as Dtr[1], composed by a historian in the reign of King Josiah, circa 622 B.C.E.[8]

6. **The last public miracle: divine fire for Elijah at Mount Carmel; followed by God's refusal to appear to Elijah at Horeb/Sinai** (1 Kings 18–19).
This story is part of a history of the kings of Israel, composed near the end of the northern kingdom of Israel, probably later than J and E, near to 722 B.C.E.[9]

7. **The last personal miracle: the shadow reverses before Isaiah and Hezekiah** (2 Kgs 20:1–11; cf. Isa 38:1–22; 2 Chr 32:24).
This story is part of a history of the kings of Judah, a work that told the story of King David's descendants on his throne, from Solomon to Hezekiah, probably composed in the early seventh century B.C.E., after Hezekiah's death and certainly before the reign of Josiah.[10]

8. **God is not mentioned in Esther.**
Dating of this book is difficult, with scholarly views varying from the late Persian period (fourth century B.C.E.) to the early Hellenistic period (second century B.C.E.), but by any reckoning it is later than any of the other works on this list.[11]

I have provided the dates and names of these works (J, P, Dtr[1], etc.) here for those who are interested in the specifics of biblical authorship. For those who are not concerned with the intricacies of that analysis, the main thing to observe here is that these stories were written at various times over centuries, and the order in which they were written has little to do with the order in which they occur in the narrative now. Thus:

Order in which stories occur:		Order in which stories were written:
1	Moses sees God at Sinai.	1
2	Moses wears a veil.	4
3	God says, "I shall hide my face."	7
4	Last time God is "revealed": Samuel.	2
5	Last time God "appeared": Solomon.	6
6	Last public miracle: Elijah at Carmel.	3
7	Last personal miracle: shadow reverses.	5
8	God not mentioned in Esther.	8

Other scholars date some of the authors differently from my dating, but the order of the stories still does not come out following the chronology of the authors. Indeed, by some scholarly models, the discrepancy is even more pronounced. What we find in my reconstruction of biblical authorship and in other scholars' reconstructions is that to some extent the order of the stories does follow the chronology of the authors (e.g., Moses' seeing God was written first, and Esther was written last), but to a significant extent it does not. The phenomenon of the diminishing presence of God does not follow the chronology of the authors' lives; it follows the internal chronology of the Bible's story itself. So no author, and no committee of authors, conceived of the hiding of the face of God. No author could know what later authors would write, and none of them knew that all their works would come to be combined into a continuous work later.

We might consider giving the credit for the continuous development of the disappearance of God to the editor who put the Bible's narrative together. But that explanation does not suffice either. First of all, there was no *one* editor of biblical narrative. The editing, like the writing, was done by several persons, separated from one another by centuries. Second, we cannot just make up omnipotent editors of the Bible, imagining that they had the power to cut or rewrite texts in any way they saw fit. In my studies of the work of the ancient biblical editors, I have found that they were as different from one another as modern editors are from each other. They all had their own ideas about the texts they handled, their own degree of respect for the texts' sacredness, and their own standards of what might be cut and what might not.[12] And so we cannot just make blanket assumptions about how these people organized the Bible. To take a single example, perhaps the most important editor was the person who finally put together the Torah (Genesis through Deuteronomy). This person is known in biblical scholarship as the Redactor (or for short, of course, R). I have argued that this individual was Ezra, the scribe whose acts are recounted in the book by that name. He combined his texts in an extraordinarily complex manner, so that frequently a single page of the Torah now contains the combined work of three different authors. But I found that if I separated these source texts from one another, each flows nearly completely. That is, you can unravel the book of Genesis or Exodus the way you can unravel the individual strands of twine that make up a rope; and then you find that you are able to read each of the main component texts as a continuous story with very few breaks. What this means is that this editor was not cutting or changing his source texts. He was trying to keep each of them as nearly complete as possible.[13] So the editors who put the Bible together did not somehow tamper with the texts they edited in order to make God disappear. The disappearance of God in the Bible is not the product of the biblical authors' intentions nor of the biblical editors' intentions.

The more we know about the people who wrote and edited the Bible, the *harder* it is to explain how it came out with such consistent developments as the hiding of the face of God and the shift in the divine-human balance. How could this have happened? Why did the authors of Esther, Ezra, and Nehemiah not include a few miracles, or an angel, or an "And the Lord said unto . . ."? Why did all of the authors of Genesis through Joshua, *no matter in what period they lived*, include revelations and miracles? How is it possible that this followed as consistent a progression as it does when it developed through the works of so many different writers, separated by centuries?

Again my fundamentalist students give me a wink. But after the wink the traditional Christian or Jew is still left with some serious concerns as well. For them the answer to the mystery may be that God is the ultimate author who dictated, inspired, or revealed the words of the Bible and that the biblical narrative is just recounting what happened. But what happened is tremendous. So for them the impressive thing, then, is that this occurred, that the face of God became hidden according to the biblical account of history, and they can contemplate why the deity chose to do this.

And for everyone else, wherever he or she may fall on the spectrum of religiosity, the mystery remains. If the disappearance of God in the Bible was unintentional, what made it happen?

RELIGION AND HISTORY

The hardest mysteries to solve are frequently those that have multiple causes. It was not the butler or the husband or the maid who done it; it was the butler *and* the husband *and* the maid working together. The now classic example of this is Agatha Christie's *Murder on the Orient Express*, in which (skip the rest of this sentence if you do not want to know who done it) no one of the suspects can have been the murderer, for each has an alibi for some crucial part of the crime; and so the detective, Poirot, deduces that all of the suspects were accomplices in the crime. I do not see any single factor that can account for the disappearance of God in the Bible, given the complexity of biblical authorship. The explanation of this phenomenon rather lies in a combination of factors: religious, historical, psychological, and literary.

The phenomenon is, in part, linked to the particular qualities of the religion of biblical Israel. This religion was a monotheism, the first enduring monotheism known. The difference between Israelite monotheism and pagan religion, though, was not a simple matter of arithmetic: one God rather than many. The pagan religion that dominated the ancient world for four millennia was tied to nature. Humans were (and are) fundamentally fearful of the forces of nature (sky, sun, earth, sea, storm, wind, fire, fertility, disease), before which our position is vulnerable and precarious. Pagan religion personified these forces, ascribed a will to them, and called them: gods. Through religious practice (prayer, sacrifice, ritual), one tried to communicate with these forces, find out what they wanted, and get them on one's side.

Having one God, who controlled all of those forces, was another (more appealing?) way to be in touch with the divine and deal with these fundamental fears. Israel's monotheism, for the first time, conceived of a God who was outside of nature, controlling its de-deified forces. If one wanted to comprehend the sun god Shamash, one contemplated the sun. If one wanted to pursue the essence of the storm god Baal, one observed the storm. But the essence of Yahweh, God of Israel, was hidden. One could not learn what this God was made of by contemplating any particular element of nature. Instead of being known through nature, God was known through His acts in history: "I am Yahweh your God who brought you out of the land of Egypt," "I appeared to Abraham, Isaac, and Jacob," "I gave you a land," and so forth.[14]

Now, *by moving the essence of divinity from the realm of nature to the realm of history, Israelite religion made it possible for a deity to recede.* The forces of nature (earth, sea, sky, sun, the storm, etc.) are always present. The sun's effects on the earth do not recede over a long span of time, and therefore the sun god cannot be perceived to disappear in pagan myth. On the contrary, nature is cyclical. The seasons come and go in order. The rivers annually flood at their deltas. The sun, moon, and stars proceed regularly through their phases. In the pagan religious view of the universe, the essential perception of time was the cyclical, eternally recurring reality of nature. A measure of the degree to which pagan religion was focused on the cyclical time of nature rather than on the linear time of history is the fact that pagans did not write history. For over two millennia before Israel was born the pagan world produced no works of history. The biblical historical narratives (specifically J, E, Samuel A and B, and the Court History of David in 2 Samuel) are the first known human attempts to write history anywhere on earth, coming hundreds of years before Herodotus in Greece.[15] Only a God who is outside of the forces of nature, who is known precisely through interruptions of their cyclical recurrence (i.e., through miracles, angels, voices from the sky) can be understood to change His relationship with humans in a linear way over time.

What direction would that change take? Few of the biblical narrators suggest that they witnessed miracles, angels, etc., themselves. Since they depicted miracles as something remarkable, seemingly outside their audience's experience, and since they depicted few if any miracles close to their own lives, the evidence from their own pens is that their life experience was probably the same as most people's experience today. They heard stories about miracles, but they never saw one themselves. Given that miracles and other signs of divine presence were not in fact occurring in any apparent way to them, their perception would naturally be that God's visible interventions in human affairs belonged to a bygone age. Whenever a biblical author lived, no matter how long after the events he or she was narrating, his or her perception would be that God's visible acts had diminished. That is, the placement of God in history, inevitably, meant departure.

RELIGION, HISTORY, AND PSYCHOLOGY

Add to this the consideration that the common human inclination may well be to see ages of power receding. The thought of contact with the ultimate power in the universe is not necessarily comforting. When the Bible speaks of *fearing* God it sometimes means this figuratively (for examples: 1 Kgs 18:3; Ps 112:1; Job 1:9), but it also can mean it quite literally (Exod 3:6; 9:20; 20:18–20; Hab 3:2). When the people of Israel hear the voice of God from the sky over Mount Sinai, they are terrified and ask that God never speak to them directly again. And it occurred to the author of that story to connect this fear directly to one of the steps in the hiding of the face of God, namely the introduction of prophecy. Even when Moses first meets Yahweh at the burning bush, his first reaction is to turn away "because he was afraid to look at God" (Exod 3:6). (Ironically, the expression in that verse is "and Moses *hid his face.*") The biblical authors seem to have shared the idea that the divine realm is glorious but also fearful. Imagine being offered a chance to know for certain that a God exists, to have the door of your room open and the creator of the universe enter and communicate with you. Most people would probably say that they would accept the offer. There is a good chance, though, that they would accept the first time but politely and reverently decline the second time. I am guessing, betting, speculating, that nearly all of us would like to see a miracle, and that nearly all of us would be terrified if we did. This may suggest a common human inclination to picture ages of power as lying in the distant past (or the distant future), but, please, not in our own day. Like the Chinese curse, "May you live in interesting times," Western thinking, too, may have reflected a fundamental mixture of fear and fascination with the nearness of power, which in the case of the Bible means the nearness of divinity. Such common human feelings could affect how writers of any period would perceive the human relationship with the divine. No matter when any given biblical author/writer/historian lived, when writing about an extremely distant event (Eden, Jacob's struggle with God, the plagues in Egypt) he or she could comfortably conceive of God in close, potent contact with humans. But the closer the period of the author's story came to the author's own time, the less the author would/could picture divine intervention in his or her world. Any Israelite author could write about God powerfully involved in creation or in the ancient universal flood. Any author could picture an extraordinary divine communication at Sinai. But as their accounts moved into the period of the Israelite monarchy, these writers — any writers — wrote of miracles that were less public, witnessed only by individuals or small groups. The combination of texts from numerous authors would not confound this trend in stories spread over centuries of history. (Actually at several junctures it enhanced it.) Given this common, possibly universal feeling of uneasiness with the closeness of the divine, the placement of God in history — once again — inevitably meant departure.

Add to this the equally common human notion of conflict with the divine. After all, one rarely encounters sacred literature, of any religion, that pictures humans and deities living together in tranquil, blissful harmony. (In the Bible we find this at the beginning, in Eden, but it is all over by Chapter 3.) There is a sense of profound tension between humans and deities, and that sense manifests itself differently in each religion. In the case of ancient pagan religion it patently relates to the realities of nature. To some extent — a large extent — the forces of nature are unpredictable. The expression of this condition in pagan religion is that the wills of the gods associated with these forces are unpredictable. The gods can be arbitrary, capricious. The storm wind (be it Enlil in Mesopotamia, Baal in Canaan, or Zeus in Greece) may come, wreaking havoc, even if one has sacrificed to him and tried to do his will. And so humans perceive themselves to be at odds with the gods.

Pagan literature reflects this in a variety of ways. In the epic of *Gilgamesh*, which was possibly the first book, that is, the first lengthy written work known to us, this was already expressed blatantly. This work, com-

posed of twelve tablets of poetry, recounts the travels and exploits of Gilgamesh and his friend Enkidu. They come into conflict first with the
goddess Ishtar. She persuades her father, Anu, to send the Bull of Heaven
against them, but they defeat it and throw a leg of bull in Ishtar's face.
The gods react to the men's hubris by causing Enkidu to die of a disease.
The rest of the epic depicts Gilgamesh attempting to overcome the common lot of human beings, namely death, which the gods have irrevocably
imposed. The accounts of his attempts are tantalizing: he brings up from
the sea a plant that has the power to rejuvenate humans and make them
young again, but *a snake steals this tree of life* from him; he meets the one
man and woman on whom the gods bestowed eternal life after this man
built a boat and took all the animal species on it during a flood that the
gods sent to destroy the earth. Tantalizing indeed, but my point for now
is simply that from the very first work of literature that our species ever
produced we have pictured ourselves in struggle with the gods. And this
divine-human contention persists as a theme through the pagan litera-
tures, from ancient Near Eastern and Homeric epic to the exquisitely
constructed expressions of it in Greek tragedy. Because the natural entities and forces of the universe were unstable and unaccommodating to
human needs, the gods who were linked to those forces were understood
to be unstable and potentially hostile.

But history, no less than nature, is precarious, inexplicable, and
marked by suffering. And so monotheistic Israel, with its belief in a God
who was known through history, shared with pagan religion the perception of tension with the divine. That tension was usually set in a context
of covenant. From our earliest prose sources in the Bible, divine-human
relations are conceived as functioning through covenant. A covenant is a
formal, legal contract with the deity. One of the most fruitful discoveries
of modern biblical scholarship was that the biblical covenants are composed in a common form of legal documents in use all over the ancient
Near East, employing standard legal terminology. The equivalent in
modern legal terms would be if we were to imagine a text that went:
"Hereafter God will be known as the party of the first part, and humans
will be known as the party of the second part . . ." The relations between
the deity and the human species were defined. The things that Yahweh
required of His human covenant partners were listed. The blessings and
curses for human success or failure respectively in keeping those require-

ments were listed as well (Leviticus 26; Deuteronomy 28).[16] The blessings included having an established relationship with God. The curses
included degrees of alienation from God, particularly in the curse of exile. Now, covenant is a model that is connected to history. The text of the
Decalogue, part of the Israelite covenant of Sinai, does not begin with
the first commandment: "You shall have no other gods before me."
Rather, like the ancient Near Eastern treaty texts, it begins with a historical prologue, and this point of history is the premise on which the
divine requirements are to be based: "I am Yahweh your God, *who
brought you out of the land of Egypt, out of the house of bondage.*"

Once a covenant doctrine was in place, Israel's historical fortunes
would naturally be interpreted in terms of the nation's adherence to
covenant. If they were suffering, it must be that they had done something
wrong, something in violation of the covenant. In a system related to
history, each new catastrophe would appear to be another degree of distancing from the original closeness to the deity as the covenant was vio-
lated and its curses realized. The Assyrian defeat of the kingdom of Israel,
the Babylonian defeat of the kingdom of Judah, the destruction of the
Temple: all of these contributed to the feeling that God and humans were
becoming more alienated from one another. "My God, my God, why
have you left me?" Given that Israel did historically suffer destruction
and exile, the placement of God in history, linked to a covenant theology,
inevitably meant departure.

RELIGION, HISTORY, PSYCHOLOGY, AND
LITERARY COMPOSITION

Add to this some literary factors, including perhaps sheer chance, as some
of the stages of the hiding of the face of God and the shift in the divine-
human balance were results of the combination of texts that were originally separate. Consider the matter of the patriarchal succession in
Genesis. I described in Chapter 2 the transition that takes place in human
direction of the succession from Abraham to Isaac and then from Isaac
to Jacob. In the first story, Abraham asks God to accept Ishmael as the
covenantal heir, but the deity refuses Abraham's wish and declares that

the heir is to be Isaac. The decision on the succession is God's, not Abraham's. In the second story, Isaac chooses his favorite son, Esau; but Rebekah and her favorite son, Jacob, deceive Isaac into blessing Jacob with the preeminence instead. Here the decision on the succession appears to be determined through the actions of the humans, and Yahweh accepts the outcome. I identified this transition as one of the significant stages in the shift of the divine-human balance. But, from the standpoint of critical biblical scholarship, this transition is in fact a result of the combination of two stories that were written by two different authors. Moreover, the stories, as they are now arranged in the narrative, are in the reverse of the order in which they were composed. The first story was written second, and the second was written first. (The first story is from P, the second is from J.) I am not so certain that the religious-psychological-historical complex I have pictured so far can account for this particular case. It is possible that the ancient authors in general could more readily imagine decisive human action in Isaac's generation than in Abraham's, but after all that is a difference of only one generation, and the era of these patriarchs is a thousand years before the time of either of these two writers. The most likely explanation in this particular case may be that the development in the text is simply a chance result of an editor's combination of two texts. We cannot even suggest that perhaps the editor intentionally arranged the two stories for the purpose of developing the shift in the divine-human balance, for the editor was bound by the chronology of his source texts. He obviously was not free to set Jacob before Abraham, because by his time the stories of the generations in the order Abraham-Isaac-Jacob had been around for centuries.

The unusual manner in which the parts of the Bible were composed and then combined may even have played a more pervasive role in the development of the hiding of the face of God. As I have said, the consensus in critical scholarship is that an editor assembled the first five books of the Bible (the Torah, Pentateuch, Five Books of Moses) by combining texts from several sources (known in scholarship as J, E, P, and D). Now, these source texts originally duplicated each other on a number of points. For example the E text included a story of Moses striking a rock with a staff in the wilderness at a place called Meribah with the result that water miraculously flowed from the rock. The P text, written somewhat later, included a very similar story, which I emphasized in Chapter 2: Moses strikes a rock with a staff in the wilderness at a place called Meribah, and water miraculously flows from the rock. The editor chose to include both stories, placing one near the beginning of the account of Israel's wandering in the wilderness and one much later in the narrative. So the biblical narrative came to include two stories of miraculous precipitation from rocks. The first now appears in Exodus 17, and the second is in Numbers 20. Such appearances of two very similar stories as a result of the combination of originally separate texts are known in biblical scholarship as doublets, and they occur very frequently in the Five Books of Moses.

Particularly revealing in this regard is the story of the plagues in Egypt, which appears in Exodus 7–12. This narrative is a combination of two originally separate accounts of the plagues. From the first account (E), there are eight plagues, and from the second account (P), there are five. Some of the plagues are the same in both accounts, and some are different, thus:

E	P
blood	blood
frogs	frogs
flies	lice
cattle disease	boils
hail	death of firstborn
locusts	
darkness	
death of firstborn	

Three of the plagues (blood, frogs, and death of firstborn) appeared in both of the source texts. Seven of the plagues (five from E and two from P) were different in each of the source texts. When the redactor combined these two texts into a single account, the result was that there was now a total of ten plagues, more than either author had originally pictured. And the accounts of the three common plagues were now twice as long as in either of the originals, because the redactor retained the texts of both in the combined version. Thus the narrative came to picture a lengthier, more numerous sequence of divine interjections into the order of nature than either source text had pictured alone.

The result of all these cases of united doublets — two rock strikings, ten plagues, and all the rest — was a magnified picture of miraculous divine involvement in the Five Books of Moses. Now it happens that the next six books of the Bible were assembled by a different editor, and the character of this editor's source texts was different as well. This editor's texts had fewer cases of doublets. When this person (known in scholarship as the Deuteronomistic historian) constructed the history of the kings of Israel and Judah, he drew primarily on one source for the kings of Israel and another source for the kings of Judah. Treating the histories of two different kingdoms, these sources rarely duplicated one another. The result was that the combination of the two (into what is now the books of 1 and 2 Kings) did not transform doublets into images of increased miraculous activity. When the Five Books of Moses, with all its doublets, and these next six books later came to be joined as a continuous history in the Bible, the result was a heightened impression of diminishing visible divine involvement in human affairs.[17]

But who is responsible for that impression? Who fashioned that phenomenon in the biblical narrative? Not the authors. Not the editors. It appears to be a side effect of the Bible's singular literary history. A fortuitous side effect.

There are, therefore, a variety of intersecting causes for the phenomenon of the disappearance of God in the Bible. Monotheism plus history plus factors of psychology meant perceiving the age of power, the great age of closeness with the deity, as behind us and always receding (or distantly in front of us, as in the apocalyptic visions of Ezekiel). No matter at what point a biblical author (and that author's audience) lived, if the author was writing about historical ages long past he or she would conceive of God as present and involved in human affairs. When writing of more and more contemporary history, the author would see God as less involved, as the evidence of contemporary events (setbacks, apparent rarity of miracles) attested. And when writing of the distant future, the author could again conceive of the deity as visibly involved. And the character of the literary composition of the Bible (plus an element of chance?) enhanced this development's formation. Through this quite amazing combination of factors, the story of the relations between God and humans in the Hebrew Bible came to include the disappearance of God.

Chapter 5

THE STRUGGLE
WITH GOD

"WHY DO YOU HIDE YOUR FACE?"

Having considered the factors that contributed to producing the disappearance of God in the Bible, we still must face the question of how to interpret this strange phenomenon. In addressing questions of history and authorship, we were, in a sense, peering behind the text, getting a glimpse of the persons, events, and forces that shaped it. In addressing the question of interpretation, we are inquiring into the meaning of the text that these persons, events, and forces have bequeathed to us. In that text's own terms, *why* does God hide His face? Probably the first answer that would occur to most readers would be that it is because of human wrongdoing. In a word: sin. After all, when Yahweh announces to Moses that He will someday hide His face, He says:

> I shall hide my face in that day because of all the wrong that they
> have done, for they turned to other gods.
>
> (Deut 31:18)

The connection to human transgression, particularly apostasy, is explicit. Nonetheless, one should not be too quick to explain this entire development as divine punishment for human misbehavior. First, I am not sure that that explanation accounts for the phenomenon of the shift in the divine-human balance, which does not appear to be an entirely negative experience. On the contrary, humans appear to be pursuing this greater participation in the divine and greater control over their destiny from the moment they reach for the fruit of the tree in Eden. Second, the next biblical reference to God's hiding His face, which comes in the following chapter of the Bible, includes the enigmatic poetic line:

> I shall hide my face from them;
> I shall see what their end will be.
> (Deut 32:20)

The words "I shall see what their end will be" could be read as divine cynicism, implying a sorry end to which these rebellious humans will come once the deity abandons them, in the sense of: "So you think you can manage without me. We'll see about that." But it could also mean that the deity really means to give these independence-seeking humans a chance to direct their own world, and that God will take an interest in seeing how they do.

Indeed, in at least one case God is said to "leave" a man, and the text expressly gives a reason other than any wrongdoing on the man's part. The individual in question is King Hezekiah, who is otherwise rated as one of the two best kings of Judah (2 Kgs 18:5).

> . . . God left him, to test him, to know everything in his heart.
> (2 Chr 32:31)

Here the divine departure is to test the man. To see what his end will be?

Another reason why we cannot explain the disappearance of God solely as punishment for sin is that sin does not necessarily call for divine abandonment, as opposed to some direct physical chastisement. The blessing-and-curse lists of Leviticus 26 and Deuteronomy 28 contain a plethora of punishment options, from agricultural disasters to military defeats to disease. Plague their crops and livestock, smite them with boils, send in the Philistines. But why *leave?!*

Moreover, some of the biblical authors themselves seem to have questioned the reason for the divine hiddenness. When the biblical poets say, "Why do you hide in times of trouble?" (Ps 10:1) and "Why do you hide your face?" (Ps 44:25; Job 13:24) and "My God, my God, why have you left me?" (Ps 22:2), they sound sincerely perplexed about the deity's hiddenness, not at all assuming that it is punishment for their community's behavior.

"A LITTLE LESS THAN GOD"

For that matter, even where divine hiddenness is traced to human violation of covenant in the Bible, that still leaves open the question of why that violation occurs. The biblical picture is not simply — simplistically — that humans are ill-behaved and so God punishes them by removing His presence. Even in the case of Adam and Eve, whom I described earlier as being like naughty children, there is the inception of something more fundamental to the divine-human relationship than disobedience and punishment. The Hebrew Bible, from the very beginning, depicts a profound disjuncture between divine and human. We can discern an essential paradox (or contradiction, or irony) in the divine-human relationship as depicted in the creation story, and it has implications for the stories that follow. God creates the humans in His image and likeness. The meaning of the creation in the image of God is one of the classic enigmas of the Bible, debated and interpreted by scholars, clergy, confirmation classes, and various laypersons. Did the biblical author imagine God anthropomorphically, having a face and hands? (What is implied, then, by the report that both male and female are created in the image of God?) Some rather take the verse to imply that humans are created in the spiritual image of God, or the intellectual image, or the moral image. The arguments are old, well-known, and unresolved; and I for one am willing to say that I just do not know what is meant (though I am tempted by the idea that it has something to do with human *consciousness* being linked to the divine, an idea to which I shall return near the end of this book). What we can say at minimum, though, is that in the Bible's picture of creation, men and women are understood to share in the divine in some way that animals and plants and stones do not. But the paradox is that, even though God has given them this special stature relative to the rest of creation, depositing something of Himself in them, He regularly treats them as subordinates. His first words to them are commands. Multiply. Fill the earth. Dominate the fish and fowl and land creatures. Eat this. Do not eat that. (They are initially created vegetarian; the deity permits them to eat meat only after the flood in their tenth generation; Gen 1:29; 9:1-3.) The deity gives them dominion over the earth (Gen 1:28), but even that is an irony: *commanding* someone to *rule.*

God's first words to the man after putting him in the garden of Eden are:

> You may eat from every tree of the garden, but from the tree of knowledge of good and bad: you may not eat from it.
> (2:16-17)

I doubt that anyone who has ever read that line did not know what the humans were going to do before the end of the story. When the snake tempts the humans to eat the forbidden fruit from the tree of knowledge of good and bad, its argument is: "In the day you eat from it . . . *you will be like God*" (3:5). Presumably, in the Bible's terms this argument would not have appealed to a mouse or a lion or an ape. Only humans are understood to aspire to the divine. The snake's temptation is specifically directed at the creatures who have something of God in them and yet are reminded that they also lack something of God and must obey His directions. They eat from the tree of knowledge of good and bad, and as a result they lose access to the tree of life, the garden, and the state of harmony with their creator (3:22-24). Their actions here are not mere disobedience; they are the obvious, essential point of the narrative, part of the very structure of the story.[1]

In biblical terms, the paradox of being human is to be enough like God to aspire to the divine, but not enough like God to achieve it. One of the most famous verses in the Bible says outright that God has made humans as creatures very close to — but still short of — the deity Himself:

> You have made him a little less than God.
> (Ps 8:6)

It is very difficult to capture the nuance of this phrase in a translation. The verb in the Hebrew (*ḥsr*) means "to lack," and the adverb (*m't*) means "a little," so that the verse would mean something like "You have made him lack [just] a little of God." The Aramaic and Old Greek translators of this verse, apparently uncomfortable with the notion that humans come this close to God, translated the line as "a little lower than the *angels.*" The Vulgate (Latin) translator followed the Greek. So do the King James Version and the Jewish Publication Society translation (1917). The New English Bible (and the Revised English Bible) make it "You have made him little less than a god." The New Jewish Publication Society translation (1985) makes it "You have made him little less than divine." The Revised Standard Version, closest to the translation given here, reads "Thou hast made him little less than God." My point in comparing these various translations is to convey the difficulty of the text. In this case the differences are not just linguistic but theological. This is an extraordinary thing to find in the Bible. While the context of this psalm begins with a humble view of humankind ("What is man that you are mindful of him?" — v. 5), it proceeds to describe the species as coming very close to divine qualities. Though the original clearly refers to humans' lacking just a little of God (Hebrew: *'ĕlōhîm*), some of the translators were sufficiently troubled by that to make it "angels" (though if my understanding of angels in Chapter 1 is correct they were not far off anyway). The larger point is that this passage from biblical poetry is consistent with the prose conception of the early chapters of Genesis. Humans are very close to divinity, close enough to be moved to struggle with it, to build a tower to it, to take what the deity forbids. They are not merely naughty children who disobey their parents. They are more like adolescents who want to be like their parents, to have a share in their parents' world, who need their parents, but who also feel their parents' presence to be intrusive and limiting and humbling. The struggle with the deity is of the very essence of human experience in the Bible's story. The more the deity commands, the more humans disobey. The closer the deity gets, the more they rebel.

As I said in Chapter 1, this is what makes the stories of human rebellion in the Hebrew Bible so remarkable. It is precisely when humans are closest to God that they rebel most blatantly. The wilderness generation has a miraculous column of cloud in front of them all day and a miraculous column of fire all night, every day and every night for forty years. Miraculous food (manna) precipitates out of the dew on the ground every morning, and birds occasionally fly over and drop dead on the ground for them to eat (Exod 16:2–35; Num 11:31–32). When there is no water, water miraculously comes out of rocks (Exod 17:1–7; Num 20:2–

13). When water is bitter, it is miraculously made drinkable (Exod 15:
23–25). When snakes bite, the victims look at a brass snake on a pole and
are cured (Num 21:4–9). Fires swallow various transgressors; an earthquake opens under others (Num 11:1–3; 16:31–35). God speaks from
the sky (Exod 19:17–20:22; Deut 5:2–23). One does not read this and
picture an Israelite asking his friend, "Do you believe in God?" This
generation is pictured as the one generation to have constant visible evidence of their God's presence. And they are pictured as the most rebellious generation of all time.

Meanwhile, at the other end of the divine-human spectrum, in the
books of Ezra, Nehemiah, and Esther, in which the deity's presence is
least visible, the people are relatively obedient. Even when they stray,
they generally submit to their leaders' authority and turn back. The contrast with the wilderness age is intriguing. The generation that is closest
to the deity is the most rebellious. The generations in which the deity is
most hidden behave pretty well. One gets the impression that closeness
to the divine, though tempting, is not tolerable.

Hence the existence of prophets. Precisely because the people are
afraid of direct contact with God they ask Moses to do the speaking to
them. They say: "Let God not speak with us, lest we die." Moses replies,
"Don't be afraid" (Exod 20:20); but they *are.*

Hence the existence of priests. The people direct their attention to
Moses and Aaron, the human agents. Moses says, "Your complaints are
against Yahweh, not us," and he says, "Aaron, what is he that you complain against him?" (Num 16:11). But the people prefer to focus on the
men. The priestly hierarchy of zones of holiness — the ark, the tabernacle, the Holy of Holies, the Holy, the courtyard — allows only the
priests in the holiest place, with the people at a safe distance. The people
never enter the Temple. Their sacrifice, ritual, and prayer take place outside in the courtyard.

Hence the existence of kings. Yahweh tells Samuel to establish the
monarchy "for they have not rejected you, but rather they have rejected
me." The people are more comfortable with a human ruler than with the
divine one.

The divine impinges on human independence. The very presence of a
superior being is frightening. The very presence of the creator whose
image humans imperfectly resemble is humbling. And this superior crea-

tor is a ruler as well. His first words to humans are commands. The one time that He speaks aloud to a large community of humans, at Sinai, He pronounces ten more commands. Through his first great prophet, Moses, he issues six hundred more commands. (According to the traditional count, there are six hundred thirteen commandments in the Torah.) Most humans resist their parents, to some degree, at some point in their lives, craving independence, seeking direction of their own lives. How much more would they resist a *divine* parent, an *all-powerful, always present* father? A father with six hundred commandments? And so they struggle with God.

"AND HE WAS GRIEVED TO HIS HEART"

On these considerations, the Bible should be a much shorter book. God and humans are on a collision trajectory from the outset. It is in the structure of the creation. Yahweh should either come to hide His face or discontinue humankind after a few generations, or at least by the end of Genesis, or certainly by the end of Numbers. The conflict and rebellions and disobedience recur. There appears to be an element of Eve and Adam in everyone. But the creator always seems to give them one more chance.

The humans acquire knowledge of good and bad, and, by the time of the tenth generation of human beings, Yahweh sees that "the bad of humans was great in the earth, and all the inclination of the thoughts of their heart was only bad all day" (Gen 6:5). He decides "I shall erase the humans whom I have created from the face of the earth" (6:7). These opening verses of the flood story would lead a reader to believe that the story of the end of the earth — or at least the end of the species — is coming. But then God selects one human family to save, along with all the animal species. They survive the flood in a giant box (the "ark"), and at the end Yahweh promises never to do this again (8:21–22; 9:11–16). What, then, was the point of the flood? Was it to start the creation over again, with the human species all to be descended from a righteous man this time? If so, then its effect is questionable, because a few generations later people are building the tower of Babel.

Similarly in the wilderness generation, there are more than a dozen accounts of rebellions. Moses tells the people at the end of his forty-year experience with them, "From the day that you went out of the land of Egypt until you came to this place you have been rebelling against Yahweh" (Deut 9:7). On at least two occasions the deity decides to eliminate the people and start over with a new nation descended from Moses (in the golden calf episode and the spies episode), but in both cases He repents.

Most explicitly, the book of Judges states the theme of the book outright in its second chapter (Judg 2:11–20). It is a recurring theme:

1. The Israelites turn to other gods, which makes their God angry.
2. God responds by causing another people to oppress them.
3. They are miserable.
4. God enables a judge to save them.
5. After the judge dies, the Israelites turn to other gods, which makes their God angry.

The book then proceeds with stories that are a series of variations on this theme. The first time they turn to other gods, the Arameans oppress them, so the people cry to Yahweh, and Yahweh establishes the judge Othniel to save them (3:7–11). After Othniel dies, they go wrong again, and the Moabites oppress them, they cry, and Yahweh establishes the judge Ehud to save them (3:12–30). They go wrong again, the Canaanites oppress them, they cry to Yahweh, this time the judge is Deborah, and they are saved again. And so on: Gideon, Tola, Yair, Jephthah, Samson.

The point is that relations between God and humans do not seem to improve, but the deity nevertheless persists in giving the humans another chance. This proceeds through over four centuries of kings of Israel and Judah, all but two of whom are rated as partly or entirely bad, until Yahweh finally brings about the destruction that his prophets have been threatening. And even then, as in the flood story, the destruction turns out to be neither total nor final. He gives them another chance around fifty years later: the exiled Jewish people are allowed to return to their homeland and rebuild their Temple. The text even makes a special point of noting that there are people who have been at Solomon's Temple and who live to see the dedication of the second Temple, which means that the destruction was followed by new hope within a single lifetime. Moreover, even though the narrative obviously concentrates on the record of rebellions and divine reprieves of the people of Israel, it is clear that in this picture the Egyptians, Phoenicians, Canaanites, Edomites, Assyrians, et al., are no great models of behavior either (see, e.g., Amos 1–2). The world that was "exceedingly good" as of the sixth day of creation has proceeded in divine-human tension thereafter, and the creator continues to give second chances. This is a God who keeps on getting angry, and who keeps on forgiving. The question is, if divine-human relations are so continuously (and perhaps inevitably) bad, what motive is attributed to God for the repeated forgiveness and new chances? And the answer is: pity.

When Yahweh decides to bring the flood, the description is:

> And Yahweh regretted that He had made humans in the earth,
> and He was grieved to His heart.
> (Gen 6:6)

This is a curious way to speak about God. The concept of God regretting something is strange enough. If God is all-knowing, how could He possibly regret any past action? Did He not know when He did it what the results would be? But even more striking (to me, anyway) than the issue of that seeming theological contradiction is the picture of the creator of the universe as "grieved to His heart." It is a picture of a God who is disappointed and angry at the beings whom He has created but still is actually pained at their condition and possibly at the idea of hurting them.[2] In a poignant parallel in the poetry of the prophet Hosea, Yahweh decries His people's turning to pagan gods but asks how He can destroy them:

> My heart is turned against me
> My compassions are kindled together
> I shall not execute the fierceness of my anger
> I shall not return to destroy Ephraim[3]
> For I am God and not man
> (Hos 11:8–9)

The first two lines express the divine mercy as an inner conflict in the deity Himself, and the final line suggests that this degree of compassion is singularly divine rather than human. This God of the Bible is torn between His justice and His mercy, between His anger at humans and His love for them (cf. vv. 1, 4). Though destruction is within His physical power, His own heart restrains Him.

To speak of "the Old Testament God of wrath" is partly right: He does get angry. But we must also recognize a counterbalance in the divine character, a compassionate, restraining side which seemingly longs for a solution to the divine-human struggle. In Deut 5:26[4] Moses reports to the people that when they asked that he be their intermediary in place of direct contact with God, Yahweh said to him:

> Who would make it so, that they would have such a heart, to fear me and to keep my commandments, always, so that it would be good for them and for their children forever?

Who would make it so (literally: "Who would give" or "Who would set [it]")? Should *God* have to ask *who* when the answer seems so obviously to be that God Himself could make it so? Indeed, all of the major English translations of Deuteronomy reword this line, eliminating the phrase "Who would make it" (Hebrew: *mî yittēn*; Greek: *tis dosei*), presumably because it seems so incongruous.[5] But we cannot translate the concept away. It is consistent with other biblical depictions of a God whose feelings for humans — pity, compassion, mercy — temper His dissatisfaction with their development. It might even suggest retroactively that the reference to the creation of humans in the image of God should be taken as implying the emotional image, because God is described in these biblical passages as possessing such very human feelings. Even if we suggest that this might be meant as a nonliteral anthropomorphism, still it is a different kind of anthropomorphism from "the hand of God" or even "the face of God." The Hebrew Bible pictures a God who is the most hidden of deities and yet the most personal. He tells you flat-out that you may not see Him, and He is not identifiable with the components of nature, yet He is grieved to His heart. Even if we suggest that it is all meant metaphorically, still, what a metaphor! The fact remains that the biblical narrative explains the continued existence of humankind, despite their inherent conflict with their creator, as owing — metaphorically or literally — to the deity's feelings for them.

"MERCIFUL AND GRACIOUS GOD"

The closest one gets to a view of the character of God in the Hebrew Bible is in the story of the closest experience of God by a human being, the story of Moses at Sinai in Exodus 34. In the moment when Yahweh passes by and Moses glimpses the deity from behind, He pronounces a formula that will be repeated on several later occasions in the Bible, expressing the essential character of God:

> And Yahweh passed before him and called out: "Yahweh, Yahweh, merciful and gracious God, long-suffering[6] and abundant in kindness[7] and truth,[8] keeping faithfulness for thousands, bearing iniquity, transgression, and sin, though He does not utterly excuse, visiting the iniquity of the fathers on the children and on the children's children, on the third [generation] and on the fourth."

> (Exod 34:6–7)

The emphasis of the divine formula is on mercy, conveyed in several different expressions: merciful, gracious, long-suffering, bearing transgression, bearing sin, and so on. The last line ("He does not utterly excuse . . .") is still a reminder that this does not mean that one can just do anything and have the slate wiped clean. There is a conflict between divine justice and mercy, but the full, emphatic point of the formula is nevertheless that Yahweh's essential nature is compassionate and forgiving.

Thus when Yahweh says He will destroy the people and start over with a new people descended from Moses in the spies episode, Moses quotes back the words of this formula as part of his case to dissuade Yahweh:

> And now let my Lord's power be great, as you spoke, saying, "Yahweh is *long-suffering and abundant in kindness, forgiving iniquity and transgression, though He does not utterly excuse, visiting the iniquity of the fathers on the children, on the third [generation] and on the fourth*." Forgive the iniquity of this people according to the

greatness of your kindness, and as you have borne [it] for this
people from Egypt until this point.

(Num 14:18–19)

Yahweh is persuaded by Moses' arguments and says, "I have forgiven according to your words" (4:20).

An almost comical variation on this occurs in the book of Jonah. Recall
that Jonah had tried to flee to Tarshish to avoid his commission to
prophesy to the Assyrian city of Nineveh, but everything from a storm
at sea to a nauseous fish has forced him to do what he was told. He goes
to Nineveh and prophesies that the city will be overturned, but — surprise — the Assyrians actually believe him and repent. So Yahweh relents
and does not do what Jonah has predicted (Jon 3:5–10). This angers
Jonah, and he complains to God, saying:

> Isn't this what I said while I was back on my land? This is why I
> set out to flee to Tarshish. Because I knew that you are a *gracious
> and merciful God, long-suffering, and abundant in kindness, and re-
> lenting of doing harm.*

(4:2)

The incongruity that stands out like the horns on Michelangelo's sculpture of Moses is that Jonah has changed the last words of the formula. He
leaves out the part about God's not utterly excusing, and he substitutes a
phrase that suggests that God always relents. The prophet Joel, who is
known as "the learned prophet" because of the many allusions in the
book of Joel to the words of other biblical prophets, quotes this formula
as it appears in Jonah rather than in its original form from Exodus (Joel
2:13).[9] Several psalms likewise refer to the mercy portion of the formula without referring to the caveat about not utterly excusing (Pss 86:
15; 103:8; 145:8). Repeatedly in the Hebrew Bible, the divine formula
recurs, with increasing focus on the centrality of the deity's mercy.
Terence E. Fretheim noted that, "No other statement can be said to occur so often in the Old Testament."[10]

In two cases this is even connected explicitly to the matter of the hiding of the face and to the idea of God's "leaving." In the first case, following the Assyrian defeat of Israel, King Hezekiah sends a message to all
the people of Israel and Judah, assuring them that their God's anger at
them will subside if they return to Him,

because *gracious and merciful is Yahweh your God,* and *He will not turn the face* from you if you return to Him.[11]

(2 Chr 30:9)

And, in the second case, in the book of Nehemiah the people are assembled as a nation for the last time in the Hebrew Bible, and their leaders give a short account of the history of Yahweh's relations with humans from creation to their own time. It is, as it were, a summary of the Hebrew Bible's story at the end of the narrative; and in the perspective of the Nehemiah summary, there is recurring reference to the "gracious and merciful" formula, tied to the idea of God's not utterly leaving. The speakers refer to the rebellions of the wilderness generation, and they say:

But you are a God of pardons, *gracious and merciful, long-suffering, and abundant in kindness,* and you did not *leave* them.

(Neh 9:17)

They trace a series of merciful divine reprieves (9:19, 27, 28), and they conclude:

But in your great mercies you did not make an end of them, and you did not *leave* them, for you are *a gracious and merciful God.*

(9:31)

The thing that delays the departure of God and offers hope when the divine face is hidden is the massive divine compassion. This is a God who, it appears, cannot stay mad. He is just but also merciful, angry but also forgiving. The prophet Micah says at the end of his book, seemingly in wonder:

> *Who is a God like you?*
> bearing iniquity and passing over transgression
> for the remnant of His inheritance
> He has not held onto His anger forever
> for He desires kindness
> (Mic 7:18)

The deity's pity for the children whom He has created in His image repeatedly yields them another chance, for millennia.

"A GOD WHO HIDES HIMSELF"

The disappearance of God is thus a complex development that derives from both the nature of God and the nature of humans — and from the dynamic between the two. God creates humans in the divine image but subordinates them. They aspire to the divine but are unable to attain it, unable to tolerate its closeness, and unable to endure their subordinate role. God commands, and they rebel. They transgress. This, in turn, angers God, but He pities humans and therefore persists in giving them another chance. No number of second chances changes the situation, however. Humans do not want to hear God. They want to be like God. Though men and women suffer for their conflict with God — and seemingly God suffers for it as well — it is pictured more as the necessary outcome of the relationship than as simple misbehavior by humankind. It is not just that God is good and humans are bad. It is rather that God is God and humans are humans. The very nature of the divine is at odds with the very nature of human beings, and perhaps they are incompatible precisely because humans have something of the divine in them.[12] And, since the Bible attributes the creation of man and woman to God, this still leaves open the question of why the deity chooses to create the species with such a nature. In Nietzsche's formulation, the Bible begins with a mistake on God's part. As Mark Twain put it, "If the Lord didn't want humans to be rebellious, why did He create them in His image?!" To the grief of both God and humans, their natures continually leave them in conflict. And so the deity becomes more hidden. It is not exactly that God makes this happen, and it is not exactly that humans make it happen. It is in the very nature of the divine-human struggle, which is to say, in the very nature of the creation.

This two-sided aspect of the hiding of the face of God is captured in a subtle grammatical ambiguity in the book of Isaiah. At one point the prophet speaks of human wrongdoing as the cause of this hiddenness, saying, "Your sins have hidden the face from you" (59:2). But at another point, the prophet says:

Indeed, you are a God who hides Himself.

(45:15)

That is how most translations render the Hebrew. The Hebrew verb (*mistattēr*) occurs in a conjugation that is sometimes a passive form and sometimes a reflexive in biblical Hebrew (the Hitpael; cf. Isa 29:14). That is, the text can mean "a God who is hidden" or "a God who hides Himself." It is not simply a question of translation, but of meaning. The grammatical ambiguity, as it happens, corresponds to the twin dynamic in the biblical narrative. It is both human actions that cause the divine face to become gradually concealed from them, and the deity Himself who chooses to conceal His face.

The grammatical ambiguity coincides even more with the corollary of the divine hiddenness: the shift in the divine-human balance. This development itself involves an essential ambiguity: In the biblical picture, does God bestow the greater human control, or do humans take it? From one perspective one sees humankind struggling to control their own lives, but there are hints in the text that suggest another perspective: that the deity, like a wise parent, gradually steps back, allowing humans to grow up and incrementally take more responsibility for their lives. In the very first scene in this development, man and woman take the forbidden fruit of the tree of knowledge. That is their own doing, from which they derive the benefit, and for which they pay the consequences. But, after all, it is the deity who is pictured as planting the garden and setting a tree of knowledge there. What is the purpose of *creating* such a fruit tree — since no one is allowed to eat from it? Shade? One might say that it is to test humans, to see if they will take that first step into independence, or one might say that it is precisely to *draw* them to take the first step. We cannot know, because the text does not go into divine motives here. It rarely does. And so we are left with this ambiguity concerning the extent to which the deity initiates the shift in the divine-human balance.

At several subsequent junctures in the narrative, the impression that the shift is a two-sided coin is reinforced. Humans do not unilaterally insert themselves into divine territory. God, as well, is pictured as involving humans in the drama of decision and action. In the case in which Abraham is able to question God's decision to destroy Sodom and Gomorrah, how does Abraham come to be discussing Yahweh's plans for those cities in the first place? The discussion only occurs because Yahweh determines that it is important to inform Abraham of what is about to be done. In a rare case of narrating the deity's inner thoughts in the Bible, the text says:

> And Yahweh said, "Shall I hide from Abraham what I am doing, since Abraham will become a big and powerful nation, and all the nations of the earth will be blessed through him? For I have known him so that he will command his children and his household after him that they will keep Yahweh's way, to do righteousness and justice, in order for Yahweh to bring on Abraham that which He has spoken about him."
>
> (Gen 18:17–19)

The deity asks if it is right to hide this matter from Abraham. That is remarkable in itself. Why, after all, should anyone have expected the creator of the universe to have to share His personal plans with a human? And the deity decides that He should not hide it from him. That is even more remarkable. The reason Yahweh gives for making Abraham privy to a divine decision is that ultimately this will have consequences for all the earth: the result of Abraham's acquaintance with the deity is that Abraham, through his descendants, is to be a force for justice among humankind. Yahweh says that He is telling Abraham what is brewing in Sodom so as to achieve this result. And it works. Abraham's exchange with God over the fate of the cities results in Abraham's recognizing and eloquently formulating the significance of justice for future generations: the good cannot suffer for the crimes of the bad; the judge of all the earth must do justice. God has successfully drawn Abraham to be a force for justice. But, in achieving this end, the deity has also drawn a human being into realms of decision and action that, prior to this point in the Bible, have pertained solely to God.[13]

At several of the junctures we have observed in which humans gradually acquire more control of the direction of events, there are such ambiguities concerning how much the deity is actually leading the humans to act. Perhaps the most subtle and intriguing case involves a remarkable bit of poetic artistry in the Jacob and Esau story. We have observed how Rebekah and Jacob take matters in their own hands and redirect the divine blessing from Esau to Jacob, and we have noted that this constitutes a significant stage in the shift toward increasing human control. But a brief episode earlier in the story raises some doubts as to whose hands are pulling the strings. When Rebekah is pregnant with the twins Jacob and Esau, she receives an oracle from God telling her about the destiny of the two boys. The oracle includes the words "the elder will serve the younger," and people have usually taken this to mean that Yahweh tells her that her younger son, Jacob, will dominate her older one, Esau (Gen 25:23). Some readers have thought, therefore, that Rebekah is not really manipulating the succession when she sends Jacob to pose as Esau. Rather, she is simply fulfilling the will of God. The decision of who is number-one son thus is still the deity's. However, this understanding is based on a mis-understanding of a subtle, exquisitely ambiguous biblical wording. The text does not in fact say that the elder son will serve the younger son. One of the complexities of biblical Hebrew that confuses students who are first learning the language is that word order in this language is more fluid than in English and most other European and Near Eastern languages. In English the subject of the sentence usually comes before the verb, and the object usually comes after it. In biblical Hebrew, the subject may either precede or follow the verb, and the object likewise may either precede or follow the verb. What that means is that sometimes it is impossible to tell which word in a biblical verse is the subject and which is the object, especially if the verse is in poetry. That is the case in this oracle to Rebekah, which is in poetry. It can mean:

"the elder will serve the younger"

But it equally can mean:

"the elder, the younger will serve"

Like the Delphic oracles in Greece, this prediction contains two opposite meanings, and thus the person who receives it — in this case, Rebekah — can hear whatever she wants (consciously or subconsciously) to hear. It can be understood to mean that Jacob will serve Esau or that Esau will serve Jacob.[14] This story therefore has an element similar to what we saw in the case of Abraham's exchange with God over Sodom and Gomorrah. God Himself draws the humans into the matter, but then the humans themselves act in such a way as to direct the course of events. In this case, it is Rebekah and Jacob who act, their actions affect a succession that will have consequences for human destiny, and God accepts the result.

In Moses' case, too, God is pictured as, at least partly, contributing to the chain of events that leads to Moses' actions. I spoke of the episode of Moses' getting water from the rock at Meribah as a major step in the shift in the divine-human balance. Moses says, "Shall *we* bring water out of this rock," and he strikes the rock instead of speaking to it, which is the first case in which a human changes a miracle. Still, Yahweh's specific instructions to Moses in that story are:

> Take the staff and assemble the congregation, you and Aaron your brother, and speak to the rock before their eyes, and it will give its water. And *you* shall bring water out of the rock for them.
>
> (Num 20:8)

We cannot take the narrative to be condemning Moses unequivocally for saying, "Shall *we* bring water out of this rock," instead of "Shall *God*." For God Himself has said here in His instructions to Moses, "And *you* shall bring water out" instead of "And *I* shall bring water out." God's own words have already planted the concept and the wording in Moses. Nor can we take the striking of the rock with the staff instead of talking to it as unequivocally marking Moses as culpable, for the deity's curious instructions are: "Take the staff . . . and speak to the rock." [15] If Moses is only supposed to speak, why does he need a staff in his hand? Is he supposed to talk softly and carry a big stick? Why does the deity put the instructions in terms that have the potential to draw Moses to trespass a divine boundary? One could argue that it is to test Moses, or that it is precisely to produce the outcome of drawing humans to take initiative. The text does not say, for, again, the motives of God are rarely stated in biblical narrative. What we know is simply that Moses' actions in response to the divine instructions constitute a new pinnacle in human direction of miracle.

The entire matter of the establishment of monarchy in the Bible reflects this ambiguity regarding the extent of divine inception as well. Gideon refuses the crown on the grounds that "I shall not rule you, and my son will not rule you; Yahweh will rule you." Yahweh tells Samuel, "They have not rejected you, but rather they have rejected *me*." And Samuel tells the people as he gives them a king, "You have rejected your God today." All of this certainly sounds as if the inauguration of kingship constitutes a human foray into divine territory. Nonetheless, the deity had already provided for the institution of monarchy in the laws that He gave to Moses back in Deuteronomy, which included the Law of the King. One cannot regard the people's desire for a king as purely a human plan when, the first time that the notion of a king in Israel is mentioned, it is God who raises it — and expressly allows it.

Interestingly, and significantly, even the idea of fighting with God is not presented pejoratively. When Jacob struggles with God, the deity does not chastise Jacob for it; and, when He bestows the name Israel ("fights with God") on him at the end of the struggle, it is done as a *blessing!* (Gen 32:25–33)

So the deity may be responsible for the shift in the divine-human balance. We cannot easily say *how* responsible. We may say that the humans are boldly grasping an ever stronger status; or we may say that the deity, like a wise parent, is drawing the humans to take ever more responsibility; or we may say that ultimately the deity is in control of all human actions, even including their rebellions anyway; or we may suggest numerous other explanations and perspectives of the divine role. Likewise, with the increasing divine hiddenness, we cannot be certain of the degree of divine determination. Is it more correctly conceived as divine parental wisdom, divine punishment for rebellion, or divine acquiescence to human wishes, as at Sinai? All of this suggests what a potentially rich source of interpretation this phenomenon of the disappearance of God may be. At the very least we can say that it is a mutual phenomenon, involving both a divine component and a human component, and we can say that it is not entirely negative.

"IT IS A TREE OF LIFE"

Thus the hiding of the face of God and the related shift in the divine-human balance are not as pessimistic a concept as one might think. They entail divine and human grief, but they also entail divine compassion and human maturation and independence. Moreover, another element occasionally surfaces in the texts, an element that one may find either comforting or troubling, but in any case mysterious, namely a suggestion of a future reunion with God. In Chapter 3 we saw several cases in which biblical poets refer to eventual reappearances of the signs of divine presence that have diminished. Isaiah and Ezekiel prophesy the reappearance of the divine "glory" in some distant future (Isa 35:2; 40:5; 60:1–2; Ezek 43:4–5; 44:4).[16] Ezekiel predicts a day when "I shall not hide my face from them anymore" (39:29). We saw in Isaiah, as well, a prophecy that:

> For a small moment I left you,
> but with great mercies I shall gather you.
> In a little anger I hid my face for a moment from you,
> but with everlasting faithfulness I shall have mercy on you.
>
> (54:7–8)

We also saw a case from the Psalms, in the very psalm that begins with the words "My God, my God, why have you left me?" in which the psalmist also includes an implication of hope or confidence that the deity's presence will once again be apparent in the future (22:25). Notably, in the time of the second Temple in Jerusalem, the time in which the face of God is hidden and humans have apparent control of their destiny, the latest of the biblical prophets quote Yahweh as saying:

> Return to me, and I shall return to you
> (Zech 1:3; Mal 3:6–7)

The idea of a possible return of humans to their lost state of harmony with their creator emerges in a tantalizing aspect of the biblical narrative as well. The biblical account begins with the humans living in a condition of closeness with God, who walks in the garden with them and talks with them. Their felicitous relationship with God is aptly symbolized by the tree of life, which Yahweh has made available to them. He has forbidden only the tree of knowledge of good and bad (Gen 2:16–17). They are free to eat from the tree of life and live forever, a divine gift. The initial condition of creation is thus that God and humans can dwell together in a paradise forever. The act that ends this and brings about the humans' estrangement from God is their eating from the tree of knowledge of good and bad. The deity then banishes them from the garden of Eden precisely to prevent them from eating from the tree of life (3:22–24). By acquiring knowledge of good and bad, humans lose access to the tree of life and, with that, access to the place where they lived in unity and closeness with God. It is significant, though, that the tree of life and the garden of Eden are not destroyed; they are made inaccessible. Specifically, Yahweh sets cherubs and a fiery sword to guard the path back to the tree (3:24). Theoretically, therefore, the possibility of a future reconciliation and return to Eden exists.

It may in fact be more than theoretical. The humans have acquired the power to make judgments of good and bad, and the power to choose between the two. It is through this channel of knowledge of good and bad, the very channel that estranged them from paradise, that mortals may have an opportunity to return eventually to the divine-human harmony associated with Eden and the tree of life. Having disobediently appropriated this knowledge, they may now cultivate it, aiming to arrive at the highest form of knowledge in the Bible: wisdom. And the book of Proverbs characterizes wisdom this way: "It is a *Tree of Life!*" (3:18). Now able to distinguish between good and bad, they can choose to be unethical or righteous. And the book of Proverbs characterizes the righteous person's contribution this way: "The fruit of the righteous is a *Tree of Life!*" (11:30). The banishment from the garden and the tree of life is not necessarily eternal. The text never states that it is unending. Though humans have rebelled and cherubs now block their path to the tree and the garden, Yahweh makes a series of covenants with them. The text of the covenant of Sinai, inscribed on tablets, is kept in a golden box, "the ark of the covenant," and on top of the ark are two golden cherubs. And when the ark is placed in the Holy of Holies in the Temple it rests under the wings of two immense golden statues of cherubs. The placement of statues of cherubs over the ark and its precious contents is singularly appropriate. The cherubs keep watch over the path to the tree of life, and their images symbolically keep watch over the keys to the path back: covenant, Torah, knowledge, wisdom.[17]

Thus the divine hiddenness is not depicted as final. It may be that the situation by the end of the Hebrew Bible is not that the divine and the human cannot coexist, but that they are not yet *ready* to coexist. Even after one has observed the disappearance of God in the Hebrew Bible one is left with the observation that this tapestry of divine-human acquaintance and divine-human balance and divine-human struggle also includes the possibility of divine-human reunion.

"THE HIDDEN THINGS BELONG TO YAHWEH"

One last point: the mysteriousness of Yahweh. From the beginning of the book to the end, the essence of God remains unknown. Shamash is the sun. Baal is the storm wind. Asherah is fertility. Yamm is the sea. But what is Yahweh? Residing outside of nature, known only through words and through acts in history, God in the Bible remains a mystery. The stuff of Yamm is the sea waters, but what is the "stuff" of the God of the Bible? Even when God in the Bible is most intimately known to humans — in the garden of Eden, at the revelation at Sinai — they are not privileged with an iota of knowledge of the substance of God. To appreciate the biblical relationship between God and humans in general, and the disappearance of God in particular, one must have a sense of the extreme mystery that surrounds the deity like the divine cloud. God is an enigma to humans when in visible contact with them and is the memory of an enigma after becoming hidden. The most that humans are allowed to know is the outward personality of Yahweh: a merciful and gracious God, long-suffering, abundant in kindness . . . But what Yahweh *is* is the Bible's unspoken, pervasive mystery.

Among Moses' last words to the people before he dies, he tells them:

> The hidden things belong to Yahweh our God, and the revealed things belong to us and to our children forever, to do all the words of this Torah.

(Deut 29:28)

The focus is not on the discovery of the essence of God but on what humans have to do, here in this world. The Five Books of Moses and the prophetic books concentrate on the kind of life they should lead. The wisdom books (Proverbs, Job, and Ecclesiastes) concentrate on the wisdom they can pursue. But the nature of God remains a mystery. That is how the Hebrew Bible ends, with a mysterious God who has hidden the divine face from humans, leaving them in apparent charge of their world. This condition was part of the legacy of that book and that age, a legacy that was received by two religions, Judaism and Christianity, and it became a part of them.

Chapter 6

THE LEGACY
OF THE AGE

In the first few centuries following the end of the composition of the Hebrew Bible, two great religious developments occurred: (1) The religion of the Jews proceeded into a new stage, which we call rabbinic Judaism. (2) Christianity was born, a new religion, which nonetheless looked back to the Hebrew Bible as its cradle. We have no reason to think that any of the early Christians or the rabbis observed the step-by-step development of the disappearance of God through the course of the Hebrew Bible's narrative. But, at the very least, we can say that both religions developed with a consciousness of the divine hiddenness. In Judaism the term for it was the Hebrew *hestēr pānîm*, which means "the hiding of the face." According to one rabbinic text, which cites God's words to Moses at the end of Deuteronomy:

> No hour is as grievous as that hour whereof it is written, "And I shall surely hide My face . . ."[1]

In Christianity, the term was the Latin *Deus absconditus*, which comes directly from Isa 45:15, the verse that I discussed in the preceding chapter as meaning either a "hidden God" or a "God who hides Himself."

Divine hiddenness was an issue in both religions. My particular concern in the context of this book, though, is perspective. Once we have observed the phenomenon of the diminishing apparent presence of God in the Hebrew Bible, how do these two great religious developments appear against this background? Or: if God dis-appears by the end of the Hebrew Bible, what happens next?

RABBINIC JUDAISM: THE TWO TORAHS

The great days of the kings, prophets, and priests were over. Especially after the Romans destroyed the second Temple in Jerusalem, in 70 C.E., the role of the priests diminished dramatically. According to the biblical law, one could offer sacrifices only at the Temple and nowhere else on earth.[2] The destruction of the Temple therefore meant the end of sacrifices, and that in turn meant the end of the primary function and the livelihood of the priests.

Meanwhile, a new group of religious figures had been forming: rabbis. The term rabbi does not occur in the Hebrew Bible, but after several centuries of the post-biblical period these figures rose to prominence. They were people who were learned in the Hebrew Bible and especially in the biblical laws. The term rabbi meant "my great one" or "my master" and indicates the respect that their adherents accorded to them. The Hebrew Bible ends with the word of God, the Torah, being read publicly in Jerusalem at the watergate — by priests (Nehemiah 8). Judaism had developed as a religion of law, dedicated to the principle that one should live one's life according to the commandments contained in the Torah. In the centuries following Ezra, the text of the Torah had come to be held sacred, and, with the diminished status of the priests, that text was now in the hands of the rabbis. That is, the rabbis had the authority to explain, interpret, and make rulings on it. There is already an irony in this. The religion was based on obedience to the law, which is to say, obedience to God, but it placed the interpretation of this law in human hands. The shift in the divine-human balance had come to the point at which the comprehension and execution of the word of God was the responsibility of human beings. But that was only part of the picture.

The Torah appears to be incomplete as a law code. A classic example of this incompleteness is the fact that it contains laws regarding the procedure for divorce but no laws stating the procedure for getting married. If it was possible to get divorced, one assumes that it was possible to get married. Nonetheless, no marriage ceremony is described. The rabbis, however, had traditions about many of the matters that were not specifically described in the text of the Torah, and they understood these traditions to be centuries old. When a rabbi gave instructions on how to become married, it was understood that the rabbi learned these instructions from his predecessors, who learned them from their own predecessors, and so on back through centuries. At some point, though, there was a metamorphosis in the understanding of tradition. A new doctrine was born, the doctrine of the two Torahs.

According to this belief, the teachings of the rabbis were not merely old traditions, not even merely ancient, sacred traditions; rather, they went back in an unbroken chain to Moses on Sinai. In the major work of rabbinic Judaism, the Talmud (codified circa 500 C.E.), the first-century C.E. teacher Hillel is quoted as saying that there are two Torahs (Hebrew: *tôrôt*), the written Torah that appears in the Bible and a second, *oral*, Torah.[3] During the time that Moses was in communication with God he was not just writing down the text that the deity dictated to him; God was also revealing to Moses a great deal of other instruction which Moses was forbidden to record in writing. Instead, Moses was to pass it on by word of mouth. According to the opening words of one of the tractates of the Talmud (Mishna Abot 1:1):

> Moses received the Torah from Sinai,
> and he passed it to Joshua,
> and Joshua to the elders,
> and the elders to the prophets,
> and the prophets passed it to the men of the great assembly.

That is, there was continuous transmission of this revelation from Moses to the "men of the great assembly," and the men of the great assembly are further identified as the forerunners of the rabbis.[4] This is remarkable in a variety of ways. First, relative to the gradually increasing divine hiddenness, when one of my students learned this passage she commented that here the word of God is "five times removed" from the people. The text does indeed convey the feeling of distance in time and directness from the experience at Sinai. (Leon Wieseltier put it elegantly, in comparing rabbinic Judaism to the biblical stage: "It was precisely when the report of a voice did the work of a voice that tradition was born," and "In

the Bible, tradition was never all there was. There was experience, too."[5])
Second, it is interesting that the list does not include the priests. Passing
from the elders to the prophets to the rabbis, the chain of authorities in
possession of the oral Torah excludes the group whom the rabbis had
once rivaled and now replaced as the chief religious authority. Moreover,
the Bible had pictured God as personally choosing the first priest, Aaron,
and establishing a covenant with Aaron's family thereafter, making the
priesthood a hereditary office. Sons followed their fathers into the priesthood, and no one who was not a priest's son could ever become a priest.
It was thus a divinely chosen and divinely ordained line. The position of
rabbi, on the other hand, was not hereditary. Based on merit rather than
paternity, one became a rabbi by choosing to be one and by possessing
the ability to carry out the task. In this sense, too, there was a degree of
enhancement of the human role.

Most important of all, though: with the doctrine of the "oral Torah"
the rabbis placed their own traditions and rulings on a par with the Bible.
Scholars differ as to when this metamorphosis took place,[6] but there is no
overestimating how momentous it was. In a classic work on rabbinic Judaism, Ephraim Urbach wrote (using the terms "fathers" and "Sages"
for the rabbinic authorities):

> The tradition of the fathers, the enactments, and the decrees be-
> came Torah alongside the written Torah.[7]

> The expositions of the Sages possess decisive authority and de-
> serve at least the same place in the scale of religious values as the
> Written Torah, and in truth transcend it.[8]

Lawrence Schiffman put it this way:

> . . . this material became the new scripture of Judaism, and the
> authority of the Bible was now defined in terms of how it was
> interpreted in the rabbinic tradition. Scripture had been dis-
> placed by Talmud.[9]

Jacob Neusner has referred to the doctrine of the two Torahs as "the
central myth of rabbinic civilization."[10] To orthodox Jews, of course, it is
no myth; but they would hardly differ on the point that it is central.
Prophecy was over.[11] Miracle was over.[12] The rabbis were open to the

possibility of an occasional prophecy or miracle; but, first, they recognized that these things had diminished (according to one text, "Rav Papa inquired of Abbaye: 'Why is it that miracles happened to the former generations, but to us no miracle happens?'"[13]), and, second, these things could not outweigh the decisions of the rabbis. "The Almighty himself is bound by them."[14]

"MY CHILDREN HAVE DEFEATED ME"

The rabbis frequently had disagreements among themselves about the law, but the existence of disagreements was explainable and reconcilable within their system. The rabbis, after all, were separated by a millennium and a half from the time when Moses was believed to have descended Mount Sinai. That is a long time to maintain a vast corpus of law from generation to generation by oral transmission with precise memory. Conflicting recollections would naturally arise, resulting in disagreements over what the law said. When there was disagreement among the rabbis about a law, the majority ruled. A piece of a biblical verse, "to follow the many" (Exod 23:2), was cited as grounds for deciding according to the rabbinic majority, even though the verse in its biblical context appears to mean something completely different. This procedure conveys poignantly how profound this new, post-biblical stage in the shift of the divine-human balance was. In this doctrine, the word of God from Sinai was subject to a democratic vote of a group of human authorities. Once that group voted, nothing could overrule them. Not even a prophet. Not even a miracle. Not even a voice from the sky.

I mean that literally. An extraordinary story appears in the Talmud, which is frequently referred to in discussions of this matter of the authority of the rabbis. According to this story, on one occasion a majority of the rabbis rejected the view of Rabbi Eliezer. Eliezer attempted every argument he could muster to persuade the majority that he was correct in a particular matter, but they rejected his view. So right there at the academy where they assembled, miracles occurred. But they still rejected his view. Then a voice from the sky informed them that Eliezer was right. And they still rejected his view, citing a piece of a verse from Deuteronomy: "It is not in the heavens" (Deut 30:12). There is a sort of epilogue to the story, in which Rabbi Nathan happens upon the prophet Elijah some time later, and Elijah informs him of what God said on that day that the rabbis overruled Him. Here is the story as it appears in the Talmud.[15] Take particular note of what God says in the epilogue.

In that day Rabbi Eliezer gave every response in the world. And they did not accept his view.

He said to them, "If the law is as I say, let this carob tree prove it." The carob tree was uprooted a hundred cubits from its place. And some say four hundred cubits.

They said, "There is no bringing verification from a carob tree."

He responded and said to them, "If the law is as I say, let the water duct prove it." The water duct turned backwards [i.e., the water reversed and flowed upstream].

They said to him, "There is no bringing verification from a water duct."

He responded and said to them, "If the law is as I say, let the walls of the academy prove it." The walls of the academy bent to fall down.

Rabbi Joshua rebuked them [the walls]. He said to them, "If scholars dispute with one another about the law, how is it your concern?" They did not fall down, out of respect for Rabbi Joshua. And they did not straighten, out of respect for Rabbi Eliezer. And they are still standing bent.

He responded and said to them, "If the law is as I say, let them prove it from the heavens." A voice emanated and said, "What [standing] do you have beside Rabbi Eliezer, for the law is as he says in every case."

Rabbi Joshua stood on his feet and said, "It is not in the heavens."

What is the meaning of "It is not in the heavens"? Rabbi Jeremiah said, "[The meaning is] that the Torah has already been given at Mount Sinai. We do not pay attention to a voice, for You have already written at Mount Sinai in the Torah: 'to follow the many.'"

Rabbi Nathan met Elijah. He said to him, "What did the Holy
One Blessed Be He do at that time?"

He said to him, "He laughed. And He said, 'My children have
defeated me. My children have defeated me.'"

In the light of the hiding of the face of God and the shift in the divine-
human balance in the Bible, this is simply an amazing next step. The
human authorities, citing a text revealed by God, ruling by the authority
of a text revealed by God, reject divine intervention and overrule God.
The rabbis have declared that their traditions, decisions, and expositions
of texts are Torah — equal to the Torah in the Bible. The Torah is now
in the hands of humans, and not even God can change it.

I do not mean to exaggerate the importance of the Eliezer story. It is
just one story out of a mass of rabbinic literature, a huge corpus that
contains a variety of views and perspectives. I emphasize it here because,
first, I think that it is significant that such a story was told and that it was
included in the Talmud and not suppressed. Second, as I have said, the
story is frequently cited or alluded to in discussions of rabbinic Judaism
and so has come to acquire a centrality in this subject. Neusner refers to
it on the first page of an explication of rabbinic Judaism.[16] When the
medievalist Isadore Twersky discusses the great medieval Jewish philosopher Maimonides, he says:

> Maimonides emphasizes that the Oral Law is a completely ra-
> tional enterprise, subject to its own canons of interpretation,
> and brooking no suprarational interference. It follows that even
> prophecy is of little relevance to the juridical process. Only the
> prophecy of Moses was legislative — and therefore unique; all
> subsequent prophecy was exhortatory, based on moral persua-
> sion, and could not create new laws. . . . A thousand prophets
> would not, therefore, outweigh a thousand and one jurists, for
> the juridical principle of majority rule, absolutely indifferent to
> claims of special inspiration or heavenly instruction, would pre-
> vail. The Torah "is not in heaven" (Deut 30:12).[17]

Allusions like these to Eliezer and to that story's conclusion that "it is not
in the heavens" are common. A third reason for emphasizing the Eliezer

story here is that I use this tale as a metaphor for what rabbinic Judaism represents against the background of the disappearance of God. The tale has particular relevance to the concept of the human struggle with God. Here the creator declares "My children have defeated Me," and this is not pictured as being said in anger or as threatening. Rather, as the deity says it, He laughs. It is reminiscent of the biblical account of the deity's changing Jacob's name to Israel ("for you have struggled with God and prevailed") as a *blessing*. What analogy would be appropriate? Is it like a parent who, for the first time, loses to his or her child at a sport, or is corrected by the child on a point of fact — and, though perhaps annoyed, the parent is also pleased at the sight of the child growing older and more capable? So in rabbinic Judaism there is a focus on showing humans how to live, on living life in accordance with the Torah (meaning with *both* Torahs). In one passage in rabbinic literature the deity actually says: "Would that you would forsake me but keep my Torah." [18] Certainly one could say that there is a catch here, because it still says, "but keep my Torah," and persons who observe the biblical laws are unlikely to forsake the deity. Indeed, the fact is that historically those who have most meticulously endeavored to keep the Torah have not done so at the neglect of their God. On the contrary, though observant persons, such as orthodox Jews, are sometimes accused of concentrating on the outward practices rather than on the spiritual, divine aspect behind those practices, the charge is usually untrue. There are, no doubt, persons of whom this is true, but, at least in my experience, religiously observant individuals and communities tend to be no less consciously, piously concerned with the deity than others. So the notion of "forsake me but keep my Torah" is arguably an oxymoron, expressing acute divine wisdom. Still, the phrase suggests a focus on the divinely prescribed way of life rather than on the divinity, and that is religiously noteworthy, especially since the identification of that way of life has been left in the hands of humans, and divine interference, such as miracles and voices, has been excluded.

Like the Hebrew Bible, the religion of the rabbinic stage of Judaism was still about God, but it was constructed in terms of a concern with the way God directs humans to live. In a classic story from rabbinic literature the single most central principle is said to be, "What is hateful to you, do not do to your neighbor." Of all the commandments that could have been selected, the one that is identified as primary is the quintessential commandment regarding humans' relations with other humans — known now as "the golden rule" — as opposed to a commandment such as "You shall have no other gods before Me" or even "Love the Lord your God with all your heart and with all your soul and with all your might," which concerns humans' relations with the deity. Post-biblical, rabbinic Judaism — the stage that prevails as normative Judaism to this day — appears to be a consistent next step to the biblical developments. It included the expression "the hiding of the face of God," it included the concept that was reflected by this expression — namely that the deity was less visibly present now than in past times — and it included the doctrine of the two Torahs, which meant a new degree of human focus, authority, and responsibility.

CHRISTIANITY: "THE WORD BECAME FLESH"

In the same period that rabbinic Judaism was forming, Christianity was born. As with my discussion of Judaism, I do not mean to mount a broad analysis of the early history and doctrines of the religion, but only to consider how the phenomenon of the disappearance of God in the Hebrew Bible relates to some essential aspects of the religion and its literature. Against the backdrop of the Hebrew Bible, one reads in the first four books of the New Testament — Matthew, Mark, Luke, and John, the four Gospels — a narrative in which, after centuries of hiddenness, the deity once again manifests His presence visibly in human form. There had been nothing like this since the Genesis accounts of Eden and Jacob's struggle with God. Over a millennium had passed since, according to the Hebrew Bible, the creator told Moses, "I shall hide My face from them," and then, in one moment, there is the most immediate expression of the divine presence on earth since Sinai. There is scholarly controversy over when the doctrine that Jesus was an incarnation of God took hold. Whatever doubt there is of incarnation in Matthew, Mark, and Luke — known as the Synoptic Gospels — it appears to be explicit in the Gospel of John, both in passages that identify Jesus as "Lord" and "God" (John 20:18, 28) and in the famous opening of the book:

In the beginning was the word,
and the word was with God,
and the word was God.

And the word became flesh
and dwelled among us.

(1:1, 14)

Whether one understands the depiction of Jesus at any point in the Gospels to be as God, son of God, messiah, expression of God, or incarnation of God, one can say minimally that the narratives picture something of the divine in human form as never before. And once the doctrine of the incarnation becomes normative in Christianity, that distinction between the gospels and the narratives of the Hebrew Bible is sharpened. Even Jacob's struggle with the deity in Genesis was understood, at least by the prophet Hosea, to involve an angel; and the notion of an incarnation certainly seems to exceed angels as I understood them in Chapter 1 or, indeed, as anyone understands them. The central being of the New Testament is child of a human mother and divine father. He is depicted as someone who looks like a man, who *is* a man, but who is also from the divine realm.

In the context we have been observing, the portrayal of God taking human form may be seen as the ultimate step in the divine-human shift. It is powerful, striking, mysterious, and ironic that, though Jesus comes from the divine realm, "the one title he constantly uses of himself, always in third person"[19] in Matthew is "son of man" (Greek *ho huios tou anthropou*, translating Hebrew *ben 'ādām* or *ben 'ĕnôš*, Aramaic *bar 'ĕnāš*). In all four Gospels, only Jesus uses this term (with one exception) and only of himself. The term is already common in the Hebrew Bible, where it occurs one hundred nine times and simply means "human being." The one time in the Hebrew Bible that it is used in connection with someone who is other than an ordinary human being is in a vision in the book of Daniel (7:13), where a cloud-borne figure is identified as looking *like* a son of man. The great majority of occurrences of the term (ninety-three) are in the book of Ezekiel, where it refers to the prophet Ezekiel himself. The question of the meaning of this term in the New Testament is an entire area of analysis and differing views, certainly too much to introduce here;[20] but, in a limited way, I note that this is Jesus' main term for himself in the New Testament, and I especially want to take note of its meaning as "human being" in the perspective of the hiding of the face of God and the shift in the divine-human balance in the Hebrew Bible. I surmise that much of the complexity and controversy of the term in readings of the New Testament owes to the fact that the authors of the Gospels picture Jesus as more than an ordinary human, yet they regularly picture him as referring to himself as "human being." It strikes me that the irony involved in his calling himself this is precisely what is so powerful. Compare it to a story of a princess who goes incognito among the masses and so calls herself by some unroyal-sounding name like "Maggie." Every time she calls herself Maggie in the story it is ironic. And after it is revealed in the end that she is in fact the princess and is actually named something like Princess Margaret Victoria, everyone who met her in the story now thinks back with awe and embarrassment about every time he or she called her Maggie. Does a story in which the deity walks incarnate among humans as a man not bear at least as much irony? Every time he calls himself "son of man" it resounds with implications, consequences, and imminent revelations, with things that the readers know but the persons in the story do not. No one in the story is depicted as realizing who Jesus is. When Pilate points at Jesus and says, "*Ecce homo*" ("Behold the *man*"), his remark is incongruous, ironic, and even pathetic. Against the background of the divine hiddenness the irony is enriched. After centuries of hiddenness the divine takes a visible form, walking on earth among humans who have struggled with the deity since Eden. And over and over this figure persists in referring to himself as a human, a "son of man."

From the perspective of the disappearance of God such ironies abound. First, in the Hebrew Bible we saw the acts of God coming to be replaced by the word of God. Then, in the Christian story, "the word[21] was God . . . and the word became flesh." The word, which I have characterized as a lesser experience of the divine than the act, has been transformed in the book of John into the most intense experience of the divine. The gradual distancing of divinity thus has been followed by the most immediate divine contact with humans since Eden, where God had walked among the humans in the breeze of the day (Gen 3:8). Second, the mystery of the incarnation, especially as it developed in connection with the doctrine of the trinity, means that while the divine is visible on earth in one aspect, the divine in another aspect — God the father, God as known in the Hebrew Bible — remains hidden. For example, as L. T. Johnson observed, "In Luke-Acts, the most important character is arguably the God who never appears but who in various ways directs the action, and with reference to whom all of the narrative unfolds."[22] Thus, in terms of the Christian conception, the phenomenon of the hidden face of God becomes more complex, emphasizing the mystery of the deity while at the same time picturing another aspect of the deity as more manifest than ever before. Third, the very concept of God taking the form of a human both responds to the rise in human status and, at the same time, shifts the balance back toward the divine. Humans have become responsible for their own world; they have prevailed in the divine-human struggle. And then a form of the deity moves among humans, *as* a human. In the Hebrew Bible, creating humans in the divine image yet subordinating them had meant an innate basis of conflict, so that the divine and the human were unable to co-exist, which ultimately led to the diminishing apparent presence of the deity on earth. Now God appears among humans, visibly bearing that shared divine-human image, and he relates to them as a fellow human rather than as a commanding master. One could say that this is the course of action that is left now that the deity has ceased using splitting seas and fire from the sky as divine manifestations. But, in any case, the actions in the life of this human become, in Christian belief, the mechanism of salvation. It is through this son of man that humans are believed to be redirected to God.

If this ironic reverse in the shift of the divine-human balance is not immediately clear, it may be more readily apparent in the matter of kingship. In the Hebrew Bible the monarchy in Israel was a key step in this shift, going contrary to the warnings of Gideon and Samuel, making a human king instead of having only God as king. The deity tells Samuel to anoint a king "for they have not rejected you, but rather they have rejected *me* from ruling over them" (1 Sam 8:7). Later the deity makes a covenant of *eternal* kingship with the house of David. Now, in the New Testament, Jesus is identified in the first verse as "the son of David" (Matt 1:1; cf. Mark 10:47f.), followed by a genealogy from Abraham to David to Jesus (1:2–16; cf.Luke 3:23–38) and reference to him as king of the Jews later (Matt 2:2; 27:37; Mark 15:26; Luke 23:38; John 19:19). The idea of the incarnation of the divine in the form of a man, joined to the idea that this man is in the royal line of David, pulls the carpet out from under the human institution of monarchy, and it returns God to the place of sole monarch. In the Hebrew Bible, the king is called "the anointed," which in Hebrew is *mǎšîaḥ*, or as we pronounce it in English: messiah. "Anointed" in Greek is *christos*, or as we pronounce it in English: christ. That is, when Jesus is identified as Christ/Messiah/Anointed (Mark 8:29) he is seen in the context of the monarchy that is established in the Hebrew Bible. Joining the doctrine of the incarnation with the messianic expectations of that period resulted in this remarkable reversal of the effect of the monarchy. Given that the monarchy is inaugurated with the prophet Samuel declaring to the people, "You have rejected your God today," (1 Sam 10:19), and given that monarchy involves humans' appropriation of some of the deity's dominion over them, the depiction of Jesus as king in the New Testament narrative involves an ironic divine reappropriation of kingship. As Jesus says in his first words in the book of Mark, "The kingdom of God is at hand" (1:14).

"IT IS ELIJAH"

The depiction of the return of visible expressions of the deity's presence in the New Testament narrative is accompanied and buttressed by accounts of miracles and other signs of presence like those pictured in the Hebrew Bible, including angels (Matt 1:20; 2:13, 19; 28:2–7; Mark 24: 23; 4:11; Luke 1:11–20, 26–38; 2:9–15; John 20:12), dreams (Matt 2: 12), visions (Matt 17:9), voices from the heavens (Matt 3:17; Mark 1: 11; Luke 3:22; John 12:28–30), and appearances (i.e., by Jesus after his death; Matt 28:9–10, 16–20; Mark 16:9–19; Luke 24:13–51; 20:14– 17, 19–23, 26–29; 21:1–23). Indeed, coming to this narrative with a consciousness of the development of the hiding of the face of God, one is struck by the great rush of miracles that one encounters in the Gospels. It is an unparalleled concentration; there has been no portrayal of so many episodes of miracles in so short a time span before. The miracles of Jesus are not of the great public sort like the plagues in Egypt or the sun standing still in Joshua's day. They are not witnessed by "all the people," and they do not involve immediate transformations of national destinies the way the scattering at "Babel" and the splitting of the Red Sea do. Rather, they are the sort of miracles that I have described earlier as personal rather than public miracles. But the sheer quantity of them in a relatively short period of time covered in the narrative (about three years) makes a strong impression, all the more so if one reads them immediately after reading Ezra, Nehemiah, and Esther, where there are no miracles at all. Suddenly, about five centuries later, there are numerous episodes of miraculous healing,

> (Matt 4:23f; 8:2–15; 9:1–8, 20–22; 9:35; 12:10–16; 14:14, 35–36; 15:30–31; 17:14–21; 19:2; Mark 1:30–31, 40–45; 2: 3–12; 3:5; 5:25–34; 6:5, 54–56; Luke 4:38–39; 5:12–14, 17– 26; 6:6–11, 17–19; 7:1–10, 21–22; 8:43–48; 9:11, 37–43; 10:1–17; 13:10–17; 14:1–6; 17:12–19; 22:50–51; John 5:5– 9; 6:2)

of casting out demons and spirits,

> (Matt 8:16, 28–34; 15:21–28; Mark 1:23–27, 32–34; 5:1–13; 6:13; 7:25–30; 9:14–29; Luke 4:40f; 8:2, 26–33)

causing the blind to see,

> (Matt 9:27–31; 20:29–34; 21:14; Mark 8:22–26; 10:46–52; Luke 18:35–43; John 9:1–41)

the mute to speak,

> (Matt 9:32–34; 12:22; Mark 7:32–37; Luke 11:14)

and returning the dead to life.

> (Matt 9:18–19, 23–26; Mark 5:22–24, 35–43; Luke 7:11–17; 8:41–42, 49–56; John 11:1–44)

Jesus multiplies loaves and fish to feed thousands,

> (Matt 14:15; 15:32–38; Mark 6:34–44; 8:1–10; Luke 9:12– 17; John 6:1–14)

turns water to wine,

(John 2:6–11)

calms the wind and sea,

(Matt 8:24–27; Mark 4:39–41; Luke 8:22–25)

curses a fig tree and it withers,

(Matt 21:18–22; Mark 11:12–14, 20–25)

and walks on the sea.

(Matt 14:25–33; Mark 6:48–52; John 6:19)

It is notable that Jesus is pictured performing the personal sort of miracles. Specifically, Jesus' miracles most closely resemble not the miracles of Moses or Joshua, but those of Elijah and Elisha: multiplication of food, curing leprosy, mastering water, reviving the dead. The narrative in fact makes the semblance to Elijah explicit, as it raises the question of who people think Jesus is. While some take him to be a reincarnation of John the Baptist, " . . . others said, 'It is Elijah.' And others said, 'It is a prophet, like one of the prophets of old'" (Mark 6:15; cf. 8:27–30). As I described in my discussion of the shift in the divine-human balance in Chapter 2, Elijah's and Elisha's wonders are the miracles that are performed in humans' most advanced control of divine powers in the Hebrew Bible. The acts that Elijah and Elisha perform that I took as marks of the shift to the human side are now attributed to Jesus in the New Testament. And Jesus performs them, at least partly, as confirmation of his identity as an incarnation of the deity. That is, the New Testament accounts once again reverse the shift in the divine-human balance and transport it back toward the divine.

"MY GOD, MY GOD, WHY HAVE YOU LEFT ME?"

I focused on the story of Rabbi Eliezer earlier as significant in itself and as a metaphor for what rabbinic Judaism can represent against the background of the disappearance of God. I want to focus in a similar way on a particular moment in the New Testament narrative that I think particularly conveys the significance of the disappearance of God as a valuable perspective for Christianity as well. I have in mind one of the accounts of Jesus' last words on the cross. While recounting the ironies of the Gospel narratives, one can hardly leave out:

> the irony that lies at the heart of the story Mark tells — the Son
> of God who is rejected and killed by the very human race he had
> come to save . . .[23]

Against the background of the divine-human struggle as traced in the Hebrew Bible from the garden of Eden to the hiding of the face of God, the story of the death of Jesus in the New Testament appears as a culmination of that struggle. An incarnation of God moves among humans on earth in the form of a human being, and they kill him. In the New Testament story it is indeed humankind who are responsible for killing Jesus, as the Catholic Church has profoundly noted, not the Roman authorities, not soldiers who perform the execution, not the Jewish authorities who turn him over to the Romans, not the crowd who request Barabbas rather than Jesus for clemency. The divine and the human have been in conflict since the former created the latter, and it is utterly consistent with that background that the first time that the deity places some aspect of Himself within the power of humans they act as they do. He says, in enormous generosity, "Father forgive them, for they know not what they do." But, consciously aware of the import of what they are doing or not, humans are acting consistently with what had transpired in the Hebrew Bible narrative. This act is more powerful, more awesome than those earlier human rebellions, certainly, but it fits comprehensibly in a linear historical sequence that has near its beginning an account in which some human form of God meets Jacob and, with no reason at all given, they fight.

Given my interest in the disappearance of God in the Hebrew Bible as a perspective here, I particularly want to focus on the last words Jesus speaks before dying (in Matthew and Mark) because the words, a verse from the Hebrew Bible (Ps 22:2),[24] are a verse that specifically played a role in our tracing of this development. He says, "My God, my God, why have you left me?" (Matt 27:46; Mark 15:34).[25] On almost any view of the doctrines of incarnation and the trinity and their relationship to the Synoptic Gospels, this is a puzzling thing for him to say. If one understands him to be the son, the second person of the trinity, speaking to the father, the first person of the trinity, why does he say *this?* What can it mean to say that one has left the other? If he is an incarnation of the divine, why does he say this? If he had foreknowledge that this was to happen, why does he say this? If this was the playing out of a divine plan, why say this?

Conscious of the entire development of the disappearance of God in the Hebrew Bible, one might suggest that Jesus can be pictured here as asking the question for all humankind, that is, as expressing the feeling of divine absence for everyone. The human part of him, now speaking as a representative for humanity which he has joined, asks the divine part: why have you left? The question thus understood would also convey a corollary of the Christian concept of the divine in the form of a man, namely that such a being paradoxically houses both sides of the divine-human struggle within him.[26] The struggle had led to a parting of ways. Now an aspect of the divine joins humans in the form of a man. In this human incarnation he experiences the feeling of the separation, and he asks the divine aspect: why have you left?

Another explanation of Jesus' words on the cross could be that, since they are a quotation, he should be understood to *mean* them as a quotation. He is not addressing God and asking why he personally has been left at this particular moment. His words are rather meant for the humans who hear (and read) them. They convey that in that moment of agony and seeming failure people should remember the words of the Hebrew Bible. People should contemplate the record of divine-human relations there, quintessentially represented by this verse, and seek meaning for this event in context. And they should look there for explanations, wisdom, consolation, and hope.

More narrowly, Jesus' last words could be a quotation of an *incipit*. The term *incipit* refers to the use of the opening line of a poem or song as an abbreviated way of referring to the entire song. If, for example, one wanted to ask a friend if he or she was familiar with Psalm 23, one could just cite the *incipit* and ask, "Do you know 'The Lord is my shepherd'?" Similarly in the contemporary United States, people commonly refer to the patriotic song titled "America" by its first line. Instead of saying, "Now we're going to sing 'America,'" they say, "Now we're going to sing 'My country, 'tis of thee.'" In this way one might understand the words on the cross to mean not just the first verse of Psalm 22; but rather, by pronouncing the *incipit*, Jesus invokes the entire psalm.[27] As I said in Chapter 3, the poet in Psalm 22 looks back to past generations, when God would answer humans' cries (22:4–5), and the poet urges those who fear Yahweh to keep the faith because God has helped in the past:

> For He has not despised and has not abhorred the
>   affliction of the afflicted,
> And He has not hidden His face from him,
> And when he cried to Him, He listened.
>
> (22:25)[28]

It thus conveys that even in conditions of deeply felt divine hiddenness, one can recall that the deity was present, listening, and answering in the past, and it suggests that the deity will be so again in the future.

The account of Jesus' last words thus relates explicitly and intriguingly to the matter of the hiding of the face of God in the Hebrew Bible, and that development in turn potentially provides a valuable perspective from which to view the story in the New Testament. For those who believe that story literally, take this element literally. For those who see it as a myth, take it as part of the myth. But, either way, take the point: In the climactic moment of the Christian story, the central being of the Christian story speaks of the departure of God.

The notion of the resurrection of Jesus after his death adds another dimension (literally?), of course, in a sense nullifying the human condemnation of the incarnate God and returning the victory to the deity after all. The execution turns out to be not a human victory but an element of a divine plan, the death turns out to be a divine sacrifice, the resurrection a channel to human salvation. But the essential fact from the perspective of the disappearance of God remains: the divine and the human have once again been unable to co-exist. They will be able to in some future day perhaps, in the kingdom of heaven, in an afterlife, but not on this earth as constructed at creation. In the New Testament account, God has reappeared, angels have been seen, voices have spoken, and miracles have abounded. And humans have rejected it.

In this account, Jesus has told and *shown* humans how to live. He has not only performed miracles. He has preached sermons, taught disciples, formulated parables, and taught by example. This notion of the divine personally showing humans how to live is a new phenomenon, a function of this ultimate closeness and ultimate anthropomorphism. "Anthropomorphism" is a cold term. To appreciate the context of this phenomenon, one has to get a feel for what it means to picture God in human terms the way the Hebrew Bible does. In the Hebrew Bible the deity is, on the one hand, the most hidden of deities, the creator, who is outside the system of nature while other gods are inside it. Yet when He meets Moses at the burning bush He does not introduce Himself as "I am the creator" or even "I am the God of Israel"; His introduction is rather, "I am the God of your father . . ." (Exod 3:6). And Abraham, Moses, and Jonah argue with Him. And He can be grieved to His heart. Indeed, one could argue that it was this already-developed feeling of God's closeness, of personal relationship, of caring, that made it possible for the Christian conception of the incarnation to be born: God in the form of a man, yet still the one and only God. Cosmic yet personal. The *logos* yet flesh. People could walk and talk with an incarnation of an infinite being who was beyond the universe.

It may also be that the feeling of the disappearance of God itself contributed to the reception of the Christian conception. It had been so long, according to the Hebrew Bible, since the time of appearance and closeness. What was left was the book and the law. It was not that the law had become such a burden. Millions of people have lived according to the law and not found it to be a burden. On the contrary, they have frequently found it to be aesthetically attractive, ethically enriching, and a source of identity, as well as a system of tangible symbols of inner faith — and, for that matter, a comfort. It was that the law, even at its most meaningful, was still not the equal of seeing fire come out of the sky or water come out of a rock, or hearing the voice of God. The Christian story said that God had come close once again, in "modern" times, and in an even more personal form than before. "Glad tidings" indeed.

From a historical perspective as well, I would say that one of the reasons for the great appeal and rapid spread of Christianity may have been the feeling of a divine void, of a hidden face of God, in that age, not only by the early Jewish followers of Christianity, but by the pagans as well. As pagan religion was, for a variety of reasons, no longer satisfying, here was a religion saying that God was close, immanent. He had walked among humans, and He would be back.

"HE CAUSES TO BE"

I have concentrated here on what is most different about the two religions — the oral Torah in rabbinic Judaism and the person and divinity of Jesus in Christianity — because that is my concern here: a perspective on the two religions as offering two different responses to the development of the hiding of the face of God in the Hebrew Bible, the scripture that both religions held sacred. For Judaism the path back is Torah. For Christianity it is salvation through Jesus Christ. Obviously there is much that the two faiths have in common which is interesting from the perspective of the hiding of the face as well. Both of them refashioned the role of miracles. After all, Jesus' miracles do not accomplish much more than Rabbi Eliezer's when it comes to convincing the authorities. Even the response of the masses is mixed; in one case, when people see and hear about one of Jesus' miracles, "they began to beg him to depart from their neighborhood" (Mark 5:14–17). And when the thief who is crucified next to Jesus asks him why he does not somehow miraculously save himself, Jesus declines (Luke 23:39–43; Matt 27:38–44; Mark 15:27–32), as he had done earlier in response to three temptations by the devil (Matt 4:1–11; Mark 1:12–13; Luke 4:1–13). It appears that he does not seek to win people by miracles. Miracles are significant but are not what the story is primarily about. Both Christianity and normative Judaism appear to be more concerned with humans' learning how to live, both with each other ("Love your neighbor as yourself") and in relation to their God ("Love the Lord your God with all your heart, with all your soul, and with all your might").

Both religions also became more concerned with what lies after this life. One of the puzzling and unexpected aspects of the Hebrew Bible is its near silence on the subject of life after death, salvation, and reward and punishment in a world to come. It is not that there are no references at all to this matter. The curious thing is that such references are so rare. These rare references are well-known, and they stand out precisely as exceptions. The best-known references are to a place called "*sheol*," the meaning of which is uncertain. It may mean some realm of the dead, where they dwell in some unspecified form, or it may simply mean the grave.[29] There are also passages in which, it has been argued, the words for earth (Hebrew: *'ôlām*, *'ereṣ*) may refer rather to something like "the underworld." [30] These and a few other references are enough to indicate that there was a belief in some kind of life after death in ancient Israel, and this is supported by archaeological evidence from excavations of tombs from the biblical period, in which bodies were buried along with possessions and food. But the evidence from archaeology and the few textual references make it all the more perplexing that this is not a more central subject of interest in the Hebrew Bible. If some or most or all of the biblical writers believed in life after death, why did they not give it attention among the most important matters in the Hebrew Bible? Whatever answer may be found to this mystery, the fact remains that the situation is different in Christianity and in the rabbinic stage of Judaism, both of which give explicit attention to these matters, to salvation in Christianity, and to "the world to come" in normative Judaism. It is notable that the explicit interest in this matter increased in the age in which the divine hiddenness prevailed. Possibly, in concentrating more on the afterlife, both Judaism and Christianity became more concerned with a realm in which divine authority still functioned completely. It was both a recognition of the hiding of the face of God and a yearning for contact with the divine. And, at the same time, it reserved this contact with the divine for the future, after one's life in this world was over, so it fulfilled the psychological need to keep contact with the divine in the past and the future but not in one's immediate experience.

Another common element of post-biblical Judaism and Christianity that plays a part in the phenomenon of the distancing of the deity is their attitude toward the name of God. As I discussed in Chapter 1, the name of God in the Hebrew Bible is more than a mere appellation or title. In the book of Exodus it represents the deity's making Himself known in the world, as the name, Yahweh, is revealed for the first time (3:13–15; 6:2–3). One of the ten commandments forbids taking this name in vain (which is commonly understood in modern scholarship to mean that if one swears an oath and invokes the name one must take care to keep that oath). And, of most immediate relevance to the matter of the hiding of the presence of God, the Temple in Jerusalem is identified as "the place where Yahweh your God chooses to cause His name to dwell" (Deut 12: 51; cf. 12:5, 21; Kgs 3:2; 8:18–20, 43, 44, 48). The name itself is understood to be a hypostasis of the divine presence, housed in the Temple;

and the Babylonian destruction of the Temple, "the house where I said my name will be there," is one of the major steps in the hiding of the face (2 Kgs 23:27). A degree of hiddenness was added in post-biblical Judaism as the practice was established never to say the name of God. Whenever the name appeared in the Bible, people said "the Lord" (Hebrew: *'ădōnāy*) rather than read the actual name out loud. When they translated the Hebrew Bible into Greek, they replaced the name of God with the Greek word for Lord: *kurios*. Christianity followed Judaism in this practice (and nearly all translations have followed this custom ever since). And the extraordinary thing is that, for all the criticism that Jews and Christians receive for frequently failing to live up to the tenets of their faiths, they were so universally careful to fulfill the prohibition against saying the name, for millennia, that it is now lost! The name appears in manuscripts of the Hebrew Bible as far back as the Qumran (Dead Sea) scrolls, but one of the features of biblical Hebrew (and some other Semitic languages) is that it is written only with consonants; most vowels are not represented. And so the name of God appears only as *yhwh*. We are not certain what the correct vowels are.

The divine name has been reintroduced in our century, mainly as a consequence of modern biblical and linguistic scholarship. The probable vocalization is Yahweh, which would mean "He causes to be." [31] (By another vocalization the name would mean "He is.") I have followed this vocalization here, but I shall share a caution against being too sure of our scholarly reconstruction, which I received from a Hassidic rabbi who sat in on my class one day. After the lesson I asked him if he was offended by my saying the name out loud in the class, and he said: "It's okay. You don't know that you're pronouncing it right." That dramatizes the situation. And this situation strikes me as a noteworthy development in Judaism and Christianity from the perspective of the hiding of the face of God. Even when the motive was to treat the name of God with reverence, as being too holy to be said aloud, the ironic result was that people forgot what their God's name was.

Both Judaism and Christianity had a sense of the hiddenness of God. I suspect that many other religions have it, too. Pascal said, "Every religion which does not affirm that God is hidden, is not true." [32] Likewise with the notion of divine-human struggle: it is not singularly Jewish, it is not singularly Christian, nor is it singularly pagan. It is simply human to feel at odds with the forces of the universe, which are mysterious and stronger than we are. In the story that I used as expressive of rabbinic Judaism, humans overrule a heavenly voice, and God says, "My children have defeated me." In the story that I used for Christianity, humans execute the incarnation of God, and he speaks of the divine departure. Literally or symbolically, these both portray humans attempting to exclude God.

The kernel of the concept of the diminishing apparent presence of God thus was present in Judaism and Christianity. It was present in the legacy of the Hebrew Bible and present in the literature that each religion added and treasured. One could assemble a history of this concept in Christianity and Judaism, looking at the various forms that it took at various times and various places, seeing when individuals and groups were sensitive to the feeling of divine hiddenness and when they were not, what language and symbols were used to express it, how it was expressed in theology, art, literature, liturgy, and a host of other interesting avenues of investigation. But I leave it to scholars in these fields, if they find this interesting, to pursue these things, which are beyond the range of my professional expertise. My purpose here has been a more limited one. I have sought to establish that in the core elements of Christianity and Judaism the sense of the disappearance of God already resides, and the perspective of the disappearance of God is already relevant, fitting, and enriching.

Ultimately the legacy of the age of the hiddenness of God was a new world, a world of churches and synagogues, and of books. Instead of contact with God directly, there was contact with His church. Instead of God directly, contact with His book. Instead of God who acts (i.e., who acts publicly, visibly, identifiably), God who speaks; or, perhaps: who has spoken. And that legacy has lasted nearly two thousand years.

The phenomenon of the disappearance of God has surfaced and taken an extraordinary shape in the present century. The second mystery that we shall investigate introduces and dramatizes the current condition and the crisis that it has brought.

SECOND MYSTERY

NIETZSCHE AT TURIN

Chapter 7

NIETZSCHE AT TURIN

"GOD IS DEAD"

It is now a millennium and a half after the formation of Christianity and
rabbinic Judaism, over two millennia after the last events in the Hebrew
Bible. And it seems to me that this century, the last century of the millennium, which is nearing an end, is profoundly the heir of the feeling of the
disappearance of God. Even those who say that they have experienced
the presence of deity must acknowledege, albeit with regret, that the vast
majority of their neighbors are not aware of having had any such encounter. The disappearance of God, which developed through the course of
the Hebrew Bible and resided in Judaism and Christianity in various
forms since their birth, has become explicit. It was a subtle development
in the Bible, so that it has never before been fully observed. But now it is
blatant. In this century, the "death of God" has come to be a commonly
known expression and idea. The second mystery relates to the surfacing
of this concept in our age.

This riddle does not unfold through a book, as the first mystery did,
but through a man. The clues to its solution derive not only from words
on pages but also from a life, the life of the person who played the central
role in making the disappearance of God a concern to be reckoned with.
That man, Friedrich Nietzsche, died in 1900, as the twentieth century
was about to be born. For much of this century his image has been veiled

by misrepresentations of his works. He was perceived to be a proto-Nazi though he criticized German nationalism; he was commonly thought to be anti-Semitic though he detested anti-Semitism. As these distortions have gradually been exposed, Nietzsche's influence has grown. Now, as the century comes to an end, we can begin to measure his impact. More than any other human being who ever lived, he brought us face to face with the idea of the disappearance of God — not with the step-by-step phenomenon that develops in the text of the Bible, but with the condition, the feeling of divine absence. People may accept or reject it, but, after Nietzsche, one cannot easily ignore it. He called it the death of God. Nietzsche made a habit of putting things in strong terms. He wrote of "doing philosophy with a hammer."

The idea of the death of God did not begin with Nietzsche. Others, including Hegel and Heine, used the expression before him. But Nietzsche is the one with whom people most often associate it, presumably because of the forcefulness of his formulation of the idea. Nietzsche *announced* the death of God. It was not a philosophical construction or analysis. He was treating it as an event.[1] He wrote his best-known work, *Thus Spoke Zarathustra,* in a form resembling a bible, and the death of God in that book is presented in the way that the Bible presents the acts of God: as an occurrence, a known fact. When Zarathustra hears an old wise man preaching about God, Zarathustra simply wonders in amazement: "Could it be possible? This old saint in the forest has not yet heard anything of this, that *God is dead!*" Like the Bible, this is a narrative, developing characters, telling stories, including poetry. Nietzsche really meant this book eventually to hold a place like that of the Bible in the destiny of civilization. In his autobiography, *Ecce Homo,* he wrote, "With *Zarathustra* I have given humankind the greatest present that has ever been made to it so far."

Not modest. But one must consider that Nietzsche was endowed (by whom?) with one of the most extraordinary minds known to our species. The quiet, polite, retired professor of classics at the University of Basel who declared the death of God was brilliant, but it was brilliance united with an exceptional sensitivity to human feelings, and an exceptional spirit. Freud said about him that "he had a more penetrating knowledge of himself than any other man who ever lived or was ever likely to live."[2] Add the fact that Nietzsche lived a life of profound loneliness and unrelenting physical and emotional suffering, which forged these gifts into one of the most remarkable souls who ever lived. He has had a strange, unique place in human history.

Nietzsche's name has been associated more than any other with the death of God, to the point that there was an oft-scribbled bit of graffiti in the 1970s that went:

"God is dead."
Nietzsche

"Nietzsche is dead."
God

One might speculate on how Nietzsche would have reacted if he had seen this. I imagine that he would have responded at first with scorn, and then a moment later, like God in the Eliezer story, he would have laughed. In any case, the interpretation of the graffito is uncertain because, after all, Nietzsche actually wrote the first line ("God is dead"), but God did not write the second ("Nietzsche is dead"). Rather, some human being had to write the line and attribute it to God — so that the graffito may ironically make Nietzsche's point rather than mock it.

Nietzsche had been insane for the twelve years preceding his death. His madness has held a fascination for many people, including both lay-persons and Nietzsche scholars, both his critics and his admirers, ever since; and there have been a variety of proposals to explain it, the most commonly mentioned one being that the cause was syphilis. Our interest here, however, is not the physical etiology of his condition but rather its ultimate connection to divine disappearance. In the writings of his sane years, Nietzsche explicitly associated madness with the death of God; and, with the onset of his own madness, he identified himself with deities who had been killed. The second mystery begins with the events on the day Nietzsche went mad. But its scope will soon expand, as mysteries tend to do, into a web of clues running through a man's life. Then it will involve another life, and then the society in which these two lives emerged. The starting focus of the investigation may seem distant from the matter of divine hiddenness, but that sort of thing is a common element of mysteries as well: at the point of entry into the maze one cannot yet see the full context of the problem. The opening scene of the mystery is a haunting image in any case, and ultimately the puzzle that it introduces is a reflection of — and a metaphor for — something larger: the unfolding of the disappearance of God as a heritage of this era.

"I WOULD RATHER HAVE BEEN A PROFESSOR THAN GOD"

In early January 1889, Nietzsche was walking in the streets of Turin when he saw a coachman whipping a horse. Nietzsche ran to the horse, put his arms around its neck, passed out, and was never sane again. When he regained consciousness he wrote several letters in which he identified himself as a god. He signed some letters "The Crucified" and others "Dionysus." In one he wrote,

> When it comes right down to it I'd much rather have been a Basel
> Professor than God; but I didn't dare be selfish enough to forgo
> the creation of the world.[3]

What was the meaning of all this? Whatever the physical or emotional cause of his madness was, why did the sight of a horse being whipped trigger his exit? How did this connect to the life he lived and the thoughts he conceived, especially his thoughts about God? The solution to the very specific mystery of what Nietzsche did that day at Turin will shed light on his work and his legacy as well.

One hint: The mystery of Nietzsche at Turin is actually two mysteries. The second one involves another genius of the nineteenth century whose impact has been important in the last century of the millennium, Dostoevsky. There is a curious relationship between the German philosopher Nietzsche and the Russian novelist Dostoevsky. Though their lives overlapped in part (Dostoevsky lived from 1821 to 1881, Nietzsche from 1844 to 1900), the two geniuses never met. Yet there are a number of interesting parallels — I would say uncanny parallels — in their works, including, most notably for our present purpose, that they both developed the idea of the death of God and the related idea that "all is permitted." I shall show enough of these intersections to demonstrate the point presently, but for now I just want to give notice that such a striking relationship between Nietzsche and Dostoevsky exists, that portions of it have been observed by scholars — and by Nietzsche himself — and that at a certain point I realized that the nature of this enigma and the solution to the mystery of Nietzsche at Turin were one.

How ironic that Nietzsche should have been the one to announce the death of God. He was the son of a pastor. His father's father was a pastor. His mother's father was a pastor. And as a boy he was called the "little pastor" by the other children and seemed destined for the ministry himself. His father, who died when Friedrich was not quite five years old, probably never would have guessed what path Friedrich would take, and his mother was horrified when he took it.[4] To understand what culminated on the last sane day of his life, one must begin with some events of his childhood and follow a rather peculiar trail of clues through his life. It may seem distant from this book's concern, the divine hiddenness, but I promise that it will all be very relevant in the end. Our first problem is to solve the mystery, and our second will be to find how it relates to the disappearance of God.

Nietzsche's father died very young, thirty-six years old, of what the physicians called "softening of the brain," leaving a wife and three children: Friedrich, a younger sister, Elisabeth, and a baby brother, Joseph. The effect on Friedrich was powerful. Years later he wrote about the funeral, "Oh, never will I get the sad sound of the bells out of my ears. . . ."[5] Six months after his father died, Nietzsche had a frightful dream experience. Here is his own report of it, which he wrote eight years later:

> I heard the church organ playing as at a funeral. When I looked to see what was going on, a grave opened suddenly, and father arose out of it in a shroud. He hurries into the church and soon comes back with a small child in his arms. The mound on the grave reopens, he climbs back in, and the gravestone sinks back over the opening. The swelling noise of the organ stops at once, and I wake up. In the morning I tell the dream to my dear mother. Soon after that little Joseph is suddenly taken ill. He goes into convulsions and dies within hours.[6]

From a psychoanalytic perspective it is reasonable to interpret the dream as the young boy's wish to be reunited with his father, whom he loved dearly, and perhaps also as the wish to expiate the Oedipal guilt associated with the death of the father. The child in the dream would be Friedrich himself. Whatever the forces that produced the dream, though, the fact is that it came true that very day with a different child, Friedrich's infant brother. Even worse, Nietzsche's father's body was exhumed, the body of the baby was placed in the arms of the father, and the two were reburied together, thus bizarrely fulfilling the dream even more closely. How does a five-year-old child comprehend such a thing?

Nietzsche received an outstanding education, culminating in an un-usual appointment to a professorial chair at Basel when he was only twenty-four years old. At that time he had not yet taken his doctoral examination or written his dissertation, so the University of Leipzig waived the examination and dissertation requirements and conferred the degree on him. He was not a Swiss citizen, so Switzerland waived the citizenship requirement for employment at the university. Nietzsche's years in school had also included a good deal of experience with horses. He enjoyed riding, was considered the best rider, and when he entered military service he was an officer in the horse-drawn artillery. Once, while trying to perform a leaping mount into the saddle, Nietzsche fell and injured himself badly as the pommel of the saddle dug into his chest, tore muscles, and broke his ribs, and he nearly died. Later he served as a medic in the Franco-Prussian war and contracted a severe and protracted illness. His health had been bad since his youth, and from this point on he suffered from intolerably ill health for the rest of his life. Meanwhile, his first book, *The Birth of Tragedy*, produced such a negative reaction to him that parents of students actually protested his presence at the univer-sity. As his physical condition deteriorated he left the university and was granted a modest pension for the rest of his life. He spent the balance of his sane years wandering as a man without a country — literally; he had given up his Prussian citizenship but never finished acquiring Swiss citi-zenship[7] — moving every few weeks or months through Italy, the Enga-dine mountains of Switzerland, France, and sometimes Germany, trying to find some place where the climate least upset his wretched condition. He suffered horrible headaches, for which he would take powerful drugs, followed by comparably horrible digestive ailments, pain, vomiting, in-somnia, exhaustion; and all the while his vision was failing, so that despite doctor's orders to limit his reading and writing, he spent much of his day painfully reading and writing his books and letters. Descriptions of his life in these years picture a continuous torture ("I had 200 days of torment in the year. . . . My specialty was to endure extreme pain, *cru, vert* [raw, green], with perfect clarity, for two or three consecutive days, accompanied by constant vomiting"),[8] some of it physiological, some of it perhaps psychosomatic; the causes are largely unknown to us and apparently were unknown to him. And this condition was exacerbated by Nietzsche's emotional state. He was producing books that he believed to be among the greatest ever written, and almost no one on earth outside of his own acquaintances was reading them. It was in this period and in this condition that he first wrote of the concept of the death of God. He was always on the move, usually separated from his family and friends. And he knew the profound loneliness of the genius, the kind of loneliness that one can feel in the middle of a crowd, conceiving thoughts that few humans, even friends, could share, including thoughts in the realm of religion that were alienating him from his family. He was in terrible pain, and he had to endure it alone.

"DON'T FORGET THE WHIP"

During the course of all this he made two new friends. The first was Paul Rée, a philosopher whose intelligence Nietzsche admired. Rée told Nietzsche about an intriguing young woman who had come from Russia, Lou Salomé, a woman of extraordinary intelligence and independence of spirit. The more Nietzsche heard about her, the more he could not wait to meet her. Rée arranged for them all to meet in Rome (in St. Peter's!) in the spring of 1882, when Nietzsche was thirty-seven and Lou Salomé was twenty-one. Nietzsche's first words to her were: "From which stars have we fallen to meet each other here?" Salomé answered, "I've just come from Zurich."[9]

Nietzsche, Salomé, and Rée became close friends. They referred to themselves as "the Holy Trinity." They decided to live together in a sexless ménage à trois, but it never worked out. At least part of the problem was that Lou was a beautiful and exciting woman, and the two men came to be competing for her. Nietzsche was the odd man out in the end. Lou and Paul ended up together, and Nietzsche lost both friendships, never saw either of them again, and was left deeply hurt and feeling more solitary than ever before in his life. Moreover, this was a pattern that seemed to keep recurring for Nietzsche. A few years earlier he had been introduced by a musician named Senger to his student Mathilde Trampedach; Nietzsche proposed marriage to Mathilde, but she rejected his proposal because there was another man in her life: Senger (whom she married). And before that Nietzsche had been practically a member of Richard Wagner's household, and he was quite taken with the woman who lived with Wagner and was later his wife, Cosima, who was also the daughter of Franz Liszt. In Nietzsche's words, "an indescribably close intimacy sprang up between me and Richard and Cosima Wagner. . . . For some years we had everything, great and small in common, a confidence without bounds." [10] Of course Nietzsche was the odd man in that relationship, and later his famous break with Wagner (who happened to be the same age as Nietzsche's father) meant the end of his acquaintance with Cosima as well. Wagner forbade everyone to say Nietzsche's name in his presence. One of the letters Nietzsche wrote in the days after he went mad was to Cosima. It went, "Ariadne, I love you. Dionysus." [11]

One episode from the lives of "the Holy Trinity" stands out for special notice. Near the end of their time together, Nietzsche, Rée, and Salomé stopped to have their photograph taken while in Lucerne. Lou posed the picture, [12] in which she is sitting in a little two-wheeled wagon (which the photographer kept in his studio for photographs of children) while Rée and Nietzsche pretend to be horses, with ropes around their arms binding them to the wagon. Lou is holding a whip over their heads, which was made by tying some strings (and flowers) to a stick. The effect is comic and also a little weird. The photograph appears on page 151. What I find especially intriguing about the photograph is that barely a year later Nietzsche wrote the section of *Thus Spoke Zarathustra* titled "On Little Old and Young Women," in which an old woman gives Zarathustra the advice, "You're going to women? Don't forget the whip!" ("Du gehst zu Frauen? Vergiss die Peitsche nicht!"), [13] the line that has long served to persuade readers that Nietzsche was an outrageous misogynist. [14] Probably nearly everyone who has ever read that line has assumed that it is the man who holds the whip. When one looks at the photograph and sees who is in fact wielding the whip there, however, one must admit

Nietzsche (right) with Paul Rée (center) and Lou Salomé (with whip)

that Nietzsche's point in his book is ambiguous and perhaps intentionally Delphic: as ambiguous and Delphic as God's oracle to Rebekah in Genesis that "the elder the younger will serve." That is, it appears that Nietzsche has administered a Rorschach test that may reveal more about his readers than about himself. I should note that when I first observed this I was proud of myself for making the connection, but I later found that H. F. Peters had already pointed out the link between the photograph and the line in *Thus Spoke Zarathustra* many years earlier.[15] I acknowledge Peters's priority on this point. His publication of this observation some thirty years ago makes it all the more noteworthy that people have gone on misunderstanding this important point in Nietzsche all this time. Nietzsche's relationship with women, both in his writings and in his life, is much more complicated and nuanced than one would expect.

The years following the "Holy Trinity" fiasco were harder than ever for Nietzsche.[16] He wrote *Thus Spoke Zarathustra* and developed the "death of God" in it while enduring an assembly of physical and emotional afflictions. His loneliness deepened, and his relations with his family were an increased source of pain to him. In a letter about his sister he wrote, "Between me and an anti-Semitic goose like her there can be no reconciliation." And his mother told him, "You are a disgrace to your father's grave." An unfortunate choice of image. Nietzsche wrote after five months had passed that he had not been able to forget even for an hour that his mother had said this to him.[17] Lou Salomé wrote in her Nietzsche biography:

> Suffering and loneliness then are the two great lines of fate in Nietzsche's biography, which become ever more pronounced the nearer one comes to the end.[18]

There were times when Nietzsche, in a sense, rose above his pain, was consciously aware that his suffering contributed to the power of his spirit, and felt a kind of appreciation for it and pride in it all. He wrote near the end of his sane life: "After all, my illness has been of the greatest use to me: it has released me, it has restored to me the courage to be myself. . . ."[19] And he is famous for having said, "What does not kill me makes me stronger."[20]

In the middle of this, Nietzsche discovered Dostoevsky.

"AN UNDERGROUND MAN"

In January of 1887, Nietzsche was in a bookstore and, by chance, happened to glance at a certain book. It was by an author he had never heard of, but he was drawn to it, and to the author, instantly and powerfully. He wrote in a letter that "Dostoevsky happened to me as Stendhal did earlier, by sheer accident: a book casually flipped open in a shop, a name I'd never even heard before — and the sudden awareness that one has met with a brother." As he read the book, "the instinct of kinship (or how shall I name it?) spoke up immediately; my joy was extraordinary. . . ." For all his suffering, he wrote, "I count any Russian book, above all one by Dostoevsky . . . among my greatest consolations." [21] And in his notebooks, which were posthumously published as a book, *The Will to Power* (821), he wrote, "How liberating is Dostoevsky!" The Danish critic Georg Brandes, who was one of the first (and few) figures to recognize Nietzsche's importance while Nietzsche was still alive and sane and able to appreciate it, wrote to Nietzsche about Dostoevsky:

> He is a great poet, but an abominable person, utterly Christian in his emotional life and at the same time utterly sadistic. All his morality is what you have christened slave morality.

To which Nietzsche responded:

> I believe every word you say about Dostoevsky; and yet he has given me my most precious psychological material. I'm grateful to him in a very special way, much as he constantly offends my most basic instincts. [22]

In print as well, Nietzsche described Dostoevsky in *The Twilight of the Idols* as:

> . . . Dostoevsky, the only psychologist, incidentally, from whom I had something to learn; he ranks among the most beautiful strokes of fortune in my life. . . ." [23]

Anyone can read Dostoevsky and see that there is much there that would be likely to appeal to Nietzsche, and much that would "offend his most basic instincts." And anyone can see the extent and well-known depth of the psychological component of Dostoevsky's work as well and understand why it would be so valuable to Nietzsche, as it was to Freud, who shared Nietzsche's fascination with Dostoevsky. But I am particularly interested here in a curious string of elements in Dostoevsky's works, which I think would have been more than mildly interesting to Nietzsche.

The book that Nietzsche flipped open in the bookstore that day was titled *The Underground Spirit* (containing Dostoevsky's *Notes from Underground* and his short story "The Landlady").[24] There were strange coincidences about the book. Just a few months, at most, before Nietzsche opened it he had written a preface to his own book *Dawn*[25] in which he said in the very first words:

> In this book you will find an "underground[26] man" at work. . . .

Which may explain why he was drawn to flip open a book called *The Underground Spirit*. The narrator in that book is generally known in Dostoevsky criticism as the "underground man." On the day that Nietzsche opened the book he was looking for a new room. The first sentence of *The Underground Spirit* was:

> Ordynov had finally decided to change his room.[27]

The character Ordynov's life is pictured as "solitary."[28] He finds a room with a strange couple, and he is quite taken with the woman, who is described as being "about twenty, and she was wonderfully beautiful."[29] She says, "I'm not from this part of the world."[30] In the end Ordynov is the odd man out, the man and woman depart, and he is left, never to see them again.

The second part of the book begins with the narrator saying:

> I am a sick man. . . . I am a spiteful man. I am an unpleasant man. I think my liver is diseased. However, I don't know beans about my disease, and I am not sure what is bothering me.[31]

And later he says:

> But, gentlemen, whoever can pride himself on his diseases and even swagger over them?[32]

In *Thus Spoke Zarathustra*, the hero has been living as a hermit in the mountains; in his fortieth year he "goes under" to humans, and most of the book is his speeches to them. Dostoevsky's underground man says:

> We underground folk . . . Though we may sit forty years underground without speaking, when we do come out into the light of day and break out, we talk and talk and talk. . . .[33]

Again I imagine Nietzsche having a good laugh as he reads that — and also when the underground man says:

> You must excuse me for being overphilosophical; it's the result of forty years underground![34]

Other parallels emerge. The lonely underground man says, "I am cleverer than any of the people surrounding me. . . ."[35] and ". . . there was no one like me, and I was unlike anyone else. 'I am alone and they are *all*.'"[36] He says, "Suffering is good."[37] He favorably quotes Heine, whom Nietzsche admired.[38] He refers to having an "overacute consciousness."[39] Chillingly, he utters, ". . . however you knock at your coffin lid at night, when the dead arise. . . ."[40] There is also a section in which the underground man discusses the idea of a man's voluntarily choosing to go mad.[41] Nietzsche had written of the idea of voluntary madness in *Thus Spoke Zarathustra* years earlier.[42]

In addition to finding "the instinct of kinship," "the sudden awareness that one has met with a brother," and his "most precious psychological material," Nietzsche was discovering in both Dostoevsky's details and concepts some curious reflections of himself.

Two more clues from *The Underground Spirit*, involving dreams and horses: First, dream images figure in the book. There is a lengthy section on dreams in which a particular dream culminates at Lake Como, which is located within about forty miles from Turin;[43] and there is a fearful image of "whole cemeteries giving up to him their dead."[44] Second, there is a strange scene involving a horse, a child, and church bells. Ordynov goes to a church, then walks outside the town and sees this: "a little horse with sticking-out ribs, its head sagging, its lower lip hanging down, stood unharnessed beside a two-wheeled cart, as though it were reflecting on something." A little boy is present. "Eventually he turned back towards the town, from which there suddenly wafted a dense rumbling of bells, summoning the faithful to evening service. . . ."[45] There is also a scene involving a pitiful horse, in which the horse's driver flicks his whip.[46]

"AS THOUGH IT HAD HAPPENED IN A DREAM"

Nietzsche read whatever was available in translation of Dostoevsky's novels. He told a friend that he had read Dostoevsky's *The Insulted and Injured* with "his eyes overflowing" with tears.[47] That novel is a sad and touching story about impossible loves and about making breaks with parents, even to the point of being willing to injure them. The narrator of the story clings closely to a couple because of his love for and loyalty to the woman, but he is left the odd man out. In the end there is a beautiful scene of reunion between the woman and the parents she had shamed, enough to move any sensitive reader to tears, let alone Nietzsche, who had been told that he was a shame to his father's grave, and who repeatedly had been the odd man out. A theme of the book has to do with the "egoism of suffering," suggesting that there is a kind of person who positively needs to suffer, who finds a kind of psychological fulfillment in anguish.[48] There is also a dark view of the egoism of virtue, placed in the mouth of the book's villain, who declares that ". . . at the root of all human virtues lies the completest egoism. And the more virtuous anything is, the more egoism there is in it,"[49] a line that one could easily imagine Nietzsche himself writing (albeit from a different perspective). Indeed, in the section of *Thus Spoke Zarathustra* titled "On the Virtuous," Nietzsche's prescription concerning virtue is "that your self be in your deed."

Three more clues from *The Insulted and Injured*: First, references to madness are strewn all through the book, about thirty in all. Second, dreams play a significant part in the book; notably, near the beginning the narrator says, "I felt as though it had happened in a dream," and near the end the woman says, "It was all a dream."[50] And, third, there are a number of cases of presentiment and coincidence that give the story a mysterious quality.[51]

This all may still seem to be a mass of unconnected clues — madness, dreams, chance, horses, carts, whips, a deceased baby brother, shaming one's parents, a sick and solitary underground man — more disparate and confused than the midpoint of a Raymond Chandler detective novel. But we are, in fact, extremely close to the culmination. First, though, we must bring a few more factors, including God, into the equation.

"HE WILL HIMSELF BECOME A GOD"

Nietzsche was familiar with Dostoevsky's novel *The Idiot* also, and he began using the word *idiot* in a number of contexts in his works and letters during the year after his discovery of Dostoevsky in the bookshop.[52] Notably he used the word in referring to Jesus, Kant, and himself. Indeed his reference to himself as an idiot occurs in a paragraph about Dostoevsky.[53]

Recent scholarship has revealed also that Nietzsche read Dostoevsky's *The Devils* (also translated *The Possessed*) and copied twenty-one passages from it into his notes, translated into German, about nine months before he went mad.[54] His special interest in *The Devils* is particularly relevant because that novel involves some patent parallels to Nietzsche's concepts of the overman and, above all, the death of God. Nietzsche had already written of the overman (sometimes translated as "superman"; German: *Übermensch*) in *Thus Spoke Zarathustra*. There he introduced the concept in a seemingly evolutionary context (though he certainly did not intend literally a Darwinian meaning),[55] with an analogy to the relationship between the human and the ape:

> And Zarathustra spoke thus to the people:
> "*I teach you the overman.* Man is something that shall be overcome.... All beings so far have created something beyond themselves.... What is the ape to man? A laughingstock and a painful embarrassment. And man shall be just that for the overman."

A few sentences later Zarathustra ties this to the idea of the death of God:

> "Behold I teach you the overman. The overman is the meaning of the earth.... Once the sin against God was the greatest sin; but God died, and these sinners died with him. To sin against the earth is now the most dreadful thing."[56]

The overman is not a particular individual, a certain type of person, or a racial or ethnic group. It is the developing legacy of all humankind, a potential product of human development, a yearning to yield something happier, nobler, wiser than ourselves, so much so that "man" (better: "human") will no longer be a fitting term; hence the need for a new term "overman." [57] The man who wrote these things now read in Dostoevsky's *The Devils* of a character named Kirilov, who has a view of history as being divided into two epochs: the first is "from the gorilla to the annihilation of God," and the second is from the annihilation of God "to the physical transformation of the earth and man. Man will be god. He'll be physically transformed." [58] Not identical, but close enough to get Nietzsche's attention. Indeed, Nietzsche wrote letters within months after reading about this division of history, saying his great task, "the revaluation of all values," "will split the history of humankind into two halves" and "I am powerful enough to break the history of mankind in two." [59] (The last letter was written less than a month before he went mad.)

One more clue: Kirilov says twice about this new man, who will "conquer pain and fear," that he "will himself become a god." [60]

An interesting passage which Nietzsche copied was Kirilov's "account of those moments of visionary ecstasy in which he thinks himself to experience the 'presence of eternal harmony perfectly attained.'" [61] Nietzsche was familiar with visionary and ecstatic experience, having discovered his central doctrine of "eternal recurrence" in such a state, according to his own report. We shall return to this later. He also had pictured such a state in a tranquil scene near the end of *Thus Spoke Zarathustra* (IV, section 10). And he would express such a feeling of joyous harmony one more time, on the day after he collapsed with his arms around the neck of the horse in Turin.

"ALL IS PERMITTED"

One more of Dostoevsky's books figures in this picture, and it is the most important of all: *Crime and Punishment*. Nietzsche referred to it in a letter as "Dostoevsky's main novel." [62] (Nietzsche never read *The Brothers Karamazov*, which was translated too late for him to have read it.) In *Crime and Punishment* the hero, Rodion Raskolnikov, commits a murder, not for profit but to act upon his belief that there are two kinds of people in this world, ordinary and extraordinary. The great majority of people — the ordinary — serve to reproduce their kind and thus to people the earth, while the very few — the extraordinary — create something new and change the course of human history. In Raskolnikov's conception, these few stand outside the morality of the masses. Turning this from an intellectual conception into an actual deed, Raskolnikov murders a callous old pawnbroker woman. Almost as an afterthought, he robs a few things from her rooms. But afterward he cannot live with his crime, and in the end (with my apologies to those for whom I am about to ruin the ending) he turns himself in and goes to serve his sentence in Siberia. Raskolnikov is pictured as being ill all through the book. He is in a state that borders on madness; there are over fifty references to madness in the book. And he is described as *pale* at least ten times.

In Nietzsche's *Thus Spoke Zarathustra*, there is a section titled "On the Pale Criminal," which is so blatantly akin to *Crime and Punishment* that it is virtually impossible for one to miss the allusion. Here is a portion of it, which I am reproducing here to convey how strong the resemblance to Dostoevsky and his pale Raskolnikov is. And, when it is joined with the other parallels, we shall see how eerie the connection is between these two men who wrote of the death of God.

> But thought is one thing, the deed is another: and the image of the deed still another: the wheel of causality does not roll between them.
>
> An image made this pale man pale. He was equal to his deed when he did it; but he could not bear its image after it was done. Now he always saw himself as the doer of one deed. Madness I call this: the exception now became the essence for him. A chalk streak stops a hen; the stroke that he himself struck stopped his poor reason: madness *after* the deed I call this.
>
> Listen, O judges: there is yet another madness, and that comes *before* the deed. Alas, you have not yet crept deep enough into this soul.
>
> Thus speaks the red judge, "Why did this criminal murder? He wanted to rob." But I say unto you: his soul wanted blood,

not robbery; he thirsted after the bliss of the knife. His poor reason, however, did not comprehend this madness and persuaded
him: "What matters blood?" it asked; "don't you want at least
to commit a robbery with it? To take revenge?" And he listened
to his poor reason: its speech lay upon him like lead; so he
robbed when he murdered. He did not want to be ashamed of his
madness.

And now the lead of his guilt lies upon him, and again his poor
reason is so stiff, so paralyzed, so heavy. If only he could shake
his head, then his burden would roll off: but who could shake this
head?

What is this man? A heap of diseases, which, through his
spirit, reach out into the world: there they want to catch their
prey.[63]

The passage is so reminiscent of Raskolnikov that Thomas Mann
wrote an essay about Dostoevsky's influence on Nietzsche here. *But Nietzsche wrote* "On the Pale Criminal" *before he had ever heard of Dostoevsky.*[64]
In a similar anachronism, Erich Heller wrote that Dostoevsky's *Notes
from Underground* was "a book that undoubtedly had prompted Nietzsche to call himself in the preface to *Dawn* — 1881, preface of 1886 —
an 'underground man.'"[65] But, as I mentioned earlier, Nietzsche did not
discover Dostoevsky until 1887; he called himself an "underground man"
a few months *before* he read Dostoevsky's book. My interest here, however, is not simply to criticize these writers, which strikes me as petty,
especially since their assumptions are perfectly understandable. My interest in this is not even the scholarly question of Dostoevsky's influence
on Nietzsche. What intrigues me is wondering what went through
Nietzsche's head when he read these things: from ape to annihilation of
God; a pale, sick, mad criminal who commits a murder and robs second-
arily but cannot live with it; an underground man; odd men out; and all
the rest — all in the works of a man with whom he had felt an immediate
instinct of kinship, the sudden awareness of having met a brother, a feeling of liberation, of gratitude, among his greatest consolations, the only
man who could teach him something psychologically. What did Nietzsche make of this?

Until Nietzsche arrived at *Crime and Punishment*, there were enough of these intersections for him to take note of them but not necessarily to take them as more than the understandable parallels of a kindred spirit, or even coincidences. With *Crime and Punishment*, however, the relationship became more dynamic and complex. There were numerous parallels besides those in "On the Pale Criminal." Raskolnikov's most commonly mentioned example of the extraordinary human is Napoleon, whose name occurs over a dozen times in *Crime and Punishment*. Nietzsche, too, had a special feeling for Napoleon and referred to him often, including in contexts involving the overman. In *On the Genealogy of Morals*, he refers to Napoleon as "this synthesis of *Unmensch* and *Übermensch* [inhuman and superhuman]." [66]

Near the beginning of *Crime and Punishment*, Raskolnikov encounters a man in a tavern who, in introducing himself, says, "Behold the man!" quoting Pilate's words about Jesus in the New Testament: "Behold the man," which in Latin is *"Ecce homo"* (John 19:5).[67] *Ecce Homo* is the title of Nietzsche's autobiography.

Raskolnikov's view of the relationship between the masses and the great individuals calls to mind Nietzsche's views in a variety of ways. Nietzsche's references to superior persons, the free spirits, and of course the *Übermensch* are numerous and are among the thoughts that are most readily associated with him. One also might well wonder how Nietzsche reacted as he read Raskolnikov's remarks on the necessity of suffering for great individuals in the same context:

> Pain and suffering are always inevitable for a large intelligence and a deep heart. The really great men must, I think, have great sadness on earth.[68]

Raskolnikov's picture of Napoleon in particular and of great individuals in general includes the notion that to such people "all is permitted." The point is stated in these words three times in *Crime and Punishment* (and again as an important formula in *The Brothers Karamazov*).[69] These words are also attributed to Nietzsche and are among his most famous. He had written them in *Thus Spoke Zarathustra* (IV, 9), where the full formula is "Nothing is true, all is permitted"; and he repeats them in *On the Genealogy of Morals* (III, 24), where he attributes the formula to the Islamic sect known as the Assassins. The phrase also occurs in his note-

books that were published as *The Will to Power* (602). Arthur Danto wrote
that Nietzsche's use of the expression "must surely be a paraphrase of the
Russian novelist he so admired."[70] But Nietzsche had written *Thus Spoke
Zarathustra* and the passage in his notebook years before he discovered
Dostoevsky. Again, my point is not to criticize a distinguished scholar
(and Danto's comment, like Thomas Mann's, has already been chal-
lenged by Walter Kaufmann in any case)[71] but rather to show that key
lines in Nietzsche are so strikingly close to Dostoevsky that scholars have
often taken them to be a result of Dostoevsky's influence, when in fact
Nietzsche wrote the lines before reading Dostoevsky. And, again, my interest is in how peculiar this must have felt to Nietzsche as he encountered these things.

Raskolnikov's family, like Nietzsche's, consists of a mother and a
younger sister, and his father is deceased; and he has one other kin in
common with Nietzsche, about whom we shall read in a moment.

"A HORRIBLE DREAM"

Our final piece of evidence is a scene in *Crime and Punishment*, a frightening picture, which emerges as a crucial piece of the puzzle. It involves
a dream that Raskolnikov has on the day before he commits the murder.
Here is the entire text of the account of the dream which Nietzsche read
(translation by Steven Cassedy).

> Raskolnikov had a horrible dream. He saw himself again as a
> child in the little town where he lived at that time with his family.
> He is seven years old, it is a holiday, it is almost evening, and he
> is taking a walk *extra muros* with his father. The weather is dreary,
> the air is heavy, the various places are exactly the way his memory
> recalled them, and even in a dreaming state he rediscovers more
> than one detail that had been erased from his mind. The little
> town appears completely bare. There is not so much as a single
> white willow around. Somewhere, quite far away, right at the ho-
> rizon, a little wood forms a black spot. A few steps from the last
> garden in town there is a tavern, a large tavern, which the child
> could never pass during a walk with his father without experienc-

ing an extremely disagreeable sensation and even a feeling of terror. There was always such a crowd there, people brawling,
laughing, insulting one another, fighting, or singing such nasty
things in gruff voices. There were always drunken men wandering about the area, and their faces were so horrible . . . When
they used to come near, Rodion would press close to his father,
and his whole body would tremble.

The cross-street that runs alongside the tavern is always covered with a black dust. Three hundred steps away, the road bends
to the right and goes by the town cemetery. In the middle of the
cemetery stands a stone church with a green cupola, where the
child used to go to mass twice a year with his father and mother,
when services were held for the soul of his grandmother, who had
died long ago and whom he had never known. On these occasions he would always get to take a rice cake with a cross made of
raisins on it. He loved this church, its old, mostly unadorned
icons, and the priest, with his shaky head. Next to the stone
marking the place where the old woman's remains had been laid
to rest, there was a little grave, belonging to Rodion's younger
brother, who had died at the age of six months. He hadn't known
him either, but he had been told that he had had a little brother.
For this reason, every time he came to visit the cemetery, he
would piously make the sign of the cross over the little grave, bow
respectfully, and kiss it.

Here is what he dreamed: He is walking with his father along
the road that leads to the cemetery; the two of them are passing
in front of the tavern; he is holding his father's hand and casting
timid glances toward the hateful house, which seems to be even
more full of life than usual. There are a great many women of
the middle classes and peasant women in their Sunday dresses,
their husbands, and all sorts of people belonging to the dregs
of humanity. Everyone is drunk, and everyone is singing songs.
In front of the steps of the tavern stands one of those enormous wagons normally used for transporting various goods and
casks of wine. Usually, one hitches strong horses with large legs
and long manes to such wagons, and Raskolnikov had always
taken great pleasure in contemplating these robust beasts, who

could drag the heaviest loads without feeling the slightest fatigue. But on this occasion there was a small, pitiably thin roan horse hitched to the heavy wagon, one of those nags that the *muzhiks* sometimes force to pull large carts laden with wood or hay, and upon which they rain blows, going so far as to whip them on the eyes and the muzzle, when the poor beasts exhaust themselves in a vain effort to disengage a vehicle that is stuck in the mud. This spectacle, which Raskolnikov had so often witnessed, had always brought tears to his eyes, and his mother in such cases would always take him away from the window. Suddenly there is a great row. Several *muzhiks*, completely drunk, yelling, singing, and playing the guitar, are coming out of the tavern. They are wearing red and blue shirts; their smocks are thrown carelessly over their shoulders. "Get on, get on, everybody!" yells a man, still young, with a large neck and a beefy face as red as a carrot. "I'll take you all! Get on!" These words provoke immediate laughter and exclamations:

"An old nag like that is going to take us?"

"You must've lost your mind, Mikolka, hitching this little mare to a wagon like that!"

"Sure, friends, the roan mare can walk even if she's twenty!"

"Get on! I'm taking everybody!" Mikolka yells again as he jumps onto the wagon before the rest, grabs the reins, and draws himself up to his full height on the front of the vehicle. "The bay horse already left with Matvei, and this mare, friends, is a real heartbreak for me. I think I ought to kill her. She's not earning her food. Get on, I'm telling you! I'll make her gallop! Oh, she'll gallop!"

Saying this, he takes his whip, delighted already at the idea of whipping the roan mare.

"Well, get on! Come on, now! He said she's going to gallop," people are snickering in the crowd.

"I'm sure she hasn't galloped in ten years."

"She'll run at quite a clip!"

"Don't spare her, friends. Each of you take a whip. Everyone get ready!"

"Great, they're going to whip her!"

Everyone climbs onto Mikolka's wagon, laughing and joking. Six men are already aboard and there is still room. They take with them a fat peasant woman with a ruddy face. This gossip, wearing a red cotton sarafan, has on her head a sort of bonnet decorated with glass beads; she is munching hazel-nuts, and now and then she laughs. In the crowd surrounding the horse and cart there is laughter too, and, in truth, who wouldn't laugh at the idea that a nag like this could pull all these people at a gallop? Two of the youths in the wagon immediately pick up whips to help Mikolka. "Let's go!" he shouts. The horse pulls with all its might, but, far from galloping, it can barely advance one step. It stamps, moans, and bends its back under the hailstorm of blows that the three whips are bringing down upon it. The laughter is growing louder in the wagon and in the crowd, but Mikolka is getting angry, and, in his rage, he hits the mare harder and harder, as if he were truly hoping to make her gallop.

"Let me get on too, lads," a young man among the spectators shouts, burning with the desire to join the joyful gang.

"Get on!" answers Mikolka. "Get on, all of you! She'll take everyone! I'm going to make her walk!"

With that he whips and whips her, and in his fury no longer even knows what to hit his beast with.

"Daddy, Daddy," cries the child to his father, "Daddy, what are they doing? Daddy, they're hitting the poor little horse!"

"Keep moving, keep moving!" says the father. "They're just drunks having fun, the idiots. Come along, don't pay any attention to them!" And he wants to take the child along, but Rodion tears himself away from his father's hands and, beside himself, runs over to the horse. The unhappy animal is already giving out. It is panting, and after a moment's halt it begins to pull once again and nearly collapses.

"Whip her till she dies!" Mikolka yells. "That's the only thing left to do. I'm going to do it!"

"You're no Christian, that's for sure, you monster!" shouts an old man in the crowd.

"Who ever saw such a small horse pull a heavy wagon like that?" adds another.

"Scoundrel!" a third shouts.

"This is none of your business! She's my property! I'll do as I please. Get on, more of you! Get on, all of you! She is going to gallop! . . ."

Suddenly Mikolka's voice is drowned out by noisy peals of laughter: the mare, overcome with the blows, has finally lost patience and, despite her weakness, has begun to kick. The general hilarity gets the better of even the old man. And there really is something to laugh about: a horse that can barely stay on its feet and that's kicking!

Two youths break loose from the crowd, arm themselves with whips, and run to lash the animal, one from the right, the other from the left.

"Whip her on the muzzle, on the eyes, on the eyes!" yells Mikolka.

"A song, lads!" shouts someone from the wagon. The whole gang at once breaks into a coarse song, accompanied by a tambourine. The peasant woman is munching her hazelnuts and laughing.

. . . Rodion has come up to the horse. He sees it get whipped on the eyes, yes, on the eyes! He is crying. His heart swells up, tears are streaming down his face. One of the tormentors grazes his face with a whip. He doesn't feel it. He is wringing his hands, letting out cries. He hurls himself towards the old man with the beard and white hair who is shaking his head and condemning all this. A woman takes the child by the hand and tries to lead him away from this scene; he breaks free and rushes back to the mare. The mare is at the end of her strength, but she is still trying to kick.

"Ah, monster!" shouts Mikolka, exasperated. He throws his whip away, bends down, and reaches for a long, heavy shaft at the bottom of the wagon. Holding it by one end in both hands, he brandishes it with some effort over the roan mare.

"He's going to knock her down!" shout the people around him.

"He'll kill her!"

"She's my property!" shouts Mikolka, and the shaft, wielded by two strong arms, falls with a crash on the animal's back.

"Whip her, whip her! Why are you stopping?" voices can be heard shouting in the crowd.

Again the shaft rises up in the air; again it comes down on the spine of the wretched nag. Under the violent force of the blow, she weakens, but she starts up anyway, and with all the strength she has left, she pulls, pulls in different directions, to escape this agony, but from all sides she encounters the six whips of her persecutors. A third and a fourth time, Mikolka hits his victim with the shaft. He is furious that he cannot kill her with a single blow.

"She dies hard!" someone in the gathering shouts.

"She won't last long, fellows. Her time has come!" observes an enthusiast in the crowd.

"Take an axe! That'll put an end to her once and for all!" suggests a third.

"Out of the way!" says Mikolka. His hands release the shaft. He rummages around once again in the wagon and picks up an iron bar. "Watch out!" he shouts, and he strikes a violent blow with this weapon on the poor horse. The mare reels, begins to drop, still wants to pull, but a second blow of the bar flattens her out on the ground, as if her four legs had just been instantly chopped off.

"Finish her off!" yells Mikolka, who, beside himself, jumps from the wagon. Several youths, red and intoxicated, grab whatever they can get their hands on — whips, sticks, the shaft — and run over to the dying horse. Mikolka, standing next to the beast, is hitting her again and again with the bar. The mare stretches out her head and breathes her last.

"She's dead!" someone in the crowd shouts.

"But how come she didn't want to gallop?"

"She's my property!" shouts Mikolka, still holding the bar in his hands. His eyes are bloodshot. He seems sorry that death has taken away his victim.

"Sure! You're no Christian!" comes the indignant response from several onlookers.

But the poor little boy is beside himself. Screaming, he forces a path for himself through the crowd surrounding the roan mare. He takes the bloody head of the cadaver into his hands and kisses it, kisses it on the eyes, on the lips . . . Then, in a sudden fit of rage, he clenches his little fists and throws himself upon Mikolka. At this moment his father, who has been looking for him for quite a while, finds him and leads him away from the crowd.

"Let's go, let's go!" he says, "let's go home!"

"Daddy! Why did they . . . kill . . . the poor horse? . . ." the child sobs. But he cannot catch his breath, and all that comes from his tight throat are rasping sounds.

"They're just drunks carrying on. It's not our business! Let's go!" says his father. Rodion squeezes him in his arms, but he has such a heavy weight on his chest . . . He wants to breathe, to scream — and he wakes up.

From the first part of the dream, Nietzsche learned that Raskolnikov had in common with him not only a mother, a sister, and a deceased father, but also a younger brother who had died as an infant. The continuation of the dream involved another image of a horse, this time being whipped and beaten hideously, an image which, it appears, Nietzsche never forgot. I should add that in another scene, which comes shortly after Raskolnikov commits the murder, a coachman whips Raskolnikov himself, so that the two scenes merge the man and the horse in a curious and obviously symbolically suggestive way. (Also in the dream scene, one of the men who are whipping the horse strikes Raskolnikov as well.) The interchangeability of horse and man was not likely to be lost, either consciously or unconsciously, on Nietzsche, the man who had once posed as a horse under a whip and who had retained the image long enough to construct it into *Thus Spoke Zarathustra* later on.

"NOTHING HAPPENS BY CHANCE"

Another important element of *Crime and Punishment* is that it is filled with coincidences, far more than in *The Insulted and Injured*, and Dostoevsky constructs this web of accidents in such a way as to create an ambiguity as to whether things happen by chance or by some powerful, mysterious design. Early in the book, as Raskolnikov is wavering over whether to proceed with the murder, he overhears that the old pawn-broker's sister will not be in their rooms the next night, thus providing an opportunity for him to be alone with the old woman. The narrator notes that it ". . . always seemed to him afterwards the predestined turning-point of his fate," and "he felt suddenly in his whole being that he had no more freedom of thought, no will, and that everything was suddenly and irrevocably decided." [72] (It turns out that the sister in fact walks in on Raskolnikov during the crime, and he takes her life as well.) And on another occasion Raskolnikov overhears a student talking about the old woman and suggesting that it would be a service to humanity to kill her and use her money for some good purpose. Raskolnikov is amazed: "But why had he happened to hear such a discussion and such ideas at the very moment when his own brain was just conceiving . . . *the very same ideas?* . . . This coincidence always seemed strange to him . . . as though there had really been in it something preordained, some guiding hint. . . ." [73] There are at least a dozen subsequent coincidences, so that this mysterious ambiguity between coincidence and fate lingers in the texture of the story.

I note this development of chance and fate because in Nietzsche's last sane weeks he made some strange remarks in this regard. On December 7, 1888, he wrote to August Strindberg from Turin: ". . . there is no longer any element of chance in my life. . . ." [74] And on Christmas 1888, he wrote to his friend Franz Overbeck: "Nothing happens by chance any more." [75] More chilling, in retrospect, is a letter he had written to Overbeck in 1883, saying, "I've always been prone to the cruelest accidents. Or, rather, I'm the one who's made horrors out of all accidents. . . ." [76] And Nietzsche said in the closing words of Book 2 of *Ecce Homo*, which he wrote in his last two and a half sane months, "My formula for greatness in a human being is *amor fati*." [77] Translation: "love of fate." [78] Nietzsche had introduced the phrase *amor fati* years earlier in his writings, saying that this was the thought that "shall be for me the reason, warranty, and sweetness of my life henceforth." [79] He elaborates on this idea there by reference to "personal providence."

And so it was that, nine days after he wrote that "Nothing happens by chance," Nietzsche saw a coachman whipping a horse in the street in

Turin, a scene from Dostoevsky, and he stepped into the picture. Perhaps his insanity was caused by syphilis, perhaps it was hereditary from his father, or perhaps it was the product of long suffering. At least as interesting and important are the form that his madness took and the mechanism that ignited it. Nietzsche had encountered a series of reflections of himself in Dostoevsky's books, from a solitary "underground" man, to odd men out in love triangles, to the idea that suffering is good, to the egoism of virtue, to the dead rising from coffins, to ordinary and extraordinary humans, to a pale criminal who murders but cannot live with the deed, to "all is permitted," to a deceased infant brother, to a whipped horse, to the annihilation of God, to feeling eternal harmony, to man becoming a god — joined to scores of references to madness, in contexts in which the difference between coincidence and fate is blurred.[80] Nietzsche was just then writing that there was no element of chance in his life. He was in a strange condition in which, mysteriously, his physical ailments had disappeared for some months, which may be a signal of his oncoming madness. I think that when he saw the horse being whipped, it was like a door opening and beckoning him to step in. Throwing his arms around the neck of the suffering horse was a synthesis and culmination of so many compartments of his life. Dreams, experiences, and ideas all merged in a symbol, and he stepped in and embraced it.

The next day he wrote a one-line letter expressing at least euphoria, if not ecstatic experience:

> Sing me a new song: the world is transfigured and all the heavens
> are full of joy.
>
> The Crucified[81]

Not just the signature indicates his identifying himself with God. The words "Sing *me* a new song," coming from a man who knew his Bible as Nietzsche did, are manifestly a rewording of a biblical verse. In the Bible the verse, which comes from the book of Psalms, reads: "Sing to *the Lord* a new song."[82] Nietzsche's madness, the form it took, and the event in which it was first manifest are remarkable in themselves, but the fact that his condition was so expressly linked to God at its outset remains for us to try to understand. We have found the immediate solution to the mystery of why Nietzsche embraced the horse in Turin, but it remains for us to reach a deeper understanding of what all of this meant. This investigation is not merely a study of a curious side-point in a biography. We are about to find that the episode of Nietzsche at Turin and the related mystery of his bond with Dostoevsky are intricately bound to the matter of the disappearance of God.

Postscript:

   During a period of his madness, Nietzsche would say certain sentences over and over: "I am dead because I am stupid," "I am stupid because I am dead," "I have a fine feeling for things," and "I do not like horses." [83]

Second postscript:

   Nietzsche died on August 25, 1900. Church bells were rung at his funeral. He was buried beside his father.

Chapter 8

THE "DEATH" OF GOD

"I AM THE GOD WHO MADE THIS JOKE"

When we were observing the shift in the divine-human balance in the Bible, I remarked on how curious it is that Jacob, after fighting with God all night, refuses to let God go unless He blesses him. In the light of Nietzsche's life and work (which are so inseparable) that story seems less surprising. The struggle with the deity takes such an effort, and such a toll, that the human who pursues it has to live with the wounds thereafter, sorely in need of blessing. Jacob limps after his exertion. Nietzsche may well have grappled with God more mightily, and he certainly suffered far more. Moving from religious belief and an anticipated life in the ministry to pronouncing the death of God was only one aspect of his struggle. It was an ongoing campaign in his life and works. In *Thus Spoke Zarathustra*, the death of God is not just a single announcement but rather a development that runs through the work. Like the Bible, *Thus Spoke Zarathustra* is composed of several books, and the death of God is pronounced in the first book, it recurs thereafter, and it is especially developed in the fourth and last book. And in Nietzsche's later work *The Antichrist*, which is more singly directed to the subject of religion, he leveled the most powerful criticism of Christianity that he could muster. He was taking God on, and both his books and his letters reveal that he felt that he was prevailing as no human before him in the match with the divine. But it

was a conflict at an enormous cost: a breach with his mother, a breach
with his loving memory of his father, a breach with his own early faith, a
solitary nomadic existence, a continuous awareness that he was shoulder-
ing something enormous, that he was saying things to a world that was
not ready to hear him. He was not toying with ideas or seeking to make
a name as an outrageous theologian. He was living his struggle with God,
and with family, church, European society, and history. It took a toll on
his physical health, and it played some part in his going insane. He said
in the days following his collapse in Turin that he would go around slap-
ping people on the back, saying in Italian, "Siamo contenti? Son dio ho
fatto questa caricatura." Translation: "Are we happy? I am the god who
made this joke." The man who had striven with the deity so profoundly
and at such cost had gone mad, and then a prominent feature of his madness was his identifying with God.[1]

Is there a relationship between madness and the death of God in
Nietzsche? It seems hard to doubt, given that Nietzsche places the first
announcement of the death of God in the mouth of a *madman*. The madman declares, "God is dead" in *The Gay Science* (also translated *The Joyful
Wisdom*),[2] a book that Nietzsche wrote about a year before he penned
Zarathustra's speeches. Walter Kaufmann, commenting on this passage
about a hundred years later, wrote that "Nietzsche prophetically envis-
ages himself as a madman: to have lost God means madness. . . ."[3] The
idea that there was something prophetic in Nietzsche's putting his words
in a deranged man's mouth is eerie. The idea that to have lost God *means*
madness is tantalizing and provocative. It does not mean that every religious person who becomes an atheist goes insane, but it does have implications for a *society* that loses its deity, as we shall see, and it has particular
implications for the case of the man who so potently formulated and developed the idea.

I believe that the Dostoevsky connection is not only the key to what
happened at Turin, but also the key to revealing the linkage between that
outbreak of Nietzsche's madness and the death of God. I did not refer to
Dostoevsky's own life and experience in the preceding chapter, not because they are not of interest. Anyone familiar with even a small portion
of the Dostoevsky biography knows that he lived an extaordinary life.
Rather, I intentionally limited myself to the Dostoevsky whom Nietzsche
knew, which was through Dostoevsky's books (plus a small number of

facts that he was able to learn from Georg Brandes and others). Interestingly, Dostoevsky spent some years in Germany and Switzerland at times when Nietzsche was in those places, and I think that the two men may sometimes have been within seventy-five miles of each other. For all we know, they could have passed each other on the street. But they did not know it. Nietzsche had not yet heard of Dostoevsky, Dostoevsky probably never heard of Nietzsche, and they never met. But we must now consider a few points of Dostoevsky's life which are particularly relevant to the matter of Nietzsche's and Dostoevsky's commonality. We should recognize, of course, that there are also differences between them, dramatic differences, and the idea is not to list and weigh the similarities and the distinctions against each other as with pans on a scale. Rather, we have observed an intriguing line of points connecting the two men, and my purpose now is to examine a few things that they have in common, which are relevant to the extent that they reveal something about this connection. As with the case of the hiding of the face of God in the Bible, the explanation of Nietzsche at Turin and its relationship to the disappearance of God lies in a combination of factors. One does not follow a single line of clues to a finish. One must rather synthesize an elaborate mosaic of elements.

"IN THE FANTASIZINGS OF DREAMS"

In tracing the shift in the divine-human balance in the Bible, we saw that the first divine power possessed by a human is the interpretation of dreams. Dreams and visions subsequently become the formal mechanism of revelation to prophets. The seriousness of the biblical attitude toward the dream realm is a marker of its special place in human experience. And this realm is significant in reckoning the common spheres of Nietzsche and Dostoevsky. After all, in a certain sense the trail between them begins and ends with dreams, in each case followed by a "fulfillment": Nietzsche's own childhood dream, followed by the death of his infant brother; and Raskolnikov's dream involving his deceased infant brother and a beaten horse, followed by the beating of the horse in Turin. And both Dostoevsky and Nietzsche were attracted by the psychological power of dreams and their relationship to waking life. In the paragraph that precedes the account of Raskolnikov's fearful dream in *Crime and Punishment*, Dostoevsky introduces the nightmare with an analysis that one could imagine Freud himself writing:

> In a sickly state, our dreams are often distinguished by their extraordinary relief and their striking resemblance to reality. The picture is sometimes monstrous, but the staging and everything else about the production are so true to life, the details are so sharp, and they present, by their unforeseeable quality, an arrangement so ingenious, that the dreamer, even if he were an artist like Pushkin or Turgenev, would not be able to invent anything so good in a waking state. These sickly dreams always remain in the memory for a long time and have a profound effect on the individual's organism, which is already out of kilter.[4]

Dreams were the subject of the first pages of Nietzsche's first book, the opening section of *The Birth of Tragedy*, and by now it should hardly even come as a surprise to us that he made comments similar to Dostoevky's, for example noting that in the creation of our dream worlds, "every man is truly an artist."[5] He also wrote of the relationship between dreams and waking life in two passages in *Human, All Too Human* (I: 12, 13) which Freud in fact cited in *The Interpretation of Dreams*.[6] Lou Salomé, who later was a friend of Freud's and a psychoanalyst herself, wrote in her Nietzsche biography:

> Dreams always played a great role in his life and thinking, and during his last years he often drew from them — as with the solution of a riddle — the contents of his teachings.[7]

She went on to tie the realms of dreaming and waking to one other important arena in Nietzsche's thought, the realm of madness:

> Nietzsche's unifying thought then emerged: under certain circumstances, dream is the revivication of everything lived in the past, while life, on the other hand, in its deepest essence is a dream whose spirit and meaning we must determine for ourselves as awakeners. The same is true of all dream-related conditions and of all that which could lead far down into the chaotic,

dark, and inexhaustible underground of life. . . . And yet, the tranquil dream is insufficient for that quest. What is needed is a much more real, effective, and even more terrible experiencing, namely through orgiastic Dionysian conditions and the chaos of frenzied passions — yes, *madness* itself as a means of sinking back down into the mass of entwined feelings and imaginings. This seemed for Nietzsche the last road into the primal depths imbedded within us.

Of course we should not accept uncritically Salomé's analysis of Nietzsche, which she wrote after Nietzsche had gone mad, but Nietzsche himself juxtaposed dreams and madness in *Dawn*, in a passage that Salomé cites: "In outbursts of passion, and in the fantasising of dreams and insanity, a man rediscovers his own and mankind's prehistory."[8] Note especially this overlap of dreams and madness, two of the areas that figure prominently in the connection between Nietzsche and Dostoevsky. We shall encounter other cases of overlap.

FATHERS AND SONS

The link between the two men involves fathers as well. Dostoevsky, too, lost his father unexpectedly and horribly. While Dostoevsky, in his late teens, was away studying at the Academy of Engineers, he received the news that his father had been murdered by his serfs. Though the very historicity of the murder has recently been thrown into doubt, the fact remains that Dostoevsky himself believed it to be true. As Joseph Frank noted in the first volume of his renowned biography of Dostoevsky, ". . . no part of his biography has attracted more attention and speculation, or been given greater importance in determining the future."[9] Freud's own interest in Dostoevsky was focused on this point; his essay on Dostoevsky is titled, "Dostoevsky and Parricide."[10] Freud was concerned with Dostoevsky's Oedipal guilt associated with his father's death. Frank characterized Dostoevsky's guilt feelings as more consciously and immediately derived from recent events: in his first year away from home at the Academy of Engineers he failed to be promoted, and when his father received a letter informing him of this he had a stroke; and Dostoevsky had been asking for, and receiving, money from his father so as not to feel socially inferior at the academy, though he knew that his father was in extremely difficult financial straits at the time. He may even have felt that pressing his father for funds because of his own vanity is what forced his father to oppress their serfs, leading them to commit the murder.[11] In short, there are grounds to believe that Dostoevsky felt his father's death keenly and that he had conscious and unconscious reasons to be burdened with guilt. In *Crime and Punishment*, Raskolnikov's father is dead, and on the night before committing the crime Raskolnikov dreams that he is walking with his father by the hand. In *The Brothers Karamazov*, the father (whose name is Feodor, the same as Dostoevky's own first name) is murdered by one of his sons, but all of the sons bear the guilt for their father's death in their respective ways.[12] Dostoevsky told his brother, "I would regret nothing if the tears of our poor father did not burn my soul."[13]

Nietzsche, as we know, felt his father's untimely death no less keenly, and the childhood dream of father and son returning together to the grave is one reflection of that. He also lived in dread of suffering a similar fate to his father's, that is, madness and early death,[14] and the year in which he attained the age that his father had been at the time of death was an all-time low point in his physical health and his spirits. He wrote: "My father died very young, at exactly the age at which I myself was nearest to death."[15] We cannot enter a full, detailed analysis of Nietzsche's and Dostoevsky's responses to their fathers' deaths here. I note it as a common point, first, because it would be irresponsible *not* to reckon so manifestly significant a factor in considering their relationship. Second, it strikes me as obvious that fathers are models who play a fundamental part in the conceptions that humans form of God — especially in two men who had religious upbringings in a faith that spoke of "God the Father" and prayed to "our Father who art in heaven." Freud argued that religion "arose out of the relation to the father" and analyzed the way in which people equate God with fathers, but one does not have to be a Freudian to perceive that there is some such connection between people's images of their fathers and their conceptions of God.[16] More particularly, the matter of these two men's fathers is relevant to our interest in the disappearance of God. While there is no rule that says that a child who has lost a father must necessarily arrive at a particular theological view as

a result, still one does not need ten courses in Freudian analysis to understand how a boy who has painfully lost his father might come to the view
that God has died.[17] I do not mean either to oversimplify or overestimate
this point, but rather just to note it for now and include it in the evidence.

We must take account of the matter of horses as well. Nietzsche was
not alone in his empathy for the whipped animal. Such scenes were frequent in Nietzsche's and Dostoevsky's world, at least as frequent as
people angrily replacing punctured tires in mine, and one such scene
made a lasting impression on Dostoevsky. On the very journey in which
he and his brother Mikhail first left home as teenagers to enter the
academy, traveling from Moscow to St. Petersburg on his "journey from
boyhood to manhood,"[18] he saw a driver of a troika being beaten by a
courier in such a way that, each time the courier struck the driver with
his fist, the driver whipped the horse in a corresponding rhythm. Frank
writes of "the primacy of the experience for Dostoevsky, and the forma-
tive role that he assigns it in his own self-development."[19] Dostoevsky
himself describes this bizarre merger of the fates of the horse and the
man in his *Diary of a Writer*; he says, "This disgusting sight has remained
in my memory all my life. Never was I able to forget it. . . . This little
scene appeared to me, so to speak, as an emblem, as something which
very graphically demonstrated the link between cause and effect. Here
every blow dealt at the animal leaped out of each blow dealt at the
man."[20] We might well surmise that this influenced Dostoevsky's formulation of *Crime and Punishment*. In fact we do not have to surmise,
because, Frank observes, Dostoevsky refers to this experience specifically
in his notebooks for the novel. Note that what was central for Dostoevsky
was the merging of the fate of the horse and the man, which, as we have
seen, materialized in the structure of the novel.

Dostoevsky brought the image back in *The Brothers Karamazov*, in the
chapter titled "Rebellion," one of the classic treatments of suffering in
literature. It is a discussion between two of the brothers: Alyosha, who is
preparing for the priesthood, and Ivan, who is an atheist. Ivan cites cases
of human infliction of suffering and rejects any reconciliation between
this and the notion of a just God. His cases involve the infliction of pain
on human beings, especially children, but he includes one case of a horse,
which a peasant beats when it cannot pull a load, whipping the horse on
its eyes. It sounds like an allusion to Dostoevsky's own scene back in

Crime and Punishment, but Ivan attributes it to a poem by Nekrassov. It has been noted that "the poem by Nekrassov had left in Dostoevsky's soul the most profound impression."[21] The point is that, both in his experience and in a literary work he had read (by an author whom he knew personally), Dostoevsky had been moved powerfully by the image that later moved Nietzsche. The force of these impressions found its way into the texture of Dostoevsky's novel. I think that the dream in *Crime and Punishment* is one of the most frightening scenes in world literature, much more powerful than the grotesque, blatantly scary episodes in current popular macabre fiction. Dostoevsky's wife Anna describes an occasion on which Dostoevsky read this excerpt from *Crime and Punishment*, the dream of the beaten horse, to an audience, and she says: "and I myself saw the people sitting pale with terror and some of them crying. I myself could not hold back my tears."[22] The very fact that Dostoevsky chose this particular excerpt to read is noteworthy as well. Both Nietzsche and Dostoevsky felt the beating of a horse to be a symbol of human suffering. Dostoevsky possessed the skill to convey it in words, and Nietzsche had the sensitivity to feel it in Dostoevsky's text and the fortune to encounter it soon after.

The horse has a double relevance in this assembly of connections because, we should recall, it is argued that horses have psychological associations with the father as well. Freud's classic case of "little Hans," the first successful application of psychoanalysis to a child, comes to mind. Hans was terrified of horses and feared to go out in the street where horses were present. The specific "precipitating cause of the outbreak of Hans's illness" was the boy's seeing a horse fall down in the street; Freud wrote that ". . . the neurosis took its start directly from this chance event. . . ."[23] And Freud related the neurosis to Oedipal tensions associated with Hans's father. It is a Freudian notion that animal phobias generally relate to Oedipal fears of the father. I can add testimony from observations of my own that I have seen evidence of such a connection; but, again, my purpose in occasional references to Freudian theories is not to win converts to Freud nor to accept general psychoanalytic notions uncritically. I mention them as grounds to consider such possibilities in the specific cases at hand. In Dostoevsky's case, he witnessed the beating of the horse just at the time that he left home and saw his father for the last time in his life. Also, one story of his father's death involved his suffocation with a pillow from a horse-drawn carriage. And then, in the dream of the horse in *Crime and Punishment*, Raskolnikov is holding his father's hand through the scene. And Nietzsche read that scene, which was preceded by the reference to a deceased infant brother, which in turn recalled Nietzsche's dream of his own father. (And recall that that dream was of his deceased father going into a *church*, and bringing a child *out of the church*. From church to grave: an interesting image for a person who would go from being "the little pastor" to announcing the "death of God.")

The horse in fact has a triple relevance to this picture in that horses have a history of curious associations with gods. This connection has been developed most recently and effectively in Peter Shaffer's remarkable play *Equus*. The drama involves a psychiatrist treating the neurosis of a boy who fashions and worships a deity of his own, "Equus," Latin for horse. The boy's pious Christian upbringing by his mother is upset when his atheist father tears the boy's picture of the crucified Jesus off the wall over the boy's bed. The boy replaces the picture of Jesus with a picture of a horse, chained by its bit, and he conceives a religion of his own, with his own rituals, including passionate night rides on horseback. The drama is replete with references to horses in religious contexts, pagan and biblical, including the image that when Europeans first came to the New World riding horses, the indigenous people perceived the horse and rider to be a single creature, like a centaur, like a god. Shaffer conveys the enigma of horses, which is known to anyone who has ever ridden one: as animals far more powerful than humans, which are nonetheless mastered by humans, they are power restrained. In this sense he compares the might of the horse, controlled by bit and reins, to Jesus, the deity bound to the cross by humans. *Equus*, besides being a stunning drama, can be read as an interesting reflection on the case of Nietzsche and Dostoevsky, drawing together fathers and sons, horses and gods, all in a tapestry of psychology and religion, that even includes the explicit notion of gods dying. My point is that there is a complex web of psychological associations (dreams, fathers, gods, horses) reflected in the lives and works of Nietzsche and Dostoevsky, which plays a part in the chain of events that connects them.

"DEVIL TAKE HIM, HE'S PARTLY RIGHT!"

The network of connections includes suffering as well. One can hardly ignore the fact that Dostoevsky had a record of anguish and loss that made him akin to Nietzsche in this all-important regard as well. He had a history of illnesses and hypochondria, and he was epileptic. The early death of his father came only two years after the early death of his mother. And later his first wife and his brother died in the same year. Above all, though, is the series of events that ripped into Dostoevsky's life just as he was beginning his career as a writer. His first book, *Poor Folk*, was extremely well received, and he was regarded as a major new figure in Russian literature. But his exceptional early success when he was only in his early twenties was cut off because of his views and associations (like Nietzsche's!). Dostoevsky was arrested for being a member of a group with revolutionary ideas, and he and the other members were tried, convicted, and sentenced to death. In December of 1849, a month before Nietzsche had his dream of his father's grave, Dostoevsky stood in line at a scaffold to be executed, but minutes before his execution was to take place he was informed that the czar had reprieved the group, and he was sent to prison in Siberia. He spent the next four years wearing irons, at hard labor, in brutal conditions, followed by five more years of exile in Siberia before he was permitted to return. One can begin to form a picture of those horrible years in prison from his *Memoirs from the House of the Dead*. Nietzsche, by the way, was aware of these basic facts of Dostoevsky's life. He wrote to his friend Gast:

> So far I know little about his career, his reputation, or his background. He died in 1881. In his youth he was in a bad way: illness, poverty (of the genteel sort), a death sentence at twenty-seven, a reprieve at the scaffold, then four years in Siberia, chained, among hardened criminals. This period was decisive. He discovered the power of his psychological intuition; what's more, his heart was sweetened and deepened in the process. His book of recollections from these years, *La Maison des morts*, is one of the most *human* books ever written.[24]

It was in prison that Dostoevsky's epilepsy began; it figured in his novels thereafter, notably in *The Idiot* and *The Brothers Karamazov*. The post-Siberia years were hard in other ways besides his epilepsy and the loss of his wife and brother. He was a compulsive gambler, frequently losing everything at the gaming tables, then bitterly reproaching himself for thus afflicting himself and his family, and subsequently returning to lose all again. He often wrote feverishly to complete novels in time for deadlines after losing the advances that had been paid. Only in the very last years of his life did he achieve a measure of success and satisfaction.

There is another aspect of the agony of both these men that is harder to capture, an element of profound internal struggle with themselves and with their pasts. It is a commonplace to point out that Dostoevsky used to create great speeches and powerful arguments for the very characters with whom he disagreed, notably Raskolnikov in *Crime and Punishment*, Kirilov in *The Devils*, and Ivan in *The Brothers Karamazov*. He was certainly aware of, and annoyed by, his ability to create such independent and effective opponents to himself. In one of his manuscripts he wrote in the margin beside one such speech: "Devil take him, he's partly right!" At least one interpreter, Lev Shestov, has argued that the real Dostoevsky — that is, his genuine beliefs and feelings — is to be found in these fictional characters rather than in the views that Dostoevsky professed as his own. In discussing the powerful speech about the egotism of virtue in *The Insulted and Injured* that I cited in the previous chapter, a speech presenting a view that was morally hideous to Dostoevsky, Shestov wrote, "When you let anyone, even in a novel, deride your holy of holies so caustically, it means you have taken the first step toward denial."[25] Other Dostoevsky scholars have rejected this view. This issue seems to me to reflect the tension that pervades Dostoevsky's novels between the views that he holds and those that he rejects but presents so amazingly effectively. One is reminded of Brandes's portrait of Dostoevsky in his letter to Nietzsche: "a great poet, but an abominable person, utterly Christian in his emotional life and at the same time utterly sadistic." And Nietzsche's own two-sided reaction to Dostoevsky may well reflect this tension as well: "I'm grateful to him in a very special way, much as he constantly offends my most basic instincts." Nietzsche, of all men, surely was able to understand how these two sides could coexist in Dostoevsky, and he

knew the psychological anguish and physical effects that were the consequences of waging an unremitting internal battle for years.

"THE GREATEST DANGER"

Most blatantly, Nietzsche and Dostoevsky shared a concern with mad-
ness. There are regular references to it in Dostoevsky's works, including
The Underground Spirit and *Memoirs from the House of the Dead*, over
thirty references in *The Insulted and Injured*, and over fifty in *Crime and
Punishment*. It is no less common in Nietzsche's works and letters. We
have already noted the portrayal of the madman in *The Gay Science*.
About a year after he composed that image, he wrote a letter to Lou
Salomé in which he described a happy afternoon in which "I wondered
in all innocence and malice if I had any tendency to madness. In the end
I said *no*." [26] He said no, but a year later, after his painful loss of Salomé
and Rée and his painful recognition of his sister's malicious part in the
affair, he wrote a rather different view of madness, relating it to his internal struggles:

> . . . there was a real hatred of my sister, who has cheated me of
> my best acts of self-conquest for a whole year . . . so that I have
> finally become the victim of a relentless desire for vengeance,
> precisely when my inmost thinking has renounced all schemes
> of vengeance and punishment. This conflict is bringing me step
> by step closer to *madness* — I feel this in the most frightening
> way. . . . [27]

While Nietzsche was expressing such feelings privately in his letters
he also was speaking of madness openly in his books. In an aphorism in
The Gay Science titled "The greatest danger," he identified the greatest
danger threatening humanity as "the eruption of madness." [28] In *Thus
Spoke Zarathustra*, he made numerous references to madness, including
the recurring line: "Thus preached madness." [29] And, interestingly, while
the densest concentration of references to madness in Dostoevsky is in
Crime and Punishment, the densest concentration in *Thus Spoke Zarathu-*

stra is in the section titled "The Pale Criminal," the section that so strikingly and mysteriously calls Raskolnikov and *Crime and Punishment* to mind.

More tantalizing is Nietzsche's — and Dostoevsky's — interest in *voluntary* madness, that is, in choosing to go insane. In Zarathustra's first speech he says:

> Everybody wants the same, everybody is the same: whoever feels different goes voluntarily into a madhouse.[30]

In the aphorism on "The greatest danger" in *The Gay Science*, Nietzsche refers to people whom he identifies as "the most select spirits" and "the explorers of *truth* above all," and he comments: "It is in these impatient spirits that a veritable delight in madness erupts because madness has such a cheerful tempo."

"A delight in madness." "Madness has such a cheerful tempo." This has a strange parallel in a letter that August Strindberg wrote to Nietzsche. Strindberg, perhaps reacting to a mad-sounding letter from Nietzsche, wrote a few lines in Greek and Latin. He began with a quotation from Greek poetry: θελω, θελω μανηναι! Translation: "I want, I want to be mad!" And he ended with the Latin words: *Interdum juvat insanire!* Translation: "Meanwhile it is a joy to be mad!"[31] It is impossible to say that this letter influenced Nietzsche's actions, but we should note that it is dated just a few days before Nietzsche embraced the horse in Turin.

Nietzsche had written in *Thus Spoke Zarathustra*, "There is always some reason in madness."[32] And most explicitly of all, Nietzsche had already written in *Dawn* eight years before his own breakdown:

> All superior men who were irresistibly drawn to throw off the yoke of any kind of morality and to frame new laws had, *if they were not actually mad*, no alternative but to make themselves or pretend to be mad.[33]

The reference to making oneself mad or pretending to be mad is all the more startling when we consider that Nietzsche's friends Gast and Overbeck both said in the period of his insanity that they were haunted by an impression that Nietzsche might be pretending. Gast saw Nietzsche in a condition that "seemed to him — horrible to say — as though he were only feigning to be insane, as though he were glad to have ended this way!"[34] And Overbeck said, "I cannot escape the horrible suspicion that arises within me at certain definite periods of observation, or at least at certain moments, namely, that his madness is simulated."[35] I am informed by psychiatrists that this haunting appearance of a pretense is a known phenomenon in certain mental conditions; and the full record of reports of Nietzsche's years following the episode at Turin leaves little room for a belief that he was faking for those twelve years. Nonetheless, the impressions of these two of the very closest people to Nietzsche set his earlier remarks in a perplexing and enticing light. They at least raise the question of whether Nietzsche fearfully but knowingly drove himself to the threshold of insanity, or whether in the end he found some relief in stepping over that threshold.

This peculiar notion of voluntary — and especially pretended — madness has parallels in Dostoevsky's fiction and nonfiction as well. In a scene in *Crime and Punishment* Raskolnikov, in the presence of the inspector Zossimov, carefully portrays himself as having been both delirious and cognizant of details on a particular occasion all at the same time.

> "A familiar phenomenon," interposed Zossimov, "actions are sometimes performed in a masterly and most cunning way, while the direction of the actions is deranged and dependent on various morbid impressions — it's like a dream."
>
> "Perhaps it's a good thing really that he should think me almost a madman," thought Raskolnikov.[36]

The idea that Raskolnikov is open to posing as crazy in order to mislead the authorities is all the more interesting because elsewhere in the book he is in fact delirious and unstable. So he may be pretending less than he thinks. Indeed, in these very lines, Raskolnikov may ironically be acting out Zossimov's scenario, because he is actually portraying himself "in a masterly and cunning way, while the direction of the actions is deranged"! The point is that the line between sanity and insanity is rendered unclear here, and the role of intention in relation to madness is especially ambiguous in Dostoevsky's formulation. In the light of our earlier observations, the fact that Dostoevsky adds the words "it's like a dream" in this context is also interesting as dreams and madness again overlap. The idea of choosing to go out of one's mind also occurs in

The Underground Spirit, as I mentioned in the preceding chapter, and elsewhere Dostoevsky wrote the chilling words: "I have a plan — to go mad."

In a short story of Philip Roth's the narrator says, "But if you chose to be crazy then you weren't crazy." [37] Perhaps for Nietzsche and Dostoevsky there was some relief from the fear of the specter of insanity in the idea of voluntarily choosing that path. But whatever the reason, the end result was that this concept was patently in both men's consciousness. Both thought about madness, wrote about it, and contemplated the idea of electing it. And, as we shall see, both of them perceived a connection between madness and the struggle with the deity.

"MUST WE OURSELVES NOT BECOME GODS?"

Regarding the connection between these two men, and in relating all of this to the subject of this book, the common facet that we must consider above all is their lifelong contention with God, in their lives and in their works. Both, equally, can be compared to biblical Jacob in this respect, for having wrestled, prevailed, and suffered the wounds of divine struggle. To these two men, religion was more than a single subject of interest among many. They did not play at it nor approach it as a set of intellectually interesting propositions. Regarding Nietzsche, Lou Salomé emphasized "to what extent the religious drive always dominated his being and his knowledge." She described what she saw as "the tragic conflict of his life — the conflict between the need for God and the compulsive need to deny God." [38] Regarding Dostoevsky — who, like Nietzsche, received a strong religious education in his youth, and whose only book in all his years in prison was the Bible — he himself said that "the problem of the existence of God had tormented him all his life." He gave the most compelling arguments to the atheist Ivan Karamazov, yet "it was always emotionally impossible for him ever to accept a world that had no relation to a God of any kind." [39]

One indicator of the way in which Nietzsche understood his relationship to the matter of belief in God to be a struggle, a test of strength of his will, comes from a remark he made as commentary on a point in *Thus*

Spoke Zarathustra. Zarathustra says, "I would believe only in a god who could dance."[40] In a note in Nietzsche's *The Will to Power* he gives a warning about what Zarathustra has said: "Zarathustra says he *would;* but Zarathustra *will* not — Do not misunderstand him."[41] The rejection of belief in a deity is a choice, an act of will. Zarathustra says, "*If* there were gods, how could I endure not to be a god! *Hence* there are no gods."[42] In an aphorism Nietzsche speaks of a lake that one day refused to run off and erected a dam to block its outlet — and ever since then the lake has been rising higher. So, Nietzsche says, humankind can rise ever higher once it ceases to "flow out into a god."[43] The issue is not simply the question of whether or not God exists, which Nietzsche claims is a question that has never concerned him; he rejects both God and atheism as gross answers.[44] The issue for Nietzsche appears to be what the implications of a god's presence are for a human. He personally is not able to be the fullest human he can be in the presence of a god. Nor can humankind be all that it is capable of being in a god's presence. From the perspective of the shift in balance between the divine and human that we have contemplated in the Bible, this is a stunning development. Recall that in the Bible the most rebellious generation is the one that is closest to God (the wilderness generation) while the generation that transgresses the least is the one in which God is most hidden (Ezra-Nehemiah-Esther). The impression there is that closeness to the divine is not tolerable. Now in Nietzsche we see a human again finding the presence of God intolerable, but it is developed more explicitly, more blatantly than anything we saw in the Hebrew Bible and, in a sense, even more than the execution of the deity in the New Testament, for here there is no issue of "knowing not what they do." In Nietzsche it is a matter of rejecting deities for the sake of humankind's own development. It is even a matter of replacing gods with ourselves. When the madman says that God is dead in *The Gay Science,* he also says, "And we have killed him." And he adds, "Must we ourselves not become gods simply to appear worthy of it?"[45] In a letter that Nietzsche wrote two weeks before his breakdown in Turin he said, ". . . since the old God has abdicated, I shall rule the world from now on."[46] And in the days immediately following the breakdown he spoke of "himself as the successor to the dead God."[47] It is the ultimate confrontation in the divine-human struggle, in which the human must exclude and replace all deities in order to be all that he or she can be.

This exclusion of the divine in order to arrive at human fulfillment is what is particularly relevant in Nietzsche's works (and in his identifying himself with God after his breakdown) in the context of the shift in the divine-human balance. In the Bible the progression toward greater human responsibility and less visible divine direction is complex, sometimes subtle, interwoven through the works of many writers, so that to observe the entire progression in all its stages is a delicate task. In Nietzsche's words the shift is fearfully visible, manifest to all: the human must displace the divine.

And we find this idea in Dostoevsky. In *The Devils* it is the view of Kirilov: after the annihilation of God, "Man will be god." He "will himself be a god. And that other God will not be."[48] And in *The Brothers Karamazov* Ivan is quoted as having said, ". . . we only need to destroy the idea of God in man. . . . As soon as men have all of them denied God . . . the man-god will appear." And he says, "Let us . . . become gods."[49] This idea of humans thus displacing God is all the more astonishing in Dostoevsky because, we must never forget, he did not profess such views himself. It is a measure of his struggle with God that such concepts occurred to him and that he could articulate them so powerfully while living the life of a pious Christian.

From the perspective of the shift in the divine-human balance in the Bible, this notion of humans becoming gods is more connected to the biblical progression than Nietzsche or Dostoevsky may have realized. Recall that the first human act of rebellion in the garden of Eden is followed by the deity's stated concern that: *"the human has become like one of us."*[50] In a sense this has been the essence of divine-human struggle all along, and these two men, in pursuing this uttermost human movement into the divine zone, reached to the limits in the experience of confrontation with the divine.

"ONCE MORE AMONG MEN"

The furthest that Nietzsche saw Dostoevsky take the struggle with God was in *The Devils*, but I think that most scholars and readers in general of Dostoevsky would agree that Dostoevsky developed it most poignantly and exquisitely in *The Brothers Karamazov*, his last novel. Given all that we have seen of Nietzsche's reaction to Dostoevsky, it is more than merely noteworthy that Nietzsche never read *The Brothers Karamazov*. This novel probably has even more in common with points of Nietzsche's life and works than any of the others, and one can barely imagine with what amazement Nietzsche would have read it. I want to focus on one section of *The Brothers Karamazov*, probably the most famous part of it, because it relates to the present point and to other main points of this study in ways that will be perfectly obvious. It is the section titled "The Grand Inquisitor."[51] Since I quoted Freud's statements of his admiration for Nietzsche, it is worth quoting his impression of Dostoevsky as well. In beginning his classic analysis of Dostoevsky, he singled out this book and this section of all Dostoevsky's works to make his point: "*The Brothers Karamazov* is the most magnificent novel ever written; the episode of the Grand Inquisitor, one of the peaks in the literature of the world, can hardly be valued too highly."[52] Dostoevsky presents "The Grand Inquisitor" as a story that Ivan, the atheist Karamazov brother, has composed; Ivan calls it a "poem in prose" and recounts it to his younger brother Alyosha, the aspiring priest. In it, Jesus returns to the earth during the Spanish Inquisition. The story is immediately set in the context of the hiding of the face of God, as Ivan says in his introduction: "It is fifteen centuries since man has ceased to see signs from heaven."[53] And now the deity appears "once more among men in that human shape in which He walked among men for three years fifteen centuries ago." The divine visitor performs miracles: a blind man sees, a dead child rises. Everyone recognizes him. And then the aged cardinal who heads the Inquisition sees him and has him seized and taken to prison. The major part of the story is the scene between this old man and his God in the prison cell.

Jesus does not speak, and the Inquisitor in fact tells him not to speak, for "Thou hast no right to add anything to what Thou hadst said of old." The Inquisitor asks (rhetorically, one presumes), "Why hast Thou come now to hinder us?" Ivan interrupts his story to explain that this is a fundamental feature of Roman Catholicism, that God cannot speak or "meddle" now because "'All has been given by Thee to the Pope,' they say, 'and all, therefore, is still in the Pope's hands, and there is no need for Thee to come now at all.'" The Church is the authority now. The Grand Inquisitor then tells Jesus that he (Jesus) erred when he resisted the devil's three temptations in the wilderness. The devil offered him miracle, mystery, and authority, and Jesus rejected them. But, the old cardinal reveals, the Church accepted them. The Church rules the masses precisely by miracle, mystery, and authority; and, he argues, that is what the masses need. Jesus did not want to win them by miraculous acts and dominate them with power; he wanted them to have freedom of choice. But freedom is too difficult and frightful for them, says the Inquisitor, and so the Church has taken the three awesome gifts from the devil, the "great dread spirit." And he concludes, "We are not working with Thee, but with *him* — that is our mystery." He declares that he will have the divine intruder burnt at the stake the next day and that the masses will hasten to follow his orders. (This is a striking return of fire as an image. We saw that fire plays a recurring part in the hiding of the face of God and the shift in the divine-human balance in the Bible. Now a human being is portrayed as planning to burn an incarnation of the deity in fire.)[54] But Jesus, still not speaking, simply kisses him on the lips. "That was all his answer." The Grand Inquisitor opens the cell door and says, "Go, and come no more . . . come not at all, never, never." And the divine visitor leaves.

Some may take Dostoevsky's story as strictly his Russian Orthodox criticism of the Roman Catholic Church, but that would be more likely if he had put the story in the mouth of Alyosha, the aspiring Orthodox priest. Dostoevsky gives this powerful tale to Ivan, the atheist, whose interest is not only in questioning Catholics but in questioning God — and all religion. Dostoevsky attributes this tale to an atheist, but it is in fact Dostoevsky's creation, and he does not give Alyosha, the believer, any comparable response to it. He simply has Alyosha get up and kiss Ivan on the lips. *Imitatio Dei*. And he has Ivan delightedly say, "That's plagiarism!" He gives the best arguments to Ivan and to the Grand Inquisitor. He gives the unstated, emotional response to Alyosha and the deity. I think that both an atheist and a believer could read this story and each feel that his or her side is vindicated in it, not because of any lack of clarity in it but because of the brilliance of its formulation, a brilliance that reflected Dostoevsky's personal experience of both sides.

The story not only reflects the matter of divine hiddenness but also the shift in the divine-human balance. It is a phenomenal parallel to the story of Rabbi Eliezer. Again the divine voice is disallowed, again the human religious establishment prevails, and again the deity acquiesces in the human appropriation of powers from the divine realm. In the old Eliezer story the deity's loving understanding of the human position is expressed by His laughing. In Dostoevsky's story, it is expressed by a kiss. We do not know who the author of the old rabbinic story was, nor can we guess how that person responded to his own conception. But we know for a fact that Dostoevsky personally agonized his way through the divine struggles that he depicted in his fiction. He and Nietzsche — albeit in utterly different ways — envisioned a stage in the relations between humans and the divine in which humans could no longer tolerate the presence or even belief in the existence of a God, an age in which humans would have to appropriate the divine role in their own direction of the world. For both Nietzsche and Dostoevsky an implication of the disappearance of God was a new step for humankind. Nietzsche embraced this view and Dostoevsky resisted it, but both conceived it and understood and conveyed its significance.

"THE MASK OF A DIVINITY"

Finally, for both Nietzsche and Dostoevsky, madness and the struggle with God overlapped. Nietzsche identified with God after he went mad, but he had understood madness to be part of the journey of divine struggle long before that. His reference to superior men having to be mad or pretending to be mad, which I quoted above, was related to divinity in context; the passage begins like this:

> When, in spite of that fearful pressure of "morality of custom" under which all the communities of mankind have lived . . . , new and deviate ideas, evaluations, and drives again and again broke out, they did so accompanied by a dreadful attendant: almost everywhere it was madness which prepared the way for the new idea, which broke the spell of a venerated usage and superstition. Do you understand why it had to be madness which did this? Something in voice and bearing as uncanny and incalculable as the demonic moods of the weather and the sea and therefore worthy of a similar awe and observation? Something that bore so

visibly the sign of total unfreedom [i.e., involuntariness] as the convulsions and froth of the epileptic, that seemed to mark the madman as the mask and speaking-trumpet of a divinity?[55]

The madman is the mask behind which a god is concealed. And he is the god's speaking-trumpet, the device which magnifies one's voice so that those who are deaf will hear it. Nietzsche wrote this in *Dawn*, which he completed a few weeks after Dostoevsky died. A year later he wrote the seemingly opposite image in *The Gay Science*, in which the madman, rather than being the mask of God, announces the death of God. And a year after that he wrote the first book of *Thus Spoke Zarathustra*, in which his reference to going voluntarily into a madhouse comes in the same speech in which Zarathustra first proclaims the death of God. Later Zarathustra, saying that he once pictured the world as the creation of a suffering god, adds, "This god whom I created was man-made and madness, like all gods!" And he refers a moment later to "that brief madness of bliss which is experienced only by those who suffer most deeply."[56] His introduction of suffering into a context of gods and madness is significant, for Nietzsche had an intense concern with two divine figures in his life and works: Dionysus and the crucified Jesus. Recall that these were the two names that he signed in the letters that he wrote after his breakdown. Their notable common characteristic is that they are both suffering deities. The point: In one of Nietzsche's images the madman could appear to be the mask concealing the deity; in another the madman could be the announcer of the death of the deity. In another the suffering of humans and of gods is related to madness, and all gods are said to be "man-made and madness." In a variety of ways in his works, in his letters, and eventually in his own collapse, Nietzsche connected the struggle with God to madness.

Dostoevsky's works contain this connection as well. Kirilov is suicidal in *The Devils*. Ivan suffers delirium and hallucinations in *The Brothers Karamazov*. In a consummate scene of psychology, religion, and irony in dialogue, Ivan sits in his room while, on the couch opposite him, sits his own hallucination or dream of the devil, and the two of them argue over whether the visitor is in fact Ivan's imagination or the real thing. They debate about God, faith, the man-god, morality (including the man-god's stepping over the old slave morality, a remarkable prefiguring of Nietz-

sche), dreams, and suffering. Ivan says, "I'll get the better of you. I won't
be taken to a madhouse!" And the narrator adds about Ivan: "He was
exerting himself to the utmost not to believe in the delusion and not to
sink into complete insanity." [57]

It is understandable that these two men who were so deeply concerned
with God and with madness should have perceived these two realms to
overlap. God represents order, especially in Western religious tradition.
God gives shape, gives laws. Recall that in the Bible, creation is the divine
imposition of order over chaos. In Genesis, initially there is only water,
in a shapeless, undifferentiated abyss, described as "unformed and void"
(Hebrew *tōhû wābōhû*). Creation is a process of distinctions, or divisions,
which turn this unformed material into a universe of things and beings:
distinctions between light and dark, between dry areas and waters, between the waters above the firmament and those below, between sky and
earth, between sun, moon, and stars, et cetera.

> And God divided the light from the dark.

> And God made the firmament and divided the waters that were
> below the firmament from the waters that were above the
> firmament.

> And God said, Let there be lights in the firmament of the heavens
> to divide the day from the night.

In each case, creation involves the deity's separating a substance and then
giving it a name. With time as with space, the deity makes distinctions,
marking days, months, years, seasons. That is creation. With God, things
have distinguishable existence in time and space. Without God, "all is
permitted." Somehow madness involves, in some degree, a return to
chaos. Distinctions break down, all is permitted. Those who can envision, truly envision, the death of God can imagine the release from order
that this involves. To put this in more Nietzschean terms: In his first
book, *The Birth of Tragedy*, Nietzsche pictured the Greek god Apollo as
representing such shape and order. Apollo was god of light, associated
with sculpture. The antithesis of this was Dionysus, who represented immediate relationship with nature. Dionysus was associated with intoxi-
cation and music. Dionysus was a god who could dance. It is natural to
compare the distinction between the Dionysian and the Apollonian to

the Freudian distinction between the id and the ego. In each pairing, the former is the inner force, the latter is the restraining, shaping force. Both are necessary components of human life. To be all Dionysian, like being all id without the direction of the ego, is to be mad. Recall Lou Salomé's reference above to "orgiastic Dionysian conditions and the chaos of frenzied passions — yes, *madness* itself." When Nietzsche went mad he signed several letters "Dionysus." He signed none "Apollo." It may be that in Nietzsche's Greek terms the triumph of the Dionysian over the Apollonian had the same ultimate implication as the death of God in his Judeo-Christian terms (he signed several letters "the Crucified"; he signed none "Christ" or "the Resurrected."): It was the triumph of un-reason, of disorder, of the kind of freedom that the Grand Inquisitor says that humans are unable to bear.

The degree of overlap in Dostoevsky in each of these areas individu-ally — dreams, fathers, horses, suffering, madness, "all is permitted," hu-mans displacing God — and especially in the merging of several of them in the association between the struggle with God and madness suggests that we are not dealing here only with an idiosyncratic matter in Nietz-sche's life. We see two geniuses, with exceptional psychological insight, suffering intensely from painful life experiences and illnesses, obsessed with their fathers' early deaths, intrigued with dreams, struck by impres-sions of horses as images of suffering, struggling with themselves and their pasts, concerned with madness, indulging in the idea of voluntary mad-ness, engaging in lifelong struggles with God and religion. This is not simply a shopping list of unrelated items that they happened to have in common. These are interconnected points that form a matrix of memo-ries, fears, thoughts, and interests that constituted a pronounced bond be-tween them, despite the boundaries of geography and language that separated them. The result is that even casual readers have thought of these two men as having much in common, teachers and writers have often grouped them in studies of existentialism or nihilism, and scholars have compared and related them to one another. And it was the fate of one of them — whose personal philosophy included "love of fate" — to chance upon the other's work. And it was further his fate to chance upon an event that symbolically brought all the points of their common matrix together: a beaten horse, suffering, dreams, fathers, God. Madness. The episode of the horse in Turin is more than a curious sidepoint in a biography. That single moment in that man's singular life is an integral element — and a perfect symbol — of the matrix. *Of course* that episode is connected to the struggle with God. There is no reason to be surprised that the most prominent moment in the story of Nietzsche's life has a relationship with the most prominent point in his work.

"THE MORE SPIRITUAL MEN OF AN AGE WHICH IS BECOMING IGNITED"

A colleague of mine uses that scene in the street in Turin in one of his courses as a metaphor for the flow of Western history. Indeed, the image of Nietzsche and the horse stands out, as some images do, as amazing and enigmatic in itself and as a symbol of something that came together in history at that moment. (Nietzsche himself was struck in such a way by the images of the death of Socrates and the crucifixion of Jesus.) Nietzsche's breakdown, and the elements that it reflected, really does fit as symbolically expressing a culture's breakdown, or at least its arrival at a critical turning point. And at the summit of that culture was its God.

This state of things had been in the making for centuries in that culture. The invention of the printing press made it possible for everyone — not just the priests and the wealthy — to have a Bible, and thus an opportunity to have informed doubts. Copernicus, Galileo, Darwin, new knowledge of the age of the earth, the triumph of science in general, all provided potent grounds for doubts. The development of the state as a challenge to the church for worldly authority also impinged on the authority of the Church and ultimately of God. (Recall that, in the Bible, on the day that the people of Israel establish the monarchy, Samuel says, "You have this day rejected your God." Nietzsche called the state "the new idol.") Open challenges to the claims of religion by respectable intellectuals from all kinds of backgrounds became possible (Hobbes, Spinoza, Thomas Paine, Mark Twain, Tolstoy, etc., etc.). Hegel could write of the death of God. Marx could call religion the opium of the masses. Even within the church, modern biblical criticism became acceptable and, in the formulation of Julius Wellhausen, the father of modern biblical scholarship, it became famous; it was the culmination of a process leading to a new feeling about the Bible, religion, and God. Philosophical, political, scientific, technological, and social forces all were challenging traditional religion and religious establishments in essential ways. All of these things were in the air that Nietzsche and Dostoevsky breathed.

I am not mentioning these things to argue for a European cultural determinism. What we have observed here is more complicated than that, especially insofar as we are dealing with such uncommon persons as these two men. Nietzsche and Dostoevsky were not the type simply to be swept up in the thought of the day. They were movers and creators. Rather, perhaps that is what creators are, living in a dynamic between their "received" world and their impact on civilization's future course. It may be that the force — the power to pronounce openly what the sacred texts of the Jews and the Christians contained but did not say systematically — had been gradually surfacing for a thousand to two thousand years, and it erupted in these two men. Europe in that era provided a soil in which such ideas were possible, where philosophy and literature were at a stage at which such views were conceivable and expressible. My field is not European intellectual history, and I have neither the space nor the expertise to trace here such a development over the preceding two millennia. My interest is in the mystery of the culmination of this brewing revolution in the human response to the divine in Nietzsche and Dostoevsky near the end of the last century. Why these particular two men? It was not that they had common views. As we have seen, Dostoevsky often put the views that Nietzsche would hold in the mouths of characters whom he opposed. Indeed it is hard to know what Dostoevsky really believed at times. ("Devil take him. He's partly right!") Nietzsche's friend Gast wrote:

> Nietzsche's high appreciation of Dostoevsky has been greatly misunderstood, as if Nietzsche had discovered similar lines in Dostoevsky as in himself. This, however, is not the case. What Nietzsche admired in Dostoevsky was his insight into the depths of certain human souls, his art and the subtlety of his analysis, and the collection of rare psychological material. Nietzsche felt that Dostoevsky instructed him and enriched him as a psychologist, otherwise Dostoevsky was repellent to his instincts.[58]

Not common views, but common sensitivities and common psychological insights. It would appear that they possessed the right formula: extraordinary brilliance and extraordinary sensitivity, as well as the literary talent to articulate it all — plus perhaps a little madness. I admit that the number of coincidences between these two men is still perplexing.

Nietzsche wrote in *Human, All Too Human*, concerning "we, the more spiritual men of an age which is visibly becoming more and more ignited. . . ." That characterization of both the individuals and the age reflects the point that I want to make: that the phenomenon of the "bursting out" of the death of God in these two men in these two places at this particular moment was a product of a combination of what was happening in their era and what was happening in these two particular, extraordinary persons. Choose your metaphor: they were the lightning rods, the beacons, the radar, the conductors, announcers, storm clouds, megaphones, catalysts. However subtle and gradual the disappearance of God was in the Bible, starting in the year after Nietzsche threw his arms around the horse it was a famous and, for many, distressing concept. That day in Turin, Nietzsche crossed over from the restraints that come with sanity into the realm of chaos, into "all is permitted." We are about to see how appropriate that image is as a symbol of the condition of society at that juncture and in the century that followed.

Chapter 9

THE LEGACY OF THE AGE:
THE TWENTIETH CENTURY

"I HAVE COME TOO EARLY"

Nietzsche had a sense of the symbolic. How symbolically perfect it was that the man who announced the death of God died in 1900, on the eve of the new century, the last century of the millennium, bequeathing, as it were, the notion of the death of God to humankind. Nietzsche, in fact, wrote in 1887, ". . . my ideas are so indescribably strange and dangerous that only much later (surely not before 1901) will anybody be ready for them."[1] Like Moses, who is allowed a glimpse into the promised land but is not privileged to live to go there, Nietzsche glimpsed the twentieth century but died on the threshold (on August 25, just a few months before the new century began). Nietzsche seems to have understood all along that he was talking to people who were not born yet. When the madman announces the death of God in *The Gay Science*, Nietzsche has him say, "I have come too early. My time is not yet. This tremendous event is still on its way . . . it has not yet reached the ears of man." When Zarathustra first preaches the death of God and the advent of the over-man, Nietzsche constructs the scene in a comic context: Zarathustra preaches to a crowd who have assembled because they have come to see a tightrope walker perform. When Zarathustra talks about the "over-man," the people think that he means the tightrope walker, who, after all, is about to walk over man. Nietzsche's ability to laugh at himself even as he presents his central ideas is remarkable. (Like God, who can laugh as He says, "My children have defeated me"?) But the joke in this case enables him to present these ideas and at the same time to convey his awareness of the problem of the lack of an audience. The general rejection or, more often, ignoring of his work during all of his sane years hurt him, but Nietzsche appeared confident that he would be read and appreciated in a coming generation and that he would break history in half. As he put it: "Some are born posthumously." [2]

And that is what happened. In the twelve years between his collapse in Turin and his death he became famous. Georg Brandes wrote within a few days after Nietzsche died:

> During those very years in which he lived on in the night of insanity, his name has acquired a lustre unsurpassed by any contemporary reputation, and his works have been translated into every language and are known all over the world. . . . This prodigiously rapid attainment of the most absolute and world-wide renown has in it something in the highest degree surprising. No one in our time has experienced anything like it. [3]

Freud wrote that already "In my youth he signified a nobility which I could not attain." [4] In those last twelve years of the nineteenth century, Nietzsche lived the irony of being unaware of having achieved the stature he had craved. Also ironically, his insanity contributed to the rapid growth of his fame, for people were curious about the genius who had gone mad. And so his embracing the horse was not only a symbol but an actual factor in bringing about the spread of his ideas. In the twentieth century Nietzsche's fame has persisted and grown, and his ideas have been used and abused among the most diverse set of persons and movements imaginable, the most famous and heinous being the Nazi transformation of the overman/superman concept into racial doctrine. The concepts of overman and eternal recurrence are readily associated with him; and, more than anyone else, he is associated with the idea of the death of God, which was the starting point in our investigation of Nietzsche, Dostoevsky, and the meaning of what culminated at Turin. He foresaw a world that would feel the absence of God, and he symbolically took leave of that world a few months before it began the last century of the millennium.

When I say that Nietzsche foresaw what the world would be like in a coming age of awareness of the disappearance of the deity, I mean it literally. Brandes wrote that "in the last period of his life Nietzsche appeared rather as a prophet than as a thinker."[5] Many other writers have spoken of Nietzsche as a modern prophet as well, including Salomé and Kaufmann.[6] He is famous for this prediction concerning that coming age: "There will be wars the like of which have never yet been seen on earth."[7] This could mean more than one thing in its context, but the world wars of this century obviously come to readers' minds. And I can feel a chill when I read this remark of his from 1881 in an essay that values the Jews' contributions to Europe and rejects anti-Semitism: "Among the spectacles to which the next century invites us is the decision on the fate of the European Jews."[8] In a variety of areas Nietzsche foresaw an age of formidable spiritual and physical struggle before humankind could hope to arrive at a happier, more fruitful plateau.

This prophetic aspect, too, has a counterpart in Dostoevsky. Frank refers to "the acceptance of his novels as an astonishing harbinger of the crisis of values that has haunted Western culture for the past half-century. . . ."[9] In Sophocles' *Oedipus the King*, Jocasta tells Oedipus to beware of prophets because they never have anything good to say, and Nietzsche and Dostoevsky have in common with the Greek and the biblical prophets this aspect of usually foreseeing the bad. Nietzsche described the condition of the prophet as analogous to an animal that reacts before an approaching storm because it is pained by climatic changes that humans do not yet feel.[10] The prophet suffers the pain of what he foresees. Nietzsche and Dostoevsky, in their respective ways, felt and developed, possibly in its most powerful form, the notion of the struggle with God and the lack of manifest divine presence: the "death of God," the "annihilation of God." And whether we accept it or reject it or weigh it or fear it or embrace it or detest it or exult in it or run to or from it, this idea is part of our legacy in the twentieth century, and soon it will be part of the legacy of a new millennium. The madman said, "I have come too early . . . it has not yet reached the ears of man." And he was right. It *was* too early. It "reached the ears of man" in the next century.

"TALKING TO MYSELF"

It is in the twentieth century that we have come to feel the disappearance or "death" of God so consciously and so intensely. I do not mean by this simply that there is a large quantity of atheists and agnostics around — though there is. I sense that the feeling of the hiddenness of the divine face is pronounced among both atheists and theists in our century. It is obvious in the case of the atheist or the agnostic, but even fundamentalist and orthodox religions reflect it as well. One can believe fervently in God and still, like Isaiah, say, "You are a hidden God." The increase in the number of adherents of devout movements in recent decades represents not that the heavens opened and rained down miracles to persuade people of religious truths; but rather, I think, the turning of many to orthodox faith was, at least in part, a response to how cold and frightening our times had become. This phenomenon looks like a grasp for hope — precisely in the face of the sensation of the hiddenness of God, precisely as an expression of the fear with which the absence of God leaves us. It will become clearer as we proceed that I do not mean this as a criticism of the sincerity of those who hold such beliefs. I mean it rather as an attempt to comprehend the forces that drew people to turn to this form of religion in this particular moment in history, and I suggest that it was, to a large extent, precisely a reaction to the age, an understandable response to a fearful condition. It represented a yearning for something more spiritual, more secure, more hopeful than the prevailing feeling.

My point for now, though, is simply that the disappearance of God has been in fact a prevailing feeling for much of the world in this century, familiar to the fundamentalist, the atheist, and the spectrum of religious conservatives and liberals in between. One can find writings about it in any bookstore: writings by Nietzsche, as well as by Hegel, Marx, and a hundred others. It found its way into literature, in fiction, nonfiction, and drama. One could read of it in Dostoevsky or other novelists, great and ordinary, and one could experience it expressed in a variety of ways in the theater and on film. The most concisely impressive portrayal to me of the union of the idea of the disppearance of God and the idea that human must become God is in Peter Barnes's drama *The Ruling Class*.

The hero, notably, is a madman who believes that he is God. When asked how he knows that he is God, he answers:

Simple. When I pray to Him I find I'm talking to myself.[11]

We could find any number of other examples of dramas that deal with the disappearance of God or the divine-human struggle that are among the well-known literary products of this century, from Samuel Beckett's *Waiting for Godot* — which almost everyone assures me is about the disappearance of God — to Peter Shaffer's plays *Equus* and especially *Amadeus*. This is not to forget that there are also books and plays espousing belief and trust in a deity. My point, as I have indicated, is simply that the disappearance or death of God is a substantial part of this century's philosophical and literary legacy. One does not have to travel very far on much of this planet to find a bookstore, library, or theater housing works that once would have been considered outrageous heresy. And the only regions in which one does not find such works are those in which the power of the state has been joined with religious powers to exclude them by force.

Presumably the most influential development affecting (and effecting) the feeling of the disappearance of God in the twentieth century is the triumph of science and technology. It will probably be hard for future generations to imagine what a wonder this has been to those of us who have lived through it, experiencing changes in our lives on a scale that no generation of our ancestors has experienced. When I was a child a computer was an element in comedies and science fiction, usually portrayed naively and cynically. Now a four-year-old child learns with one. When I was a child, when we went on a long family trip, we drove. Now we fly. They taught me that the smallest known thing was an atom; now we are chasing quarks and neutrinos. We *looked* at space; now we travel in it. Now we can treat the diseases from which my father and his father died.

And so on. There are people whose religious feelings have not been diminished by the scientific revolution. There are individuals who would declare that their faith is even enhanced by it. There are religious scientists. But in global perspective this explosion of knowledge has played an obviously powerful part in challenging our species' beliefs about divinity in two ways. First, scientific discoveries have provided explanations of phenomena that were formerly explained by reference to gods. Weather, disease, the heavenly bodies, music, birth. As the Grand Inquisitor said, people expect and need mystery as one of the components of religion; and science has swept much of the mystery away. One may argue that the scientific advances in describing the phenomena of nature still do not disprove the possibility of divine causation; but my purpose now is not to argue the theological point of whether scientific explanation theoretically, necessarily, must diminish belief in divine causes, but only to recognize the fact that science has indeed had this demystifying effect on religious belief. Scientific explanation has diminished the awe of the universe, but *awe*, a term that connotes both fear and wonder, was an essential element of our feeling the presence of divinity. Second, science, united with technology, has contributed to an increase of human control of our environment on a scale that feels enormous. It is not only that we can explain things empirically that were formerly explained as deriving from deities; it is that we have a new feeling of our own increased power over our lives and over the other animate and inanimate entities of the world. The flourishing of science thus has not only contributed to the feeling of the disappearance of God; it has contributed to the feeling of the shift in the divine-human balance of control more than anything or any time in our history. Freud observed that certain advances in knowledge were blows to the human ego; Copernicus informed us that we were not at the center of the universe but were a small element on its periphery. Darwin informed us that we were descended from "lower" beings. And Freud himself informed us that, like icebergs, our feelings and motives are ninety percent below the surface, hidden from ourselves as they affect our thoughts and actions. But most of the path of science in this century has had the opposite effect, offering us new powers and new grounds for confidence in our ability to discover further solutions and cures in the future. Right or wrong, for better or worse, the advances of this age have functioned in such a way as to nurture the feeling of the disappearance of God and the growth of humankind's control of their destiny.

"A PUBLIC EVENT"

The strangest, and in a sense the ultimate, expression of the disappearance of God in the twentieth century, though, was not in science or literature or philosophy but in theology. Theologians could be heard speaking of secularity, of the coming of age of humankind. Some used terms such as the "absence" or "eclipse" or "deprivation" or "departure" of God. And in the middle of the century came a movement known as radical theology, in which theologians spoke of the "death" of God. The death-of-God theology was extremely visible for a short time, debated in a variety of books and articles, discussed in the press, probably the subject of a great many sermons. Now, near the century's end, that movement appears to have been short-lived and not very successful in terms of attracting large numbers of adherents or a new generation of leadership. Nonetheless, the very fact of the movement, the fact that the notion of the death of God had found its way even into theology, is worthy of attention. It is a marker of how conscious and well known this idea had become. Thomas J. J. Altizer, one of the leading proponents of radical theology, could write, "If there is one clear portal to the twentieth century, it is a passage through the death of God."[12] Another main figure, William Hamilton, could declare, "The death of God is a public event in our history."[13] This was not Nietzsche speaking — though nearly every book or article in the field referred to him. These were Christian theologians. They varied in their approaches and their views of the implications of the death of God, but they all remained within the fold of Christian theology.[14] The Jewish theologian Richard Rubenstein was also frequently associated with this current in twentieth-century theology. He wrote, "No words are entirely adequate to characterize a historical epoch. Nevertheless, I believe the most adequate theological description of our times is to be found in the assertion that *we live in the time of the death of God.*"[15] And he added in another context two pages later, "In the time of the death of God the Jewish radical theologian remains profoundly Jewish as the Christian radical remains profoundly Christian."[16]

The seeming contradiction of holding such a view while remaining within the discipline of theology brought considerable criticism of the individuals and the movement and presumably contributed to its failure to flourish. Early on, one writer reported, "It is widely being asked whether theologians ought not to close up shop altogether, or let others take over and mind the store."[17] Switch to philosophy. Sell shoes. Go into politics. But why be a *theologian* if God is dead?! If people stopped wearing shoes, a shoe-store owner would have the sense to switch to another line. The same applies for any other product that became unavailable. Only a theologian would stay in business even in the absence of the product.

Rubenstein wrote in 1966, "Radical theology is no fad. It will not be replaced by some other theological novelty in the foreseeable future." He appears to have been both right and wrong. In terms of its public face, the theology of the death of God has all but disappeared from the scene. No other theological novelty has replaced it, though. The *thought* of the death of God was present before this movement arose, and the thought persists. The significance of the development of that thought even within theological circles is that it is a measure of just how much the hiddenness of God has been felt in our century. More important than that brief phenomenon in theology was the real fact of our century's experience of the absence of God: (1) The idea had become widely known , and (2) it was being asserted within religious circles.

"AFTER AUSCHWITZ"

All of these elements that contributed to the feeling of the disappearance of God in this century derive from the realm of the intellect; but also fueling the sense of divine abandonment, and in a more immediate way, was the ghastly abundance of catastrophes in this century. Though great catastrophes of war, disease, and natural disaster occurred in every other century as well, at least two things were different in this era. First, the sheer numbers were staggering. Our century had two world wars. The populations involved were enormous. The capabilities of the weapons were incredible. The count of deaths and suffering by disease and natural disasters in this century is no less a horror. The Black Plague wiped out a larger *percentage* of the population in the fourteenth century, but, in plain arithmetic terms, the *quantity* of human death and suffering filled our planet's surface as never before. And, second, the notion of the death of God now existed through which to interpret these things. To doubt God in the wake of a calamity could not so easily be dismissed as the shortcoming of the insufficiently faithful. There was a well-developed, brilliantly articulated doctrine of the death of God that was famous by the dawn of this century. Formerly heretical, it was now a real option to feel, in the wake of catastrophe, that the deity of former belief was absent. It is thus meaningful symbolically that the book that Rubenstein contributed to the death-of-God theology was titled *After Auschwitz*. It stands out among the titles of those books as being the one most linked to history, and it predicates the feeling of the death of God not on a general malaise or a rampant secularity, but rather on a nightmare.

The Holocaust happened specifically to the Jews, but it has also become a symbol of suffering, a quintessential expression of human inhumanity. It stands out, first, because it was systematic, a planned nightmare; and second, because it was not for clear military or even economic advantage but for dark psychological motives. The number of murdered souls, six million people, makes most attempts at description, let alone interpretation, appear pathetic; and it makes interpretations of it as "God's will" appear obscene. In Ivan Karamazov's questioning of God in terms of suffering, he excludes adults from the argument so as to dispense with any claims that the victims might have deserved their fate. ("They've eaten the apple, and to hell with them," he says.) He limits the discussion of human suffering to cases of children to make the issue clear. If we apply his standard to the Holocaust, that means one and a half million children, just the victims under the age of twelve. One can then add to that all of the other millions killed in the two world wars and the victims of all the cataclysms in the half century since the last world war: famines in Africa producing millions of children in agony whose pictures one can no longer bear to watch, deaths of millions in war in Afghanistan and Armenia and Bangladesh and Biafra and Bosnia. And I am only up to B.

Suffering in unprecedented, inconceivable quantity has been part of our lot in this century; and, without denying that these disasters have moved some to seek explanation or at least consolation in religion, one must admit that they have also contributed to a widespread feeling that God is not present and that humans are left on their own, responsible for their own fate. Even among people who believe in the existence of God, who attend churches and synagogues, even among clergy of my acquaintance, the feeling of the deity's absence is known. No new theological formulation has emerged that has proven adequate as an explanation or as a comfort. On the contrary, the most famous theological innovations of the twentieth century have been precisely those of secularity and the death of God, which, if anything, underscore the pain and ostensible meaninglessness of the catastrophes of the century.

This is not to ignore the fact that there are sincere people alive today who feel that they have experienced the presence of God, or that there were those among the faithful in past centuries who had their doubts. I am speaking, though, of broad characteristics of whole centuries. In its experience and in the interpretive possibilities available to it, this century singularly has received the death of God as part of its legacy.

"THE UNIVERSAL BINDING FORCE
OF A FAITH"

It is a commonplace to read about this century as experiencing a crisis, usually identified as a crisis of culture, a crisis of values, or a spiritual crisis. To some eyes the world has gone crazy in this century. On one hand, it is the century of the near end of slavery, of a dramatic shift in the status of woman, and of a technological revolution that we can still barely estimate, so that we each amaze people who are just a decade younger than we are when we tell them what has been new in our lives. But, on the other hand, it is a century in which Nietzsche's prophecies came true, a century of such violence, of attempts at genocide, of such waste and stupidity, of *multiple* threats to the survival of our species — and other species with us. One might respond that the earth was always this bad, and I would not want to debate the point, because I think that it is a dead end to get caught up in a debate over whether this century is better or worse than any other. But, at the very least, (1) the *scale* is much greater, as a function of an extraordinary burst of population; (2) the risk is much greater — planetary survival, nothing less — and yet as a species we behave as if it were not; and (3) we have, like every century, one hundred years more experience than our predecessors. We have the literature, philosophy, and art of the nineteenth century; we have the historical experience of the nineteenth century; we have a psychological revolution in the understanding of the human mind, an archaeological revolution in understanding the biblical world and other civilizations that preceded us, a scientific/technological revolution in understanding and controlling what is going on around us; yet we still do these insane things that degrade us and threaten our survival. It is indeed a spiritual crisis. Is there anyone who does not know that something is wrong here? that something is missing? And, I am suggesting, it is a something that used to be addressed primarily by beliefs concerning God.

The point of speaking of the *death* of God is: it does not simply say that God does not exist. Nietzsche was not an atheist in the sense that we usually mean that word. Death rather implies that a situation that used to exist has ended, that God used to be present — or was perceived to be present — but is not any more. While "the death of God" does not necessarily mean exactly the same thing as the terms that I prefer — "the disappearance of God" or "the hiding of the face of God" — these terms all have at least this much in common: a situation that used to exist has ended. Humans' perceptions of the presence of God have changed. I think that fundamentalists, atheists, and most of those who lie between them on the religion spectrum can agree at least that, for better or worse, our century is enduring a spiritual crisis. And all of us, fundamentalists, atheists, and everyone who lies between them on the religion spectrum, are affected by this crisis. Something is missing. One has to be cut off from nearly all of the world in order not to have noticed.

In the course of investigating the first mystery in this book I dealt with the matter of human fear in the face of the great forces of nature. In pagan religion humans sought to personify, communicate with, and placate these forces. In monotheistic religion they sought to communicate with the deity who was the creator and controller of these forces. The feeling of the disappearance of this deity left one with the question of how to come to terms with this feeling of the precariousness of our existence. The second mystery introduced the matter of basing morality on the deity. The notion that God, as pictured in traditional religion, had died left one with the question of what can be the basis and authority for morality: "If God is dead, all is permitted." At the beginning of the twentieth century we were left, more blatantly than ever before, with these two problems: the underlying fear associated with our vulnerability, and the loss of a recognized basis for morality.

To give up God is frightening. To contemplate really what it means to live in a world without divine protection from the forces of nature is fearful. In Chapter 5, I suggested that the origin, or at least a primary function, of beliefs in gods was to deal with fundamental human fears. To relinquish the belief in divine protection is to have to live with those fears, consciously or internally. The covenant model in the Bible provides an antidote. The covenant is expressed in a fixed legal text, laying out everything explicitly, defining the relationship between God and Israel in formal, statutory terms, stating exactly what Yahweh expects of humans and what they can expect of Him. Fulfilling the terms of the covenant in one's life thus provides *security*, the feeling that instead of all of this uncertainty one can really know what God wants, and one can know what one is supposed to do. Don't murder. Don't steal. Honor your parents. Cease working on the seventh day. Don't eat bread on Passover. Don't eat pork ever. Love your neighbor. Love the stranger. Leave the corner of your field for the poor. Don't worship images. One who does these things can live feeling the security of knowing that he or she is fulfilling what the creator of the universe wants. The other monotheistic religions do not require so extensive a list of commandments as does biblical (and especially post-biblical, rabbinic) Judaism, but they offer some mechanism by which one enters into a relationship with the deity and learns how to behave in accordance with the deity's will. And this provides stability and security and meaning. Its absence leaves an arbitrariness, an ambiguity, concerning which even Nietzsche himself forewarned. When he said that the greatest danger lurking is madness, the full context of that remark was one of madness as the opposite of *faith*:

> The greatest danger that always hovered over humanity and still hovers over it is the eruption of madness — which means the eruption of arbitrariness in feeling, seeing, and hearing, the enjoyment of the mind's lack of discipline, the joy in human unreason. Not truth and certainty are the opposite of the world of the madman, but the universality and the universal binding force of a faith; in sum, the non-arbitrary character of judgments.[18]

Nearly a hundred years later, while some of the death-of-God theologians concentrated on the liberating aspect of the doctrine,[19] others were intensely aware of the psychologically troubling side of what they were pronouncing. Altizer wrote of ". . . a new chaos, a new meaninglessness brought on by the disappearance of an absolute or transcendent ground, the very nihilism foreseen by Nietzsche as the next stage of history."[20] And he added, "No honest contemporary seeker can ever lose sight of the very real possibility that the willing of the death of God is the way to madness [and] dehumanization. . . ."[21] Rubenstein wrote of ". . . the ambiguity, the irony, the hopelessness, and the inevitable meaninglessness of the time of the death of God." And he added, "If I am a death of God theologian, it is with a cry of agony."[22]

We noted that Freud posited that religion "arose out of the Oedipus complex, out of the relation to the father,"[23] and that Nietzsche and Dostoevsky, the two who were the most sensitive to the death of God, both lost their fathers early, particularly painfully, and with explicit expressions of guilt ("I haven't been able to forget for one hour that my mother called me a disgrace to my father's grave"). The Freudians among the readers of this book will be especially aware that the shift in the divine-human balance, culminating in the apparent triumph of the humans alongside the disappearance of God, is, in Oedipal terms, the defeat of the father. ("My children have defeated me.") The Oedipal complex involves an element of guilt and related tension and insecurity over the defeat of the father. If we could find a couch big enough for our century to lie on, we would be likely to find this element present as well.

The point is that the idea of existence without the deity is a visceral as much as an intellectual conclusion. It is fearful. I think that it is significant in this regard that the death-of-God theologians chose not to leave Christianity or Judaism. Appreciating fully what the implications of the death of God were, Nietzsche was not afraid to leave Christianity. The radical theologians were. "The Jewish radical theologian remains profoundly Jewish as the Christian radical remains profoundly Christian." I do not say this to denigrate them but to illustrate the point that confronting the death of God really is terrifying. In the face of such fears Nietzsche took on the tension of living without God, while Dostoevsky held on tenaciously to a belief in God. In the twentieth century we see both of these responses as well: Some cling to faith. Others live with the stress.

A third response is to ignore the whole thing. But this condition has implications for all — fundamentalist, atheist, and everyone in between.

"A REALLY GOOD QUESTION"

It is fairly common to hear someone say that there is no morality without God, that everything is then relative, that what one person or society says is good another says is bad. One hears this proposition expressed in the most simplistic ways and in sophisticated philosophical terms. Some declare it in a sentence without apparently thinking that any elaboration or defense is necessary, and some fill book-length works with their analyses. The essential formula found in variations in both Nietzsche and Dostoevsky is: in the absence of a deity "all is permitted." Nietzsche confronted the critical moral implication of the death of God early on, even before *Thus Spoke Zarathustra*. In the section of *The Gay Science* that I quoted earlier which refers to the death of God as the greatest recent event, he went on to speak of

> . . . how much must collapse now that this faith has been undermined because it was built upon this faith, propped up by it, grown into it; for example, the whole of our European morality.[24]

Dostoevsky's less brilliant character Smerdyakov in *The Brothers Karamazov* says more simply, "If God doesn't exist there's no such thing as virtue — virtue is useless." A more immediate case comes from a discussion I had a few years ago with a colleague on the university faculty who was a Marxist. I asked him, given his philosophical rejection of a deity and religion, on what he based his morality. At the simplest level, what prevented him from kicking out canes from under old ladies? He responded that he would discuss this with his comrades (his term) and get back to me. He later told me that he had discussed it with them, and they had all agreed that: I had asked *a really good question*.

Am I paranoid for being troubled by that?

Moralities were constructed in association with deities for millennia. What must happen to those moralities in an age of the hiding of the face of God and the shift to human responsibility? And how is it possible to

construct any morality that will have substantial acceptance in the absence of appeal to a God? There is, in the first place, an issue of the
absence of a standard. It is not that atheists are immoral. There are righteous atheists; and, God knows, there are unprincipled theists. But the
condition of humanity is such that there is no standard, nothing to which
one can appeal in order to persuade anyone else. The present condition
is uncertainty. The moral debates of this generation have the unfortunate, absurd, frustrating, annoying quality that, frequently, the two sides
do not engage one another. Each side rather *insists*, proceeding from its
particular moral starting point; but few on either side argue head-on the
validity of each other's moral starting point. They concentrate more on
the opponent's last claim, or they challenge his or her statistical points,
or his or her character. Abortion stands out as an example, being an issue
of the present generation which began as a result of a technological
breakthrough and which will probably end as a result of future technological breakthroughs and not as a result of either side's utterly prevailing, much less persuading the other side. Similarly, capital punishment,
control of guns, legalization of drugs, obscenity in art, freedom of speech
versus racist or other derogatory language, freedom of the press versus
trashing offensive newspapers, and a host of issues of religion and state,
and more — in all of these the sides generally do not engage each other;
they draw battle lines. My point is not that we argue badly but rather that
the unfruitful way in which we argue is a reflection and symptom of our
moral predicament. Altizer claimed that ". . . modern man has known a
moral chaos . . . which is unequaled in history." And, whatever my criticism of radical theology, I, regrettably, recognize that he was largely right
when he said this about thirty years ago, and things seem to me to be
dramatically worse now.

Ironically, even some otherwise positive developments may have contributed to this sense of the relativity of morality. There has been an increase of people's familiarity with world religions in this century, owing in
part to developments in education, in part to media advances, especially
in television, which make foreign cultures more accessible to one another, and in part to world political developments; for example, Middle
East economics and politics have made Europeans and Americans begin
to know more about Islam. A dramatic development in ecumenical atti-
tudes has also taken place, most famously in the Second Vatican Coun-

cil, but also involving noteworthy openness and exchange in biblical studies among Catholics, Protestants, and Jews, and a variety of conferences and interfaith programs involving other major world religions as well. The irony is that more knowledge, appreciation, and respect for other religions — which is an act of enlightenment and a blessing in many ways — also means more feeling of relativity of morality. Oddly, it was easier to believe in the absolute correctness of one's moral rules when one believed that other religions were just plain wrong. The fading of belief in the manifest active presence of God, joined with the increased openness to other religious views, was a powerful combination, contributing to the feeling that there was no single moral standard.

The connection between divinity and morality is not only one of relativity but of authority. Whatever strides there have been in the shift in humans' control of their destiny, no human or group of humans in this age has arrived at a degree of authority at which he or she could declare moral rules that would have any lasting acceptance. Those who came the closest were presumably totalitarian dictators — Mao, Lenin, Hitler — and their dictates were undone speedily upon their respective demises. Without divinity there has been no moral authority either from the powerful or the wise. The fact remains that if one believes in a God one has an authority on which to construct morality. But in an age in which the deity is not present in apparent ways and is felt by many to be "dead," then on what is one to base a morality?

The other element of the connection between divinity and morality should be obvious enough: enforcement. When it comes to effective enforcement, there is nothing like omnipotence. A glance at the blessing-and-curse lists in Leviticus 26 and Deuteronomy 28 will reveal a host of reward and punishment options that a deity may wield, and that list does not yet include heaven and hell. The feeling that the deity is not actively present, engaging in one-to-one treatment of human behavior leaves the individual free to act with impunity, without fear of punishment, without hope of reward. So why be good? Not that one can say what *is* good in a way that is guaranteed to persuade anyone else. Why is morality thought (in Western civilization) to have to be based on a God? Because of reasons of absoluteness, authority, and enforcement. In the current absence of these things, we have arrived at an age of moral cacophony. I hope to make some contribution to this matter by the end of this book, but for now my purpose is only to recognize the condition, the legacy, of this age in the wake of the development of the disappearance of God by the end of the last century. To the extent that the feeling of the presence of God provided (1) some security in the face of human fears and (2) a basis for morality, the legacy of confronting the hiddenness of God has included (1) insecurity and (2) moral tumult.

"COMING OF AGE"

In describing and interpreting the phenomenon of the hiding of the face of God in the Bible, I several times used the metaphor of parent and child, an old and obvious analogy for demonstrating points concerning the relationship between God and humans. The image of humankind as children is especially relevant given the link between the hiding of the face of God and the shift in the divine-human balance. The gradually diminishing apparent tending of humans by the divine parent requires that humans, in turn, grow up. Freud used the parent-child metaphor as well in discussing the crises that humans must face when they let go of God:

> They will have to admit to themselves the full extent of their helplessness and their insignificance in the machinery of the universe; they can no longer be the centre of creation, no longer the object of tender care on the part of a beneficent Providence. They will be in the same position as a child who has left the parental house where he was so warm and comfortable. But surely infantilism is destined to be surmounted. Men cannot remain children for ever.[25]

We have seen texts from the Bible and elsewhere that picture the increase in human direction of their own destiny as not entirely unwelcome to the deity. When He changes Jacob's name to Israel, "one who struggles with God," it is as a blessing; He laughs when he says, "My children have defeated me"; He kisses the Grand Inquisitor. The idea that humans must come of age as they learn to face the world without appealing to a divine parent to solve their problems is an integral corollary of the concept of the disappearance of God. Interestingly, many of the writings concerning the death-of-God theology cited the theologian Dietrich Bonhoeffer, even though Bonhoeffer himself preceded that movement and did not hold that view. But Bonhoeffer did develop the idea of humans' "coming of age," the notion that even if God does exist humans must live in the world, self-subsisting, as they would if there were no God:

> So our coming of age leads us to a true recognition of our situation before God. God would have us know that we must live as men who manage our lives without him.[26]

In both biblical and contemporary terms, the two go together: If we live in an age of divine hiddenness we also live in an age of human responsibility.

In discussing the divine-human struggle, I noted that the key force that binds the deity to humans even though they continually rebel and violate His covenants with them is pity. They survive their rebellions and continue their striving for increased direction of their fate because the creator feels compassion for them. And so the deity gives them ever more chances, becoming more hidden and ceding more control to them. Thus, ironically, they owe their success, at least in part, to their weakness. Nietzsche took this another step. When Zarathustra asks what God died *of*, he is told: "Pity. God died of his pity for man." Both in the Bible and in Nietzsche, humans do not arrive at the hiding of the divine face and the shift in the balance of divine-human control entirely out of strength but, at least in part, out of their frailty. From that perspective, the legacy of the age, now that God is perceived to have dis-appeared, would be that we are left weak. Scientific advance has made us feel stronger, but still it certainly does not *seem* like our age has come of age. Perhaps we need a couple of hundred more years. Lately it does not seem as though we are wrestling with God, but rather that the wrestling match is over, we have prevailed, and we are left wondering, "Now what?" We observed in Chapter 6 how Judaism and Christianity each arrived at a *response* to the feeling of the divine hiddenness that was the legacy of their age. Our society, however, has become aware of the feeling of the absence or death or eclipse or disappearance of God but has not developed a response, at least not one that has been successful and comforting on a broad scale. It is with no pleasure that I see the image of a man embracing a horse, slipping into chaos, as a symbol of this age. At the end of a chaotic century, we are left with immense questions. Where is one to go from here if one still has a need for something spiritual? How are we to deal with our fundamental fears? On what are we to base our morality if not on the deity?

The place where the answers may lie will come as a surprise to most people.

THIRD MYSTERY

BIG BANG AND

KABBALAH

Chapter 10

BIG BANG AND
KABBALAH

"I CAN'T EXPECT TO UNDERSTAND
ABOUT GOD"

The third mystery concerns the relationship between religion and science. We have already begun to consider the significance of the revolution in science that has occurred in this century. In the entire time from the era of the first mystery to the era of the second, from Moses to Nietzsche, about three thousand years, our knowledge of the universe did not grow nearly as much as it has in this one century. In our age there has been a big bang of knowledge. The battles of evolution versus creation and of geology versus the biblical depiction of the age of the earth were almost minor matters in comparison to what is happening today in science in general and in the field of science known as cosmology in particular — though in this arena science and religion are not necessarily opposed to one another. The study of the cosmos — cosmology — has involved the union of astronomy and physics, the relating of the conclusions of theoretical physicists like Einstein, Planck, and Heisenberg to the observations of astronomers like Hubble and Penzias and Wilson. Through this union of insight and observation, scientists have come to speak seriously of the origin of the universe in a way that has brought them into the territory of religion.

There has been a wave of books by scientists attempting to bring this knowledge into the public realm, from George Gamow's *One Two Three . . . Infinity* [1] to Stephen Hawking's *A Brief History of Time*, [2] as well as books by gifted science writers, most notably Timothy Ferris (*The Red Limit, Coming of Age in the Milky Way*), [3] who have the intellect to understand what the scientists are doing plus the writing skill to convey it to laypersons. The success of Hawking's book in particular — over two years on bestseller lists, spin-off books, even a motion picture — is notable for what it reflects about this phase in the relationship between science and religion. I think that this success is based partly on people's fascination with the man Hawking himself, living with Lou Gehrig's disease for over two decades while contributing to a sequence of some of the most extraordinary discoveries in human experience. And I think that another reason, and probably the larger reason, for the reception of Hawking's book is that people thought that it really might reveal something about God. At the beginning of the book Carl Sagan says in his introduction, "This book is also about God . . . or perhaps about the absence of God. The word God fills its pages" — and at the end of the book the last word is "God." Passages that relate cosmological research to God in one way or another are common in the popular literature. The physicist Steven Weinberg includes in a recent book, *Dreams of a Final Theory*, a chapter titled "What About God?" [4] The physicist Alex Vilenkin, speaking of the birth of the universe, says, "The bubble pops into existence in accord with the laws of physics. The laws of physics are already there." "Where?" asks the science writer Dennis Overbye. Vilenkin answers, "In God's mind." [5] Hawking ends his book with the now fairly famous last sentence "Then we will know the mind of God." The physicist Paul Davies follows with an entire book titled *The Mind of God*, with sections titled "Is God Necessary?" and "Does God Have to Exist?" [6] The astronomer Robert Jastrow contributes a frequently quoted book titled *God and the Astronomers*. [7] Astrophysicist George Smoot reports a satellite's observation of unevenness in the formation of matter in the universe, an important component of the Big Bang theory of origin, and says, "If you're religious, it's like looking at God." [8] Astronomer Alan Sandage says, "Newton's laws are God in a sense." Overbye refers to the "singularity," the starting point of creation in the model of Hawking and his distinguished colleague Roger Penrose, and says, "In a sense, the singularity was the closest a physicist could get to God. It was God." Science writer Dick Teresi, reviewing David Lindley's *The Myth of a Unified Theory*, notes, "The quasireligious search for a unified theory by Einstein, Heisenberg, Pauli, Weinberg, and others, Mr. Lindley says, has propelled physics into the realm of theology." In the *New York Times*, Peter Steinfels refers to "Big Bang theology." A famous cover of *Time* magazine in 1965 asked: "Is God Dead?" and was regarded as a sign of the arrival of the death-of-God theology, but a *Time* cover in 1992 asks: "What Does Science Tell Us About God?" The journalist Charles Krauthammer writes, "In the age of science, physics is a form of revelation."

The point of all of these examples is that, in a very public way, from a variety of quarters, people are looking to physicists — seriously, hopefully — for answers about God. I have learned from physicists, including James Hartle (in a personal communication) and Steven Weinberg (in *Dreams of a Final Theory*), that physicists in this era do not generally concern themselves with this theological element. One does not find it in their published papers in the field or in their exchange at professional conferences. It appears that a number of them have come to introduce the theology into their popular books and lectures and statements to the media for a variety of motives, noble and ignoble, ranging from the influence of the media upon them to a desire to make an impression to the wish for fame and wealth. But there is another reason as well, and that is that their work really does relate to the concerns of religion, regardless of whether the individual scientist happens to be religious or not, or even interested in such matters or not. These people are speaking with theoretical and experimental sophistication about nothing less than the origin of the universe. In my own experience this current overlap of science and religion was impressed upon me when I addressed the Council for the Advancement of Science Writing a few years ago. I was there to discuss my research on the authors of the Bible, and I felt the need to impress that national gathering of science writers that I respected and worked in the scientific method, and so I made my lecture as manifestly empirical and objective as possible. Later I listened to another guest at the same meeting, an astrophysicist who was lecturing on cosmology. As he lectured, I exchanged glances with several of the science writers. We all had noticed that the scientist sounded as if he was talking about religion while I, a biblical scholar, sounded like a scientist. That bit of irony may not be all that uncommon, for I later read of an incident in which the astronomer Alan Sandage, overheard talking in a restaurant, was mistaken for a minister.[9]

For most of us mere mortals, the actual work of cosmology is simply incomprehensible. The mathematics involved are extraordinarily difficult. The scientists who have tried to convey it to laypersons deserve an enormous quantum of credit for their efforts, but the matter remains beyond the understanding of all but a few among nonspecialists. The suspicion that cosmology may offer a whole new source of information about the deity and creation may be tantalizing and exciting, but it is also frustrating insofar as it is outside of most humans' grasp. Dostoevsky, over a hundred years ago, when Einstein was one year old, had his atheist Ivan Karamazov say:

> There have been and still are geometricians and philosophers, and even some of the most distinguished, who doubt whether the whole universe, or to speak more widely the whole of being, was only created in Euclid's geometry; they even dare to dream that two parallel lines, which according to Euclid can never meet on earth, may meet somewhere in infinity. I have come to the conclusion that, since I can't understand even that, I can't expect to understand about God.[10]

Most laypersons approaching physics, even through books written for laypersons, in this era must feel like Ivan. If one has to comprehend singularities, black holes, inflationary models, and superstring theory to understand about God, one may as well go back to either leaps of faith or agnosticism. Moreover, while these scientists' work has taken them into the territory of religion, many of them seem to be struggling unsuccessfully with the essentials of that territory, which itself requires an expertise which they do not possess. They do not appear to be able to make the connection between their own discoveries and what those discoveries imply if one takes religion seriously. I suspect that those persons who were looking for meaningful answers about God in Hawking's book were disappointed, as I was. But the third mystery, which we are about to explore, may be useful, as a metaphor to some, as more than a metaphor to others, in relating this century's discoveries concerning the origin and nature of the cosmos to the quest for knowledge of the divine. And its implications are alluring when seen against the backdrop of the disappearance of God.

This mystery concerns the curious parallels between the scientific model of the formation of the universe known as the Big Bang and the conception of the universe in the mystical movement known as Kabbalah.

"THE MOST CRUCIAL DISCOVERY
EVER MADE IN SCIENCE"

To discuss this requires that I review at least a few essential elements of each of the two systems. The story of the formation and acceptance of the Big Bang theory has been told many times, with various emphases. As a layperson I mean to convey it in laypersons' terms; and as a biblical scholar who is interested in the manifestation of divinity, I mean to convey it in terms that I can relate later to the subject of God and religion as it has begun to be addressed in the sort of works I cited above.

The Big Bang theory of the origin of the universe has come to wide acceptance because of three discoveries in particular. The astronomer Edwin Hubble made the first, observing the universe through the telescope at Mount Wilson in California in 1929. Aside from all the technical information concerning red shifts and velocities — which Hawking, Ferris, and others have endeavored to explain in layperson's terms — the key point about Hubble's discovery is that he saw that, in whatever direction one looks, the galaxies of the universe are moving away from us. And the farther away from us they are, the faster they are moving away. That meant: the universe is expanding.

Theoretical physicists had predicted this. The starting point was Einstein's formulation of the general theory of relativity. The Russian mathematician Alexander Friedmann had theorized, based on Einstein's theory, that the universe must be expanding (or contracting, but could not be static) in 1922. The Belgian Georges Lemaître, unaware of Friedmann's work, had reached almost the same conclusions in 1927. And now Hubble, who was unaware of both of them, was actually watching it happening in 1929. Since then, there is barely any limit to the significance that various persons have attached to this prediction and its confirmation. The prediction that the universe is expanding has been called "the greatest prediction in the history of science." [11] Hubble's confirmation of it has been called by John Barrow "the greatest discovery of twentieth-century science," and by Sandage "the most crucial discovery ever made in science." [12] Hawking calls the expansion of the universe "one of the great intellectual revolutions of the twentieth century." [13] Overbye expands this judgment to "the *prime fact* of the twentieth century, the most amazing scientific discovery of all time — the first one pointing beyond science altogether." [14] Even if we allow for a degree of hyperbole in any or all of such remarks, we should appreciate the significance of this discovery, both in itself and for where it led us.

From theory to observation. And then back to theory. Theoreticians deduced that, if the universe is expanding, it used to be smaller than it is now, and that in fact all the matter and energy in the universe used to be located in one place. That place was small. It had to be *infinitely* small. It was a single point. At a particular moment, fifteen billion years ago, for reasons unknown to anyone, that point burst out, forming all the matter that became the stars, planets, stones, and living things of the universe.

And then back to observation. The story of the second key discovery is one of those classic science stories that make the history of science as interesting a field for some scholars as the *doing* of science. How is it possible to construct a test to determine if such a "Big Bang" ever happened? The physicist George Gamow and his associates Ralph Alpher and Robert Herman, who were at the center of the formulation of the Big Bang theory, also conceived of the domain in which such a test could be constructed. In 1948 Alpher and Herman calculated that, if the universe began with such a burst, a residue of the tremendous heat of that explosion should still exist. It would be a cosmic background radiation, pervading the entire universe. [15]

In 1964, the Russian scientist Yakov Zeldovich and his associates I. D. Novikov and A. G. Doroshkevich proposed that the existence of the cosmic background radiation might be tested by means of radio astronomy. A radio telescope might be able to detect it. They noted that there was a particular radio telescope in the United States, a horn antenna in the Bell Laboratories in Holmdel, New Jersey, that would be suitable for such a project. [16]

Meanwhile: at Princeton University — which happens to be located about twenty-five miles from Holmdel, New Jersey — two scientists, Robert Dicke and James Peebles, unaware of the Russian scientists' work and of the work of Gamow and his associates, proposed similarly that there might be a cosmic residue of the Big Bang and that it might be detectable by a radio telescope, and they set about preparing a horn antenna to attempt the project.

Meanwhile: in Holmdel, New Jersey, at the Bell Laboratories, two astronomers, Arno Penzias and Robert Wilson, unaware of the work of any of these scientists, were annoyed because their work on the horn antenna was being disrupted by a mysterious static that they could not explain nor eliminate. They discovered pigeons nesting inside and removed them, they found a layer of pigeon (what is an appropriate term?) remnant and cleaned it out, they taped all the joints of the antenna, all of which helped, but some of the noise persisted. The strange thing was that the sound did not vary, no matter in what direction they aimed the antenna, no matter what the time of day, no matter what the season of the year. What Penzias and Wilson were hearing did not change in relation to the position of the antenna, or of the earth, or of the solar system, or of the entire galaxy (the Milky Way). It appeared to be coming from the whole universe. Even those who are reading this story for the first time can guess what that static was. Penzias complained about the mystery noise to a colleague who happened to know something about what Dicke and Peebles were working on at Princeton. And the rest, as they say, is history. Penzias called Dicke. Dicke drove to Holmdel. The two teams put it all together,[17] and, gradually, each came to grips with the fact that what they were hearing was nothing less than the vibration of the birth of the universe.

(Punch line: the Nobel Prize was awarded to Penzias and Wilson, who had found the cosmic background radiation but did not know what it was. None of the others, who knew what to look for but did not find it themselves, received this recognition.)

The identification of the cosmic background radiation was supportive good news for those who had maintained the Big Bang theory, and it persuaded many others, but it was bad news as well. The evenness of the sound from every direction was evidence that it indeed pervaded the entire universe, but it was also a bit *too* even. After all, the universe, as we observe it, is not perfectly symmetrical. In the Big Bang theory, the universe initially would have been uniform. Following the explosion, matter would have spread out in every direction without variation. But we do not live in such a smooth broth of a universe. There are stars and planets and moons, the stars cluster into galaxies, the galaxies cluster into great walls and bubble-like configurations in which they surround vast, apparently empty expanses of space. If the universe changed early on from a smooth soup to a lumpy unevenness in which matter could then consolidate into stars and galaxies, this should have left some remnant in the cosmic background radiation, but there was no sign of it. The background radiation was apparently the same from every direction.

Then the third key observation was made via a satellite, launched in 1989, which was capable of detecting this sort of unevenness in the cosmic background radiation. The satellite was called the Cosmic Background Explorer. A quirk of timing in the press unintentionally dramatized the significance of the third observation for me. Following a meeting of prominent cosmologists in Irvine, California, about an hour's drive from my university, the local newspaper published a feature article in April of 1992 with the title "Big Bang Bashing," suggesting that the Big Bang theory could be in serious trouble and might have to be abandoned. The article's starting point was this problem of the formation of the galaxies. It began:

> The Big Bang theory of the origin of the universe has developed a glaring shortcoming: It cannot convincingly explain how the galaxies formed or how huge clusters of them, stretching across the universe, assembled.
>
> Even the strongest Big Bang supporters acknowledge that something fundamental is missing from the story, and barring a solution, the theory . . . might be in jeopardy.[18]

The article quoted Peebles as describing this as "a deep embarrassment." Further on, it mentioned that the Cosmic Background Explorer satellite was out there searching for variation in the smoothness of the background radiation but noted, "No such variation, or signature, has been seen."

Two days later, the announcement came that the Cosmic Background Explorer had detected the ripples, the variations in the temperature of the background radiation, that had been sought. The next day, that same local newspaper carried the Associated Press story of this "momentous discovery." In the place of "Big Bang Bashing," the headline was now:

"Big-Bang Theory: Scientists Offer Proof." In the place of "a deep embarrassment," the physicist Joel Primack was quoted as calling it "one of the major discoveries of the century. In fact it's one of the major discoveries of science."[19] Hawking, likewise, was quoted as saying, "It is the discovery of the century, if not of all time."[20] This observation, which was so new that it did not figure in the wave of cosmology books by Hawking and others just a few years earlier, was immediately receiving the kind of enthusiastic evaluation that the observations of Hubble and Penzias and Wilson had received. It was in reference to this observation of the ripples in the cosmic background radiation that George Smoot, the leader of the Cosmic Background Explorer research team, said, "If you're religious, it's like looking at God."[21]

Questions and challenges concerning the Big Bang theory remain, but over the course of this century it has come to be the dominant model, the view that commands the consensus in the field. A good deal of fine tuning remains to be done. Notably, specialists debate the question of where the universe is headed if this model is correct. One possibility is that it will expand forever. Another is that the expansion will eventually slow down, the universe will then begin to contract, and it will eventually collapse back into an infinitely dense point: the Big Crunch. After that, who knows? One possibility is that then another Big Bang occurs, and it all happens again. And again? I shall return later to this question of whether the universe is open or closed or oscillating, eternally recurring. For now I simply wanted to describe some essentials of the theory and the role of key observations in bringing this theory to prominence.

"ONE HIGH AND HIDDEN POINT"

Kabbalah is the term for a mystical movement in Judaism that goes back at least to the rabbinic period and which particularly developed in medieval times, starting in the twelfth century, and continued to unfold and grow in the centuries that followed. Christian Kabbalah developed as well and was most successful in Europe in the sixteenth and seventeenth centuries. (The spelling *qabbālâ* would be consistent with the system of transcription of Hebrew words that I have used until now in this book, which is the common system used among biblical scholars at present. The term is more commonly rendered Kabbalah in English by scholars in that field of mysticism, and so I shall follow their spelling conventions of this and other terms in this section.) Its root meaning is "receive," and the term is understood to refer to an ancient received tradition. The best-known work of Kabbalah is the Zohar, thought to have been composed by Moses de León between 1280 and 1286.

To the layperson, the Zohar and Kabbalah may seem as incomprehensible as cosmology. Composed in an idiosyncratic Aramaic-Hebrew combination, the Zohar is joined by tens of thousands of other Kabbalistic texts, using a vast range of metaphors, and involving extremely difficult concepts, all constructed in a model that assumes a degree of experience on the part of the person reading and studying it. There is an often-quoted tradition that one is supposed to be at least forty years old and married before studying Kabbalah, presumably so as to have an anchor in this world while pursuing this course of study and action, a course that is directed toward nothing less than "the human need to contact God." [22]

A central concern of Kabbalah is the nature of the creation of the universe, which in Kabbalah is particularly inseparable from the nature of the deity. This inseparability is crucial. God is not pictured in this system as creating a world on a table before him the way a carpenter makes a chair. The creation is a process that occurs within God. The founding father of scholarship on the Kabbalah, Gershom Scholem, put it like this:

> To the Kabbalist the fundamental fact of creation takes place *in* God. . . . The creation of the world, that is to say, the creation of something out of nothing, is itself but the external aspect of something which takes place in God Himself.[23]

How does this happen? The doctrine in Kabbalah is that prior to the creation the deity became concentrated into a *point*. The point comes from the realm of the infinite. That realm is called in Hebrew *Ein Sof*, which translates literally as "infinite," "without end." This "one high and hidden point" is the beginning of all things — at least, all things that human beings are capable of knowing. At a particular moment, for reasons unknown to anyone, this point burst out, forming a group of ten emanations. In some texts the process of creation includes a ray of light that enters the space within the *Ein Sof* and fills it with the emanations.[24]

The emanations from the point, which are called the *Sefirot*, contain all the matter that became the stars, planets, stones, and living things of the universe. The universe expands out from the point and becomes differentiated into all these things. This is the essence of creation, as expressed in one Kabbalistic text:

> With the appearance of the light, the universe expanded.
> With its concealment, all individual existence came into being.
> This is the mystery of the act of creation.
> One who understands will understand.[25]

The last line is a reminder that these are understood to be mysteries that only a small number of persons can comprehend. At most they are expressed in the language of metaphor, through which one hopes ultimately to reach an acquaintance with the actual things that the metaphors represent. The infinite aspect of the deity, the *Ein Sof*, is unknowable; but the emanations, the *Sefirot*, which contain everything we know, express the divine personality, the aspect of God that a human is capable of experiencing. In Scholem's words:

> ... the emanation of the Sefiroth is conceived as a process which takes place *in* God and which at the same time enables man to perceive God.[26]

The doctrine of the emanations is not simply one interesting aspect of this mystical system among many. It is central to Kabbalah and to scholarship on the Kabbalah.[27] The *Sefirot* are everything in the universe, and they are an expression — the only knowable expression — of God. They are also called the "inner, intrinsic, or mystical Face of God."[28]

Now, even though all the contents of the universe, from sand to human beings, precipitate out of the emanations, something of God remains in all things. One metaphor for this in the texts is a skin wine bottle. Pour out all of the wine, rinse the bottle any number of times, but some residue of the wine always remains, which one can smell, however faintly. So the "smell of God" remains on — in — everything and everyone. Some remnant of the divine light that burst in at the moment of expansion persists. There is "a residue of divine manifestation in every being."[29]

If there had only been the explosion from the point, resulting in the entry of the deity into a space, the universe would have been more perfect than it is. There is another doctrine in Kabbalah which is quite enigmatic, in which the emanations are regarded as vessels that were to contain the light of the divine presence. The light proved to be too powerful, however, and the seven lowest emanations, unable to contain it, were shattered. This was a cosmic catastrophe, but it gave birth to the world that we know, a material world that even contains evil, which formed out of some of the fragments of the broken vessels.[30] This is known as the doctrine of the shattering of the vessels.

And so Kabbalah contains central doctrines concerning God and creation, in which the universe began as a single point; in a great flash the point expanded into the universe; the process involved a shattering of the structure that would otherwise have been perfect, bringing about unevenness and differentiation of matter; and a residue of its origin remains, pervading all things.

This sounds familar.

"THE WATERS ABOVE THE FIRMAMENT"

These elements of Kabbalah have enough in common with the Big Bang conception to make it worthwhile to see if there is something we can learn from this. I should say at the outset that I am aware that comparisons have been made before between various religious systems (especially Far Eastern systems) and contemporary cosmology, of which the best known are probably Fritjof Capra's *The Tao of Physics* and portions of Gary Zukav's *The Dancing Wu Li Masters*.[31] These have been received well by some and disdained by others.[32] Hawking, for one, has dismissed the various attempts to compare New Age systems to the work of astrophysicists as "fashionable rubbish."[33] I am not sure that he should be so quick to dismiss them, but his harsh view is valuable at the very least as a caution. Whatever one's judgment of such efforts, I should say that I have something somewhat different in mind here, of more limited scope, which I trust will prove to be interesting and useful while also being responsible in its analysis and conclusions.

I do not mean to make a simplistic comparison between two systems and then make supposedly profound judgments about the similarity, and I want to caution readers against rushing to such conclusions. I am particularly sensitive on this point because I have seen some well-intentioned but sadly uninformed attempts to do that sort of thing with the Bible itself. Attempts to reconcile the biblical creation accounts with Big Bang cosmology have been failures. Perhaps the best known of these is a book by a physicist, Gerald L. Schroeder, called *Genesis and the Big Bang*, which makes claims such as:

> An understanding of both physics and biblical tradition shows that the opening chapters of the book of Genesis and the findings of modern cosmology corroborate rather than dispute each other.[34]

and:

> The biblical narrative and the scientific account of our genesis are two mutually compatible descriptions of the same, single, and identical reality.[35]

and:

> The implications of general relativity and Doppler shifts in light are an essential part in understanding the opening chapters of Genesis.[36]

The author may be a knowledgeable physicist, but he simply lacks the knowledge of the Bible and biblical scholarship necessary for his project. He is insufficiently trained in biblical Hebrew grammar, so that he writes, for example, that the

> seeming contradiction between the incorporeality of God and making man in God's "image" is resolved by the root meaning of the Hebrew word for *image*, which modifies the word *likeness* in the biblical text (Gen 1:26). That meaning is "shadow."[37]

The Hebrew word for "shadow" (*ṣēl*; root: *ṣll*) and the word for "image" (*ṣelem*; root: *ṣlm*) are unrelated.

He writes of the consistency of existing manuscripts of the Hebrew Bible, apparently unaware of the entire field of textual criticism of the Bible and of the extremely numerous differences between the Qumran

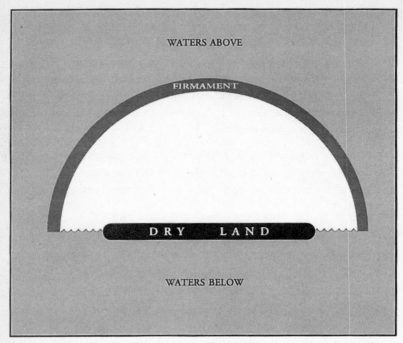

FIGURE I

(Dead Sea Scrolls) texts of the Bible and the text with which he is familiar (the commonly used version of the Masoretic text), or of the numerous differences between these texts and the Hebrew text that stands behind the Greek (Septuagint) manuscripts.[38]

He ignores all of the biblical scholarship of the last seven centuries, using instead only medieval commentaries, on the grounds that thus "we avoid the folly of using interpretations of tradition that may have been biased by modern scientific discoveries." With due respect, a scientist should have more regard for the human ability to pursue knowledge than to exclude the whole of the last seven hundred years of learning. He should rather, as in his own field, try to evaluate the research critically. And, in any case, does he really need to be afraid to consider, for example, the work of Julius Wellhausen out of concern that Wellhausen's work,

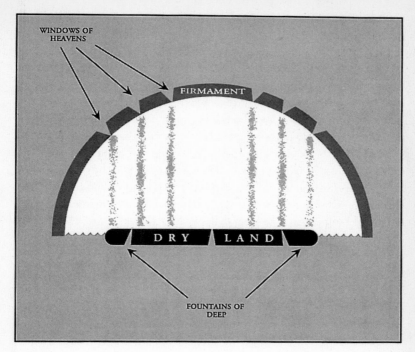

FIGURE 2

published in 1878, was biased in ways that have anything to do with Big Bang theory?

Most basically, though, he does not seem to be aware of the way that Genesis pictures the cosmos. It pictures an initial state of watery chaos, in which the deity creates a habitable bubble, in which humans and animals can live, by making a firm substance (the "firmament," Hebrew *rāqî'a*) which holds back the waters above. That is, the biblical picture of the cosmos, like the ancient Mesopotamian picture, reflected the understanding that the sky is blue because there is water up there. (See figure 1.) Thus in the biblical flood story, which comes a few chapters later, the waters pour in from above and below as the deity opens "the windows of the heavens" and "the fountains of the deep." (See figure 2.)

If Schroeder was unwilling to learn that this is what is pictured in

Genesis from a modern biblical scholar, he could have learned it from the best-known medieval scholar whom he cites, Rashi, who described it in his commentary on Genesis in the eleventh century.[39] Whatever one makes of this picture, whether one is an orthodox or reform Jew, a fundamentalist or liberal Christian, or a nineteenth- or twentieth-century critic, one cannot exactly say that it is manifestly consistent with Big Bang cosmology. Someone who wants to argue the consistency of Genesis and the Big Bang must at least *address* this most basic point.

In another book that attempts to reconcile the biblical creation account with modern cosmology, *The Genesis Answer*, by William Lee Stokes, the author at least understands that this is a problem and attempts to address it.[40] He argues that the water above the firmament is to be explained by quantities of interstellar matter that includes water molecules (H_2O) which have been found in space. He identifies the center of our galaxy as the biblical firmament and suggests that the reference to waters above and below the firmament corresponds to the two opposite spiral arms of the galaxy. Regrettably he apparently does not read biblical Hebrew, so that he relies on the *Oxford English Dictionary* for his understanding of the firmament, on which he is confused. And he does not recognize the relationship of the biblical flood account to the biblical creation account, which makes clearer that the text pictures water as we know it above the firmament, and not some matter in space that includes some molecules of H_2O.

I intend a criticism but no discourtesy to these physicists and their efforts. I assume that they are sincere and well-meaning, but I would advise them to stop trying to adapt the Bible to contemporary cosmology. To claim that the Genesis creation account reflects Big Bang cosmology is ultimately a disservice to both the Bible and cosmology.

Some readers may regard such analyses as not even worthy of being discussed in a serious treatment of relationships between science and religious traditions, but I have commented on them, first, because they (especially Schroeder's book) have been publicized and occasionally cited recently; second, to dissociate myself from that sort of work and clarify that my purpose here is different; and, third, to set these attempts at making parallels as a background so as to convey how much more marked and provocative the parallels of Kabbalah and contemporary cosmology are. These attempts to make the Bible fit the Big Bang have involved a degree of stretching, reinterpreting, and misunderstanding of the biblical text. No one would just read Genesis and right away recognize a relationship to the Big Bang. Though these attempts to uncover such a relationship may be sincerely and positively motivated, they are mixing apples and galaxies. The Kabbalistic concept of an infinite point that expands into the universe, which then retains a kind of divine radiation, is more directly parallel and striking in such a way that one is at least reasonably attracted to look into it, to see if it is merely a neat coincidence or if there is any way in which the parallel can be revealing or instructive, about the cosmos or about the way the human mind works or in some other way.[41]

"WHERE OUR UNDERSTANDING HAS REACHED ITS LIMITS"

The Kabbalah speaks of a universe that began from a single point. There was a flash in which the point began to expand. That expansion contains the universe in the form that we know it. An element of that initial event persists, pervading the universe. Very early in this process there was a breaking of the essential structures that composed the cosmos, and, without that fracture, the universe would be more perfect but would not be the universe that we know. Some may compare this last element, "the breaking of the vessels," to the change in the early universe from a smooth broth to a lumpy unevenness, the transformation that the Cosmic Background Explorer satellite detected, which is thought to have occurred at the relatively early juncture of three hundred thousand years after the Big Bang. Others may regard the breaking of the vessels as more analogous to the breaking of cosmic symmetry, another crucial element of the Big Bang theory, an event which is thought to have occurred within a tiny fraction (a trillionth) of the first second after the Big Bang. In Ferris's description:

> . . . a picture emerges of a more or less perfectly symmetrical universe that fractured its symmetries as it expanded and cooled, creating the particles of matter and energy that we find around us today and stamping them with evidence of their genealogy.[42]

As in the Kabbalistic model, without this rupture, the universe would be a perfectly symmetrical structure, like a crystal perhaps, but certainly not the universe in which we find ourselves. There would be no differentiated objects. Among other things, there would be no *us*. In the physicist Heinz Pagels's words:

> From the view of modern physics the entire world can be seen as the manifestation of a broken symmetry. If the symmetries of nature were actually perfect we would not exist.[43]

In Kabbalah, that perfect stage that preceded the shattering of the vessels is also known as *'ayin*, meaning "nothing," "nonbeing." Our existence is only possible because of the break. Ferris could almost be talking about Kabbalah when he describes the disruption of cosmic symmetry:

> It may be, then, that the universe is comprehensible because it is defective — that because it forsook the perfection of nonbeing for the welter of being, it is possible for us to exist, and to perceive the jumbled, blemished reality. . . .[44]

As for the primordial point, it has more in common with Big Bang cosmology than the simple fact that both systems begin with a single point. What Hawking and Penrose demonstrated was that, on the basis of the general theory of relativity, the universe must have had a beginning as a point which was a "singularity."[45] A singularity is a stopping point, a barrier, at which one arrives at the answer "infinity" and thus can go no farther. In Penrose's words:

> . . . space-time singularities are regions where our understanding of physics has reached its limits. [46]

and:

> . . . if one is trying to be scientific, it is understanding that appeals. And here, at the singularity, you just have to give up. . . .[47]

The laws of science break down, human intellect is stymied, and one simply cannot speak of what came before the Big Bang. Cosmologists speak of the point as infinitely dense and of space as infinitely curved. Laypersons can barely comprehend what that means, and the scientists who do comprehend it still also comprehend that it means the final barrier, that beyond this point nothing can be known.

The primordial point in the Kabbalistic conception likewise comes from the infinite (*Ein Sof*), and, as the Big Bang point is beyond inquiry through scientific channels, the Kabbalah point is beyond inquiry through religious channels. So Scholem says:

> ... *Ein Sof* cannot be subject to religious investigation, which can conceive of God only in His external aspect.[48]

Isaiah Tishby speaks of:

> The absolute concealment of *En-Sof*. . . . As far as *En-Sof*, the hidden God, is concerned, the mystery is one of non-knowledge and non-perception.[49]

Daniel Matt says:

> *Ein Sof* is inaccessible to thought. . . .[50]

And the Zohar itself says:

> Beyond that point, nothing is known.
> So it is called Beginning.[51]

Speaking for myself, I find the parallels in the essential elements of these two systems to be intriguing and mysterious. Davies warns that "Most scientists have a deep distrust of mysticism."[52] And, as if to demonstrate that point, he covers mysticism (which he combines with inspiration) in three and a half pages. Distrust and skepticism are necessary and appropriate tools of honest inquiry, but one also should not exclude the possibility that there is something to be learned from this. I realize that many persons may be satisfied to dismiss the similarity of Big Bang and Kabbalah as coincidence, which it may be; but, even if we were to assume that it is strictly coincidence, we must admit that, as coincidences go, this is a multifaceted and fascinating one. At the very least, I believe that it can be instructive. And at most, well, the sky's the limit.

Chapter 11

RELIGION AND
SCIENCE

How are we to explain the similarities between Big Bang and Kabbalah? One possible explanation is that they are coincidence, plain and simple. Another approach to account for the resemblance is that there is a finite number of conceivable and feasible models for the formation of the universe, and it is only natural that every now and then, among the many systems that humans have formulated, two of those systems should be similar. A third explanation is that any two models will have a certain number of similarities among the hundreds of elements they comprise, and so it is within the realm of probability that the Big Bang and Kabbalah systems should intersect on some elements; after all, there are numerous elements in the two systems that do not specifically match as well. A fourth possible explanation: there appears to be a human attraction to unity, which, after all, is reflected in the dominance of monotheistic religions in Western civilization and of religions in which unity plays an important role in Eastern civilization. Indeed, there is no reason why, theoretically, religions with one god are "higher" than religions with two or more, yet monotheism has triumphed over polytheistic religions in much of the world (with the notable exception of Hinduism) and has been regarded by its adherents not only as true but as an ascent for humans. If humans are in fact attracted to unity, for psychological, aesthetic, or whatever reasons, this, too, might figure in explaining the similarities of Big Bang and Kabbalah, perhaps in conjunction with one of the other possible explanations. Perhaps the solution lies in some combination of several or all of these possibilities.

These explanations, singly or combined, are possible; but, having said this, I still must add that, to my mind (and my gut), none of these explanations, singly or combined, is entirely satisfying. An innate or acquired attraction to unity is fine, and one can imagine that humans, confronted with the multiplicity of nature, might be attracted to formulate a model in which there is an original oneness that subsequently divides. But that still does not necessarily require that the oneness be a *point*. And even if we allow for the point, it still does not require an *infinite* point, beyond which all knowledge stops, plus a fracturing at an early stage, plus a residue that continues to pervade all the parts of the system. And the probability of intersection of a few elements among many still does not account for the fact that it is the *central* elements of the two systems that overlap in this case. The notion of a probable similarity among a finite number of systems, likewise, does not seem adequate to explain this degree of similarity of central structural elements. And simple coincidence seems even more unsatisfactory to explain it. These relatively banal explanations are all possible — and I learned from one of my teachers that the most banal solution is usually the right one — but there is value nevertheless in pursuing this further, both to consider another type of solution and to see what we can learn from the parallels of Big Bang and Kabbalah no matter what the explanation of their similarity is.

"THERE IS NO THERE THERE"

My starting point involves a proposal made by Hartle and Hawking in 1983 that, in a certain sense, ran counter to the work that Hawking and Penrose had done on singularities earlier. It was a construction of a history (actually, in the terms of quantum physics, a family of histories) of the whole of space and time.[1] Space-time is a four-dimensional conception: time plus the three dimensions of space. It is difficult to depict four dimensions on a page of a book, and so Hawking and others following him have attempted to convey this four-dimensional scheme with a three-dimensional representation, drawn or described on the two-

FIGURE 3

dimensional page.[2] The representation looks like a picture of a globe. A single point at the top of the globe signifies the Big Bang. A single point at the bottom of the globe is the Big Crunch. The expansion of space from the instant of the Big Bang is conveyed by the widening surface of the globe as far as its equator. The contraction back to the Big Crunch is conveyed by the comparably contracting surface down to the bottom of the globe. (See figure 3.) In this model, the point of the Big Bang is no longer a singularity. As the North Pole is just a point on the earth like any other when one looks at the whole earth, so the Big Bang is just a point like any other when one looks at the whole of space-time. The Big Bang is no more the starting point of space-time in this model than the North Pole is the starting point of the earth. Space and time have a closed surface, as pictured here, but they do not have any boundary, that is, no point at which they start and no point at which they end.

I have considerably oversimplified what Hawking has already considerably oversimplified in his presentation of this in laypersons' terms; I have omitted discussion of such elements as quantum fluctuation, wave function, sum over histories, and imaginary time. The reason for omitting them is not that I do not fully comprehend them (though I do not) but because my present concern is not so much the explication of the Hartle-Hawking construction as the way in which Hawking has attempted to relate their proposal to God and creation. He says that this idea "has profound implications for the role of God in the affairs of the universe." If you wonder why, look at the first words of the Bible. This construction leaves no room for "In the beginning."[3] And in Hawking's view:

> So long as the universe had a beginning, we could suppose it had a creator. But if the universe is really completely self-contained, having no boundary or edge, it would have neither beginning nor end: it would simply be. What place, then, for a creator?[4]

Recall Sagan's introduction to Hawking's book: "This is also a book about God . . . or perhaps about the absence of God." Hawking returns to this idea of the self-contained, unbounded universe in the last pages of his book, combining it with the possibility of a unified theory of the four forces in physics, and concludes again that it "has profound implications for the role of God as Creator." Hawking's finish is remarkable, curious, and disappointing. He still seems to be picturing a simple, traditional notion of God: *separate* from the universe. Responding to a famous comment of Einstein's, he discusses whether this God had freedom of choice to create the universe differently, or not to create it at all. And he asks about God: "And who created him?" He may have some more sophisticated conception of the deity in mind, but he formulates the question in the way many people have posed it even as children. It is as if Hawking himself does not fully appreciate the terrain he is in. He has conceived a nonclassical view of the universe, but he still relates it to a classical view of God, a God who is someplace else from the creation, a "him" who can only create from outside. We used to imagine gods on some mountain — Olympus, Zaphon — someplace else. Then we imagined a God in heaven — someplace else. Now Hartle and Hawking have imagined *every* place: all time and all space, yet Hawking still speaks in the manner of people who imagine God someplace else. But there *is* no place else in this model. From Hawking's presentation, he gives an impression of being unable to imagine — or at least to include the idea of — a God who inheres in the universe. Relating such a conception to the idea of a self-contained universe may involve a change in one's picture of creation: it is not only the production of a first event, but rather the generation of the whole of time and space. But the conception does not rule out a role for a creator. In fairness to Hawking, I should say that at other points he sounds as if he means something more complex than a classical religious view. He speaks more of whether the creator had any choice in the laws by which the universe runs, as opposed to a choice of the initial conditions of the universe. But it still seems to me like a problematic formulation of the question. The deity still sounds like a person, a choosing being, still somewhere else. The deity is still perceived as over there, "but," as Gertrude Stein said to Ernest Hemingway, "there is no there there."

Now, one intriguing aspect of Big Bang and Kabbalah is that Kabbalah conceives of such a thing — a God who inheres in the universe — precisely in a structure that resembles the cosmological model. In Kabbalah, as in Hartle and Hawking's conception, the whole of space and time is imagined (though in a different sense, of course), but one does not look someplace else for the deity. The deity is *here*. Hawking speaks of God's creation as a thing that is somehow *apart* from God. But what Big Bang and Kabbalah suggest is that it may rather be *a part* of God.[5] If the Kabbalistic view of creation really is, in some way, in tune with what we have learned through cosmology, that fact is fascinating, momentous, and worth pursuing. But even if it is just a coincidental overlap of images, we learn from it that, in the model that we now have from science, the deity need not be looked for *outside* of the universe. In the Kabbalistic conception, God is *in* the universe (and the universe is in God).

"COSMIC RELIGIOUS FEELING"

I hasten to add that, as Scholem especially emphasizes, this is not simple pantheism. Some would say that a pantheistic conception of God, a God who is in everything, is no God at all. But in Kabbalah the deity has an independent existence from creation yet still inheres in it. ". . . not a single kabbalist school of thought ever claimed that God has no existence apart from created beings."[6] The deity is not simply the sum of the parts of the universe. Rather, the creation is something that takes place within God. The creation involves the emanation of vessels, which are the outward, perceivable garments of the unperceivable actual substance of the deity, but "it is necessary to distinguish between the substance of the Emanator, which clothes itself in vessels, and the substance of the emanated."[7] The deity is not someplace else, as far as humans are concerned, because there *is* no place else that is knowable by us. But at the same time, the universe that we know is an outward, emanated expression of the hidden deity.

The implications of the cosmology of recent decades for theology are indeed profound, but they do not necessarily involve an exclusion (or rendering superfluous) of a creator deity. Rather, they are an urging toward certain kinds of concepts of what — and where — the deity is. An old joke that I heard as a child seems metaphorically relevant here. It involves a factory worker in a country with an oppressive regime. Every day the worker comes out of the factory, and the secret police search his wheelbarrow over and over. They know that he is stealing something, but they can't figure out what it is. And, the thing is, he's stealing wheelbarrows. I suggest that a lesson of Big Bang and Kabbalah may be that those who seek God might be advised to look under their noses as well. The Big Bang theory tells us that we are literally made of stardust. Kabbalah suggests that it is literally divine stardust.

The cosmologist Alan Sandage seems close to this idea of a God who inheres in the universe when he says to Timothy Ferris:

> The world is incredible — just the fact that you and I are here, that the atoms of our bodies were once part of stars. They say I'm

on some sort of a religious quest, looking for God, but God *is* the way it's put together.[8]

Perhaps he just means a kind of pantheism, in which case he is not in the zone that we are considering at this point, but he sounds as though he means more than that. Perhaps Hawking, as well, means more by "God" and "creator" than I have understood from his context. One science writer has said, "Of course when Hawking says God, he doesn't mean *God*."[9] But one would not readily guess this, either from Sagan's introduction or Hawking's own concluding pages. Again in fairness to Hawking, though, I should note that Einstein, too, is famous for expressions like "Subtle is the Lord, but malicious He is not" and "*He* does not play dice" and "What I'm really interested in is whether God could have made the world in a different way; that is, whether the necessity of logical simplicity leaves any freedom at all!" Yet Einstein did not hold the view of a personal, possibly anthropomorphic God that these remarks might imply. He wrote of a stage of religious experience which, he suggested, was at a higher level than conceptions of a personal, localized deity. He called it "cosmic religious feeling." Einstein described the cosmic religious feeling like this:

> The individual feels the futility of human desires and aims and the sublimity and marvelous order which reveal themselves both in nature and in the world of thought. Individual existence impresses him as a sort of prison and he wants to experience the universe as a single significant whole.[10]

It sounds more like the writing of a mystic than a physicist, but Einstein claimed that "the religious geniuses of all ages have been distinguished by this kind of religious feeling. . . ." and, impressively, he added a page later that "the cosmic religious feeling is the strongest and noblest motive for scientific research."[11] He did not exclude a belief in God, but he did not accept a traditional, personal concept of God. He rather expressed an awe before the universe which he perceived to be religious. I noted in Chapter 9 that for many people science has taken away some of the awe of the universe, but Einstein derived such awe precisely from his comprehension of the implications of science. Einstein (like Kabbalah) abandoned the notion of a personal God and felt instead the experience of the cosmic.

"WHERE WERE YOU WHEN I LAID
THE FOUNDATIONS OF THE EARTH?"

The experience of the cosmic is the realm in which I wish to propose an alternative explanation of the similarities of Big Bang and Kabbalah. I have in mind more than "to conclude rapturously that we are all part of the cosmos and the cosmos is part of us," as the physicist Leon Lederman characterizes works that compare science and Eastern mysticism.[12] With or without the rapture, that much is now obvious. I am proposing as another possible explanation that the reason the two similar conceptions developed is that, *given* that humans are part and parcel of the cosmos, the way in which the universe formed is part of our own composition and experience. Every bit of every one of us was present at the Big Bang, not figuratively or metaphorically, but actually. When the deity asks Job, "Where were you when I laid the foundations of the earth?" Job might answer, truly and reverently in a way, "I was there." To the extent that the universe still reverberates with the Big Bang, it reverberates in all beings; and those beings with the furthest developed state of consciousness — which on this planet includes humans — may be capable of being in touch with that part of our formation: through tools of the intellect if they are cosmologists (including observation, deduction), through tools of mysticism if they are Kabbalists (including meditation, introspection). And there are, no doubt, some tools that the two have in common as well (aesthetics, logic, instinct).

I hasten to recognize nakedly that I am not in the realm of the scientifically established here. I am simply posing a possibility. But this speculation does not come entirely *ex nihilo* either. I note that aspects of this possibility have occurred to others in related contexts. Especially since the formation of quantum physics, scientists and science writers, as well as philosophers and psychologists, have been addressing the relationship between the human mind and the universe that this mind studies. What moves humans to pursue the mystery of the origins of the universe? What moves scientists to ask the particular questions that they do? Timothy Ferris has written of the extent to which we are bound up with the wider universe, commenting in terms of quantum physics that "we are . . . unavoidably entangled in that which we study," and in terms of

Darwinian evolution that "we are such stuff as worlds are made of." [13] Coming closest to the point that I am developing here, he poses the question: why does science work, and he speculates that: "Perhaps it is because our brains evolved through the workings of natural law that they somehow resonate with natural law." [14] Paul Davies expresses a similar idea, asking:

> Is our success in explaining the world using science and mathematics just a lucky fluke, or is it inevitable that biological organisms that have emerged from the cosmic order should reflect that order in their cognitive capabilities? Is the spectacular progress of our science just an incidental quirk of history, or does it point to a deep and meaningful resonance between the human mind and the underlying organization of the natural world? [15]

And he concludes that:

> We who are children of the universe — animated stardust — can nevertheless reflect on the nature of that same universe, even to the extent of glimpsing the rules on which it runs. How we have become linked into this cosmic dimension is a mystery. Yet that linkage cannot be denied. [16]

The idea that I am considering is that if our brains do in fact somehow resonate with natural law, this resonance might find expression in more than one form of human enterprise. It finds arguably its most precise expression in scientific inquiry. But the parallels between the Kabbalistic picture of creation and the model that has been formulated through scientific probing tempt me at least to contemplate the possibility that the same force finds a form of expression through this mystical mechanism as well.

One might object that most of each person's matter was present at the formation of the planet earth, which was more recent than the Big Bang, but we do not "remember" that. Nor do we collectively remember any other events from before our birth. So why should we think that humans might have such primal memory of events that occurred billions of years before the formation of the earth? There is, however, a qualitative difference in dealing with the Big Bang event because we are talking about the *constitutive* event, the formation of the very components of our structure. Everything after the very early universe is, so to speak, mere re-shuffling of the cards. The idea is that we might resonate with essential natural law, not with specific episodes in the history of the universe. It is not "memory" so much as expression of something that is part of our structure.

One might ask: if there is any validity to this possible explanation, then why didn't more mystical systems include the parallels to Big Bang? Why did Kabbalah arrive at a primal point and a subsequent expansion, and so on, while various other mystical systems did not? The answer might be that other mystical systems may have arrived at different aspects of the nature of the universe. Thus there may or may not be something to Capra, Zukav, or Castaneda, to the teachings of the Sufis or other mystical traditions. One can only take each of them and analyze it. Even if several or all are valid, the adherents of each may have perceived different aspects of the whole. We must keep in mind that, even if there is some intersection of certain elements of mysticism and science, still mysticism is not science. It involves an admixture of other materials and historical and literary concerns that do not follow scientific method. So every mystical system, by its very nature, should include some material that looks familiar and some that looks wrong and even nonsensical to a scientist. And every mystical system will necessarily have elements that have no correspondence in other mystical systems that are no less valid. And this is all presuming that we are talking about mystical systems that have validity. Some mystics may be charlatans, and others may be sincere but wrong.

I am a bit fearful in even proposing this possibility of a relationship between natural law and human composition as an explanation of the parallels in the formulations of Big Bang and Kabbalah because this idea may be seized upon as a rationalization for every crackpot scheme in which there is some similarity to some scientific theory. But, in the end, the judgment of such comparisons must be made on the basis of the degree of parallel to the scientific theory, the character of the persons and processes involved in arriving at the parallel systems, and the quality of the scholarship involved in the study of these parallel systems. In the case of Kabbalah we are at least dealing with a centuries-old institution, involving many thousands of texts, and a highly respected, rigorous record of scholarship, at least since the work of Scholem. It is still seriously practiced by Kabbalists and seriously taught in universities. And, as we have seen, the degree of parallel to the consensus in contemporary cosmology is striking.

The feeling of a divine presence inside human beings itself has deep roots in civilization. Nietzsche suggested that the very origin of the belief in gods in pagan antiquity was such a feeling, especially as it was experienced by artists and musicians. Even contemporary musicians sometimes have the experience in which, in the midst of performance, they feel as if they are not producing the music themselves but are rather the instrument, the means, as some force causes the music to pass through them. Nietzsche suggested that the ancient artist experiencing this would be struck by the impression: "Not me, but a god moving through me." Nietzsche knew that sensation firsthand, for he once wrote: "I think of myself as the scrawl which an unknown power scribbles across a sheet of paper, to try out *a new pen*." [17] Compare Joseph's and Moses' disclaimers in the Bible: "Not I. God." Compare the words of the composer Salieri in Peter Shaffer's drama *Amadeus* as he first hears the music of Mozart: "It was the voice of God." Davies describes a similar intuition experienced by some mathematicians.[18] Athletes also have encountered this feeling. What both Big Bang and Kabbalah tell us is that, whatever has been going on in the universe since the explosion of origin, it is not just out there in the distance; it is here in us.

"THE GALAXY'S WAY OF EVOLVING A BRAIN"

Bound up in all of this is the entire matter of consciousness, the realm in which the cosmic process rises into thought. Many of those who address issues in cosmology have introduced consciousness into the discussion. Since the birth of quantum physics and the uncertainty principle, it seems virtually impossible to ignore. Questions of the relationship between human consciousness and reality *out there* have long been on the table. Modern philosophy is generally reckoned to begin with Descartes' questions of whether our minds can be trusted to know what is happening out there. It occurs even to children to ask whether, when a tree falls in a forest where there is no one to hear it, it makes a sound out there. Such questions, which were guaranteed to turn any dinner conversation into a bore, were mere Tinkertoys compared to those that arose with the uncertainty principle. Now there was the two-slit experiment, in which an electron's behavior seems to depend in a magical way on whether a human is observing it or not; or, to put it differently, what a human mind can know about the location and movement of tiny particles appears to be *necessarily* limited by the very nature of the universe. Now there was the thought experiment of Schroedinger's cat, in which a cat in a sealed box is both alive and dead — or suspended between life and death — unless and until a human opens the box and observes it. The complexity of this realm of science, which makes almost anything else in human experience look simple by comparison, is intimidating. Quantum physics and especially the uncertainty principle sound not only impenetrable but crazy to laypersons when they first hear of them. Niels Bohr is supposed to have said that anyone who does not feel giddy when learning this field has not understood it. Laypersons must at least recognize that it is not some fringe view, but rather it is an essential component of physics. And for our present context we must at least recognize that the implication of quantum physics to many persons is that our consciousness is fundamentally bound up in the universe. We are related in an essential way to what we observe. The idea of a connection between quantum physics and consciousness is extremely speculative, and we must acknowledge this as well. My concern for now, in a very limited and tentative way, is to note that it has been suggested, notably by Roger Penrose, that this may be the province in which the jump between the material realm and human consciousness takes place.[19]

This has raised a series of strange questions in science, questions that sound as if they more properly belong to the field of philosophy. (This suggests a curious reunion of science and philosophy, which, after all, were practiced as a single field in ancient Greece. The early Greek philosophers were also scientists and mathematicians, as were Descartes and Kant.) Scientists and philosophers have come to consider whether the nature of the universe requires that conscious beings exist. They have formulated various versions of what is known as the anthropic principle, suggesting that the existence of conscious beings like us is a necessity that limits the possible nature of the universe. They have questioned whether our consciousness is algorithmic, that is, the sum total of the functions that our brains perform, so that a computer that could perform the functions of the human brain would be aware as we are. Try these as dinner conversation, and you will learn to eat alone. But the essential issue of the relationship between our thoughts and the universe is not just an intellectual exercise. Roger Penrose, who has particularly brought this matter to wider circles of readers, and who argues that consciousness is not merely algorithmic, has conveyed that:

> Consciousness . . . is the phenomenon whereby the universe's very existence is made known. One can argue that a universe governed by laws that do not allow consciousness is no universe at all.[20]

He put it less formally in an interview:

> When it comes down to it, the question has to do with conscious perception of one's own existence in the world. A world that has no people in it is pointless. A universe that is just chugging away by itself with nobody in it is, in a sense, pointless.[21]

The universe coagulates into solar systems, which produce planets and moons, which blossom with living beings, some of which become conscious. Thus, in one of the great mysteries (or phenomena, or qualities, or miracles, or wonders) of the universe, some portions of matter acquire the property of being aware that all of this is going on. Some of these conscious beings can even communicate with one another, learning and advancing their common understanding of what is happening. And they can produce offspring who can preserve and advance this knowledge after their own consciousness has ended. Thus, in Davies's words, "The universe has organized its own self awareness."[22] In Ferris's words, "Life might be the galaxy's way of evolving a brain."[23]

There are those who regard the role of awareness, and especially human awareness, as even more immediately integral to the universe, from the physicist John Wheeler's "participatory universe" (in which all of the events leading up to our species' formation do not quite exist until we arrive and our consciousness calls them into existence)[24] to those who advocate the strongest versions of the anthropic principle (in which the universe cannot exist without us conscious creatures). And there are those who see our consciousness less crucially: as interesting but incidental, or coincidental, to the universe. To some, a universe chugging away unconsciously is just fine. In the present stage of our knowledge, I do not know if those of us who are attracted to this notion of an essential role for consciousness are (1) just engaging in species chauvinism, or (2) have insufficient imagination or courage to accept the idea of a universe rolling along without thinking or feeling anything, or (3) correctly suspect that our awareness participates in some *fundamental* way in the matter and energy of the universe. Nor do I know to what extent it might be possible that a common human embodiment of natural forces and universal history could come to be consciously perceived and articulated. Nor am I certain that evolving through natural law can actually have the result of resonating with natural law. But among the other possible solutions to the mystery of Big Bang and Kabbalah this strikes me as tantalizing and worth pursuing.

In the meantime, we have seen that the similarity of Big Bang and Kabbalah is instructive in any case. And I believe that it can be enlightening in other ways as well. Notably, Kabbalah shares this notion of the central role of consciousness. In Kabbalah, the emanations from the divine primordial point are reflected in humans, and a human can come to be aware of this essential aspect of his or her nature and act in such a way as to redirect these forces back to the deity. In Scholem's explanation:

> . . . the process of creation involves the departure of all from the One and its return to the One, and the crucial turning-point in this cycle takes place within man, *at the moment he begins to develop an awareness of his own true essence and yearns to retrace the path from the multiplicity of his nature to the Oneness from which he originated.*[25]

In Kabbalah there is a "Big Bang" and a "Big Crunch": everything started from the single point, and the goal is to bring everything back to that state of divine unity. And a key mechanism in bringing about this return is the human being because of the advanced degree of the human consciousness, spirituality, and free will. This element of Kabbalah attributes a significance to the human role that even transcends the views of scientists with the strongest conceptions of the place of human consciousness. But we should note, first, the commonality: that both regard consciousness as a fundamental aspect of existence. And we should note, second, the difference: that in Kabbalah there is actually a determinative role for humans to play, by their minds and actions, in the destiny of the universe.

"THE RESTORATION OF THE UNIVERSE"

To appreciate the central function that humans perform according to Kabbalah, one must first recall the Kabbalistic idea of the breaking of the vessels: The present state of the universe represents imperfection, a defect, a loss of harmony. The original perfection of existence was fractured at creation, leaving broken shards that make our particular universe and its components, including evil, possible. But humans, being a part of the universe that is aware and that can *act* on that awareness, can thus, by their thoughts and actions, participate in the course that the universe takes. In Kabbalah *the task of humans in this world* is to do this: to restore the universe to the original harmony that was lost with the breaking of the vessels.[26] This is called in Hebrew *tikkun*, a term whose range of meaning includes restoration, restitution, reintegration, mending. This is an enormously important and influential idea in Kabbalah from the sixteenth century on.[27] It involves both thought and action. The idea of intention is directly related to it. Lawrence Fine especially emphasizes the contemplative aspect of *tikkun*, that is, that it involves both action and conscious thought.[28] Yehuda Liebes notes that not only actions but also Kabbalistic discourses on the Torah bring about *tikkun*.[29] Scholem notes the importance of spiritual actions, especially prayer.[30] Deeds, words, thoughts — all contribute to the perfection of the world and the restoration of cosmic harmony.

This restoration thus involves the conscious direction of our behavior toward a universal goal. The mystic is not concerned only with himself or herself but with the repair of the universe.[31] Since there is a residue of divine manifestation in each human, the deeds which he or she performs play this crucial part in the cosmos. If they are deeds that purge evil and contribute to mending and restitution, they are bringing the universe back to its unity.[32] I am not sure that everyone would find this restoration to be an attractive goal since it means the end of this world, the world that we know, the collapse of history.[33] But the comfort is that it means the arrival of something better, the ultimate return into the oneness of the deity. And if that is not sufficient comfort there is also the fact that, if there really is any relationship between Kabbalah and the findings of contemporary cosmology, the ultimate return to unity (corresponding to the Big Crunch?) would be estimated to be, at the very least, over fifteen billion years away.

Tikkun has no *formal* parallel in contemporary science. It does, however, have a parallel in *fact*. The concept in Kabbalah is that the way in which humans think and behave has implications for the destiny of the world. One of the ideas that I mean to address in the next chapter, concerning the legacy of the age, is that this crucial role for humans applies, in a different way, to the realm of science as well.

I said in the beginning that mysteries are interesting both in themselves and as metaphors. Each of the first two mysteries — and the historical conditions for which they were metaphors — bequeathed a legacy for the age that followed. Usually one is constrained to judge a legacy in retrospect, from the perspective of a later time in which one can observe historical development. But the possible legacies of this age are so momentous that it is worthwhile at least to consider what all of this implies. I think that it implies the possibility of a reunion with God.

Chapter 12

DIVINE-HUMAN
REUNION

"IN THE IMAGE OF GOD"

We have probed three mysteries: the disappearance of God in the Bible, Nietzsche at Turin, and Big Bang and Kabbalah. In the first mystery, God disappears through the course of the Bible. The Bible recounts a gradual movement from a world in which God is publicly, manifestly involved in human life to a world in which the face of God is hidden. This biblical picture reflects and in turn bolsters a feeling that the age of power and contact with the divine lies distantly behind us. This development's legacy is that, in various ways, Judaism and Christianity come to include and respond to it; it is embedded in the thought of Western civilization. In the second mystery, the disappearance of God surfaces bluntly in the nineteenth century, most notably in Nietzsche and Dostoevsky, most powerfully in the formulation "God is dead." Major human voices tell our species that we are finally, utterly on our own. Some proclaim the moral corollary that "all is permitted." The legacy of this development is an age of insecurity, moral ambiguity, and spiritual lack. And then the third mystery materializes, involving an advance in science with intimations of arrival at a threshold of new comprehension of God and creation. Parallels in a centuries-old mystical system offer a tantalizing support to the sense that science has now intersected with religion.

The three are all fascinating, but the purpose of this book is not just to fascinate you. These mysteries have some of the qualities of detective stories, but, as I forewarned on the first page, I did not present them as an entertainment or an intellectual exercise. We are a generation of profound moral lack. Nothing has come to replace the direction and security that a more widespread reliance upon God once provided. The condition, the legacy, that I described in Chapter 9 is not a temporary malaise but rather a real crisis in the destiny of our species. Most other issues are subconditions of it. In terms of the obligation to deal with this state of affairs, it does not matter whether one is religious or not or on which side one stands on any particular social or political issue. The crisis is everyone's. I left off the discussion of it and turned to Big Bang and Kabbalah because I think that the content of this third mystery offers us an answer.

In order to arrive at that answer we must recognize how much the three puzzles are related even though they cover a span of thousands (arguably, billions) of years and involve a mosaic of disciplines and languages. The uniting point is obviously that they all relate to the human feeling of the presence or absence of God. Also, all three mysteries have two sides: each is about deity but has a human face as well. The disappearance of God in the Bible goes hand in hand with the shift in the divine-human balance, in which men and women must take greater responsibility for their lives. Nietzsche's notion of the death of God involves a new age for humankind, bringing about new burdens and responsibilities, and offering the eventuality of the superhuman (*Übermensch*). And Big Bang and Kabbalah include the ingredient of restoration (*tikkun*), in which there is a fundamental role for human beings to play in the destiny of the universe. All reflect the fact that our concept of the deity — or of the deity's absence — has implications for human behavior.

The relationship of the mysteries, though, is more consequential than the mere sharing of a common theme. The three illuminate one another. First, aspects of Big Bang and Kabbalah may shed light on the disappearance of God in the Bible. We considered the idea that the similarity of the conceptions of the origin of the universe in the scientific and the mystical models may exist because we embody and "resonate" with natural law: we were literally present at the explosion of origin, and our bodies and our consciousness are part and parcel of the physical structure of the universe. This notion of a cosmic resonance may also help to explain the common feeling of ages of power being behind us, which we considered in connection with the disappearance of God in the Bible. I raised the possibility that such a common human perception might be part of the explanation of how biblical authors from so many different periods contributed pieces that form such a consistent picture of a gradually diminishing manifest presence of God over many centuries. And I suggested that we have this perception of moving ever further from the age of close contact with the Almighty because we have an essential fear of the immediacy of power. Perhaps I was recognizing only half of the picture. We may well have such an intrinsic fear of closeness to power, but we also may well have a correct perception that we are moving away (in time and space) from the explosion of origin, which reflects the fact that that event reverberates in us and in all things. In scientific terms that means receding ever farther from the unity of all things, from the power and heat of the Big Bang. In the mystical terms of Kabbalah that means moving ever farther from the original oneness with God. At the very least this is another fruitful point of commonality between the first and third mysteries, and it may also be a way in which the two elucidate one another: the Bible reflects a sensation that we are getting farther from our powerful source because factually, literally, we *are* getting farther.

Contemporary cosmology may enhance one's appreciation of the Bible in other ways as well. In this cosmology, creation involves the formation of distinctions out of what was originally an undifferentiated broth. Our existence only became possible when this break from the unformed, smooth early universe occurred, and distinctions began. This generates a novel perspective on the Genesis creation account, which, as we saw, pictures an initial condition of undifferentiated, shapeless fluid, a mass that is "unformed and void." Creation involves a series of divisions, between light and dark, between dry land and water, between waters above the firmament and below; God separates matter into heavenly bodies, plants, animals, humans. As in the contemporary cosmological understanding, our existence in the biblical narrative is a function of these cosmic distinctions. This parallel strikes me as more interesting and enlightening than the attempts that I mentioned earlier by some writers to see the Big Bang in Genesis. And I do not mean to make a simplistic claim that the Bible is scientifically right, nor to make any claims about the insight of, or revelation to, the author of Genesis 1. I do not know if the similarity of this particular aspect of the biblical creation account to the contemporary scientific view is coincidental or another product of the resonance of cosmic structure in the human consciousness, or if the explanation lies elsewhere. I simply recognize that the parallel is there and that it suggests a hitherto unappreciated profundity to the biblical picture, no matter how that profundity is to be accounted for. For whatever reason, the Bible and scientific observation and deduction both reflect a common underlying human feeling about order and arrangement over chaos and lack of form.

This in turn has other parallels in human experience, some of which we have already encountered. In the Mesopotamian creation story, the wind god Enlil (or Marduk) defeats the goddess Tiamat, who is the waters, and makes the heavens and the earth out of her. Note: Tiamat is defeated but is not destroyed. The universe is fashioned out of her. The universe is order that is *made out of chaos.* By chaos I mean a formlessness. As we learn in school to characterize liquid as a substance that has no fixed shape but rather takes the form of its container, so the watery Tiamat is understood (along with other olden gods) to represent chaos, or shapelessness. In the pagan creation story, the universe is an orderly structure, forever holding back chaos.

Compare Nietzsche's notion of the Apollonian and the Dionysian. The Dionysian is the inner chaotic force, which is present in all humans. The Apollonian is the restraining force that imposes limitations, definition, and shape upon the Dionysian. Every human is a product and expression of this tension: a functional structure that is constantly holding back powerful chaotic forces, forces that, if released, would render the individual dysfunctional.

Compare this in turn to the Freudian notion of id and ego, whose similarity to Nietzsche's concept we have noted already. The ego (and superego) are rational structures restraining the powerful force of the id, giving it shape while drawing lines and imposing limitations upon it and thus making a person functional.

The ancient works, Mesopotamian, biblical, and Greek, were expressing, each in its own way, this inherent human sensation that we are creatures of reason who are holding back potent chaotic forces of emotion and instinct. And thus we, in turn, appear to be microcosms of the universe, insofar as the universe, too, is a formation of order and structure, differentiation and limitation, out of undifferentiated matter. It is constructed of four forces that powerfully impose distinct shape upon matter that is by nature shapeless. The universe in its way and the individual humans in their way each embody a tension between order and chaos. Who knows at this point: perhaps we have arrived at our cosmology of symmetry-breaking and of shape-giving forces precisely because we experience existence this way. Or perhaps we experience existence this way precisely because such a cosmic structure echoes in us.

This relates to another way in which our present state of learning in cosmology might open new perspectives affecting our appreciation of the Bible's opening chapters: the matter of the creation of humans "in the image of God." On one hand, from the perspective of the parallels of Big Bang and Kabbalah that we considered, we could conceive of a picture of the entire universe as being in the image of God; that is, everything derives from the primal, divine point and is an expression of it. In this sense, one might take the way in which we understood biblical angels (as a hypostasis of the deity) and understand the entire universe that way. But if everything is thus understood to be in the divine image, what then does it mean to single out humans from among all created things as Genesis 1 does? The answer might lie in the way in which both Kabbalah and some scientists single out humans: namely, in terms of consciousness. I hinted in Chapter 5 that I am tempted by the idea that creation *in imago Dei* has something to do with human consciousness being linked to the divine. In both the Kabbalistic and scientific circles we found the idea that conscious beings participate in more than an incidental way in the course of the universe. In this conception, it is through consciousness that some quantities of matter rise toward oneness with the divine. And, from this perspective, one might view human consciousness as the element through which humans could be quintessentially in the image of God. They would bear the stamp of divinity that all of the universe shares, and they would also hold the pivotal element — awareness — that enables them to participate in a unique way in the ongoing divine activity. Again, I do not mean to make a simplistic claim of biblical accuracy. As I have said, we really do not know with certainty what was originally meant by creation in the divine image in Genesis. My point is rather that, whatever one's feeling about the Bible — as literature, as history, or as revealed truth — one can appreciate and respond to its concept of creation in the divine image in a richer way in the light of this element that emerges both in mysticism and in science.

Even Einstein's sense of the cosmic religious feeling and his rejection of a personal God were not so far from the biblical picture of God as he might have thought. We saw that Israel conceived of a God who was outside of nature. But "outside" does not mean "someplace else." It means: not limited to any individual elements of nature, but rather *beyond* nature, unknown and unknowable. This quality, though consistent with cosmological and Kabbalistic models as we have seen, does not make the biblical conception of God and creation identical with Big Bang (there is still all that water to consider); but, in a more sophisticated way, it means that the biblical conception of God includes this important element, which might help Christians and Jews in this era to relate their understanding of the cosmos to biblical conceptions. Namely, in the Bible God is both: cosmic and personal.[1] And, as we saw in our investigation of the hiding of the face of God in the Bible, the deity is pictured in the Bible as gradually moving from the personal toward the cosmic as humans gradually mature.

"WHAT HAS BEEN WILL BE"

Surprising as it may seem to some, familiarity with Nietzsche, too, can enhance one's appreciation of the Bible. Notwithstanding his criticism of beliefs concerning God, nor his criticism of aspects of ancient Israelite thinking (which led some readers to think, incorrectly, that he was anti-Semitic), he held the Hebrew Bible in exceptional esteem among the great works of civilization. He wrote that in the Old Testament one encounters "human beings, things, and speeches in so grand a style that Greek and Indian literature have nothing to compare with it."[2] Coming from a scholar who was, in the first place, a classicist, this favorable comparison to the Greek works especially is striking. Coming from a man who wrote that "God is dead," it is remarkable. To Nietzsche: "the taste for the Old Testament is a touchstone for 'great' and 'small.'"[3]

There is another aspect of Nietzsche's life and work that relates both back to the Bible and forward to Big Bang and Kabbalah. Nietzsche considered stopping all his other work and reeducating himself to become a physicist at one point.[4] His motivation was not a general interest in the subject. He had something specific in mind:

> The doctrine of the "eternal recurrence," i.e. of the uncondi-
> tional and infinitely repeated circular course of all things . . .[5]

The eternal recurrence is not just a single element among many in Nietzsche's work. It is, in Nietzsche's own explanation: "the basic idea of *Zarathustra*."[6] All of this has happened before, and it will all happen again, exactly the same — an infinite number of times. Time and space are infinitely circular.

Interestingly (and perhaps we should almost expect it by now), this idea occurs in Dostoevsky as well. In *The Brothers Karamazov*, Ivan contemplates:

> "But our present earth may have been repeated a billion times."

> ". . . and the same sequence may have been repeated endlessly
> and exactly the same to every detail, most unseemly and insuffer-
> ably tedious. . . ."[7]

The idea is known in several religious and mystical traditions, and it seems to have come to Nietzsche in a manner that is reminiscent of mysticism. Nietzsche wrote that the idea struck him while on a solitary walk at a mountain lake. It was this occurrence that I had in mind, among others, when I alluded to Nietzsche's experience with moments of spiritual revelation. His plan to pursue eternal recurrence through scientific method never was fulfilled, or even begun; and Lou Salomé wrote: "What was to have become a scientifically proven truth assumed instead the character of a mystical revelation. . . ."[8] That is fascinating because the idea of eternal recurrence occurs both in contemporary science and in Kabbalah. I referred to the question in cosmology of the fate of the universe. One possibility is that the universe continues to expand, not having sufficient density ever to be slowed down by the force of gravity. Another possibility is that its expansion does eventually slow down, and the universe starts to collapse back to a single point: the Big Crunch. The question, in that case, is what happens after the Big Crunch? On one hand, that question, and the parallel question of what happened before the Big Bang, are unanswerable, for all known laws break down at the infinitely dense point. It is a "singularity." On the other hand, cosmologists are moved to wonder what the possibilities are. One possibility is that the Big Crunch is followed by another Big Bang, so that the universe bounces back: an oscillating universe. Then what? One possibility is that the universe is different in each cycle. Another is that the course of the universe is identical every time: eternal recurrence. I understand that most cosmologists would consider this last possibility to be conceivable but unlikely, so I do not want to push this idea beyond the limits of our present state of knowledge. I mean only to note, with the appropriate cautions, that Nietzsche's perception has indeed a counterpart in the alternatives that are contemplated in physics. Recall Einstein's conception that space is curved, bending back to join itself, and recall that in the no-boundary proposal of Hartle and Hawking, time is pictured as a sphere, on which the Big Bang and all other points are equal. One could think that one is reading a poetic formulation of these concepts when one reads in Nietzsche: "The center is everywhere. Bent is the path of eternity."[9]

The doctrine is present though somewhat different in Kabbalah. It is known as the doctrine of cosmic cycles (*shemittot*), and it is traced to Greek and Arabic influences.[10] It is not a central doctrine comparable to the doctrines of the emanations (*sefirot*) or restoration (*tikkun*), but it is significant and of interest, and it takes a number of forms. There are worlds before this one in which we live. According to some Kabbalists, there is a new creation out of nothing every fifty thousand years. In one formulation, these cycles lengthen and become enormously longer. In another view, it is forbidden to inquire into what comes after the end of the present cycle. We should note that no Kabbalist spoke of an infinite number of cycles, so it is not identical to the doctrine of eternal recurrence. It is similar enough to be of obvious interest, though, in the present context.

Intimations of this idea appear in the Bible, as well, in the most philosophical biblical book: Ecclesiastes. In its opening passage, the book's speaker (called "the preacher" or "Qohelet") says, "What has been, that is what will be; and what has been done, that is what will be done; and there is nothing new under the sun" (1:9; cf. 3:15). As philosophy composed in poetry, Ecclesiastes must always be interpreted with circumspection. The idea in Ecclesiastes may be eternal recurrence, or it may rather mean that, within the terms of the world that we know, life involves a constant replaying of familiar patterns of behavior and events. The former meaning is not only contextually possible and interesting in itself; it is also interesting as a common element, albeit found in various forms, running through the works and lives we have considered in this book.

There is another reason for raising Nietzsche's deep concern with eternal recurrence here. We have had a glimpse of how deeply and personally Nietzsche felt the matters he confronted in his work. Even to say that he was no armchair philosopher would be so obvious an understatement as to be laughable. In the face of all his suffering he was committed to his work, with the conviction that he was a destiny, an event in the course of civilization. Yet he was willing to leave all of his work on history, philosophy, religion, psychology, music, et cetera, et cetera, et cetera, to pursue *this*. That indicates that he understood that eternal recurrence in particular and physics in general related in an essential way to the things that interested him. Physics, and science broadly, was not a soulless enterprise, unconnected to matters of the human spirit, as some people imagine it. It was linked to religious, moral, philosophical, and psychological matters. A hundred years ago Lou Salomé wrote that "Nietzsche's teaching of the eternal recurrence has not yet been sufficiently emphasized and acknowledged, although it constitutes to a certain degree the foundation and coping stone of his ideas,"[11] and its centrality for him remains to be comprehended. For now, whatever our view of eternal recurrence, we should note that we are presently seeing the recognition of the relationship that Nietzsche perceived. Science, particularly cosmology, is coming to be widely regarded as intersecting with religion, as we have observed. People understand scientific discoveries concerning the birth of the universe to relate to questions concerning God and creation. Hubble observes that the galaxies are rushing away from us, and Hawking tells us that ultimately we could know the mind of God. Various writers have related all of this to theology, but Nietzsche understood that the consequences of science are still broader, having implications for the human condition and human behavior. These implications are becoming apparent in this century.

"THE HEAVENS TELL THE GLORY OF GOD"

The intersection of cosmology with theology means that each advance in knowledge through the work of physicists and astronomers has some potential of advancing our millennia-old pursuit of the nature of deity. Insight into the initial conditions of the universe, the explosion of origin, or the differentiation of matter is potentially insight into creation. The stunning fact that has been impressing itself upon us in the last decade is that scientific inquiry is a possible path back to our source, which may (or may not) turn out to be what people call God. It is ironic but appropriate that science should be the possible path back. Science probably did more than anything else to take away the wonder in nature that we associated with the divine, as I discussed earlier, and now it is through science that we are getting it back. Awe is an integral element of religious experience. For some, the existence of God is the justification of morality, but it is the awe of God that is the actual *motivation* for morality. That is, it is their experience of wonder and fear before the God in whom they believe that moves them to behave in certain ways. Rightly or wrongly, scientific description of nature eroded the feeling of awe, which was in large part grounded in the mystery of nature, by chipping away at the mystery. As the Grand Inquisitor points out, the feeling of mystery is a necessary part of religion. Reduce the mystery, reduce the awe. In the present age, a religious believer may not want to agree that God has disappeared or that God has died; but he or she can acknowledge, albeit sadly, that the awe has disappeared, or at least diminished dramatically, both among religious and nonreligious persons.

In southern California, where I am writing this, we use the word "awesome" in ordinary daily slang to describe anything that is good. ("That movie was awesome." "Your hair looks awesome." "That is totally awesome.") It is precisely because the world has lost so much of its authentic awe that we can use the word in this idiotic, trivial way. But the series of discoveries concerning the origin of the cosmos that we considered in the preceding chapters is *truly* awesome: picturing the origin of the universe, listening to the echo of the explosion, watching the galaxies rushing away from us, calculating the astonishing numbers of stars and distances between them, grappling with the significance of our consciousness in all of this — one must admit that science is paying back the debt that it had incurred by taking so much wonder away. Einstein's cosmic religious feeling is now within reach to anyone who can consider and appreciate the magnitude of these things.

The phenomenon of science's bringing back the feeling of wonder is dramatized by another matter of terminology, the use of the term "Big Bang" itself. On one hand, calling the origin of the universe the "Big Bang" was unfortunate. It was coined by the English cosmologist Fred Hoyle, who did not (and does not) accept this view of our origin. The term is catchy — but too catchy. It does not reflect what an awesome thing this term represents.[12] But a curious irony has occurred. The thing has such grandeur, such an effect on our imaginations, that it has bestowed some awe and grandeur on the term "Big Bang" retroactively. So who has the last laugh: Hoyle, for sticking our origin with this minimizing name, or the phenomenon itself, for overcoming the name and elevating it?

People sometimes say that the daily phenomena of nature are miracles, evidence of the existence of God: "The heavens tell the glory of God" (Ps 19:2). The fact remains, though, that people are more likely to be impressed by what we usually mean by a miracle, namely an event that seems to be contrary to the daily patterns of nature (like biblical Gideon who says, "If Yahweh is with us then where are all His miracles?"). But it may be that the present course of science will take us to a point at which we really shall see the kind of spectacle in nature that will leave us feeling the sort of awe that our ancestors felt. And the legacy of Big Bang and Kabbalah is that we may find that this awe will relate to the realm of God and religion. The main implication of this business may be that science is in fact a path back to, not away from, the deity. A hopeful passage in a work by one of the death-of-God theologians in the 1960s acquires a strange relevance in this regard. Richard Rubenstein wrote:

> The last paradox is that in the time of the death of God we have
> begun a voyage of discovery wherein we may, hopefully, find the
> true God.

This comes from an essay that he originally wrote in 1955 and then revised for inclusion in *After Auschwitz* in 1966.[13] Just one year before that

book appeared, Penzias and Wilson had first listened to the cosmic background radiation. Probably unknown to Rubenstein as he published this,
the voyage of discovery that he mentioned had already taken off in a way
that few humans on earth could have imagined.

What, exactly, do we expect to find on this venture? The chance that
it will be an elderly male human-like figure on a throne seems small.
What we encounter may or may not fulfill what we have historically
sought or needed from a God. It may or may not be what anybody means
by God now. It may not be a personal God. In the light of the discoveries
concerning the origin of the cosmos that we have made already, we can
anticipate that, whatever we find, it will be everywhere, function everywhere; it will be in us, and we will be in it, as conceived in Big Bang and
in Kabbalah; it will be in stars and in stones and in light and in flesh; it
will determine everything, and explain everything, it will relate to our
consciousness in some way; and it will impart awe. And this approaches
what we, in Western civilization, call God. It may turn out to be something closer to the concepts of Eastern religions, which are not centered
in a deity the way Western religions are. Or it may be a deeper force, to
which both Western and Eastern religions respond in their respective
ways. In the perspective of the disappearance of God in the Bible, and of
the death of God in Nietzsche, this would be a reunion with God.

"I SHALL HIDE MY FACE FROM THEM. I SHALL SEE WHAT THEIR END WILL BE"

We have seen that the Bible occasionally embraces this idea of a future
reunion. The divine hiddenness is not depicted as final. "I shall not hide
my face from them anymore" (Ezek 39:29). I observed that it may be
that the situation by the end of the Hebrew Bible is not that the divine
and the human cannot coexist, but that they are not yet ready to coexist.
And recall that knowledge in the Bible is the path back. It is through
acquisition of the fruit of the tree of knowledge of good and bad that
humans lose access to the tree of life and residence in the garden where
the deity walks, and it is through knowledge that humans are to find the

way back. That would mean, in present terms, not only knowledge of good and bad, but knowledge broadly, in its fullest sense, including scientific inquiry.

This idea of a divine-human reunion also would pertain to the central aim of Kabbalah, in which "The final goal is the reunification of the divine and the human wills."[14] And in Kabbalah there also is the notion that humans must do their part to arrive at such a point of reunion.

The question of whether or not humans are ready for reunion, or at what point humans would be ready, in turn recalls the notion of "coming of age." Bonhoeffer used this phrase in a theological context. Meaningfully, Ferris used the same phrase in scientific context in his supremely timely title: *Coming of Age in the Milky Way*. Coming of age, in the context of our present concerns, may mean being worthy to meet the deity. We saw that, in the biblical development, the hiding of the face of God (and the shift in the divine-human balance) derives from both the divine and the human side, and that it is not entirely negative. The deity wants to see humans grow up and wants to see how they will end up: "I shall hide my face from them. I shall see what their end will be." (The word "end" here, Hebrew *'aḥărît*, does not mean their finish, but rather their distant future.)

This may even have a relevance to Nietzsche's work. I observed earlier that the issue for Nietzsche appears to be what the implications of a God's presence are for a human: humankind cannot be all that it is capable of being in the presence of a God. That is more consistent with the biblical development than probably even Nietzsche himself knew. In the Bible, humans repeatedly find themselves in conflict with their very powerful parent. And their very powerful (and very wise) parent determines to let them go out on their own, to see what their end will be. In context of the disappearance of God in the Bible and in context of Nietzsche's thought, our proper conclusion may be that we humans need a period of divine hiddenness, out of the manifest presence of God, to become all that we can be. And, after that, we shall be able to meet our God, whoever or whatever that may be. I should add, similarly to what I said in the biblical section, that this is not to disparage any individual who believes that he or she has encountered divine presence in any form — miracles, revelation — already. Such experiences remain personal, though. Unlike the biblical account of the revelation at Sinai, they are not shared or witnessed by the masses. Therefore one might say that in the experience of the species as a whole, including those who believe in a deity and those who do not, there still prevails a feeling that divine presence is not manifest. For the human species, the idea of reunion with our source, whatever that may be, remains in the future.

Nietzsche foresaw an age of formidable spiritual and physical struggle before humankind could hope to arrive at a happier, more fruitful plateau. We have experienced the madness that, according to Nietzsche, accompanies the widespread feeling of the disappearance of God. We have had a hundred years of violence, suspicion, ambivalence, *inhumanity*. It would appear that now it is time to rise above the madness, time for our species to grow up. As Freud said (quoted earlier) in a context of religious development, "Men cannot remain children forever."

A helpful metaphor for this condition occurs in a popular work, one of the best-known works of science fiction, with another timely title, Arthur C. Clarke's *2001*. Begun from a short story titled "The Sentinel," then made into a motion picture, then written as a novel, the work has been the object of a variety of understandings and interpretations.[15] My understanding is this:

Beings of high intelligence visit the earth in an age in which humans are in an apelike stage of their development. Finding the early humans not yet at a stage at which meaningful communication is possible, these superior beings deposit a monolith on the earth which functions as a sort of antenna, conveying some fundamental skills and rudimentary powers of thought to the ape-humans, thus giving human development a beneficial push. The extraterrestrial beings then bury a monolith in the moon. It is designed to give off a homing signal when the lunar soil over it is removed and it is exposed. The idea is that, when humans will have progressed sufficiently to be able to travel to the moon and discover the "antenna," then humans will be ready to meet and communicate with this advanced life form. Following the discovery of the lunar monolith a party of humans is sent to follow the signal (which leads to Jupiter). One human arrives, and he is transformed by whatever it is that he encounters into a being who can move at will through space, back to earth (which is on the brink of global war), and who has godlike qualities.

The story is a useful expression of the idea that I am pursuing here through the Bible, Nietzsche, cosmology, and Kabbalah. It captures the human feeling of having once been in contact with a great power, from whom we learned but with whom we were not yet ready to communicate, so we were left on our own, our task being to become worthy to be reunited with that power. Note also in the story that for the first communication the superior beings come to us. They leave basic information on how to grow, mature, and act, and then they leave. For the next communication, we must go to them: find them and communicate with them. So in our pursuit of these mysteries, the mystery of the disappearance of God in the Bible concerns how the deity first communicates with humans, gives them basic information, and then leaves. The mystery of Nietzsche at Turin concerns how we came to face the fact that the deity had left. And the mystery of Big Bang and Kabbalah suggests that for our next communication we must go to God. Take it literally or as myth or metaphor, as philosophy, science, or science fiction. The common point is that we have a sense of an extraordinary origin and of having grown through a period of tribulation, which is not quite over, and of being on the brink of discovery of what underlies our origin and probably our destiny. And we must be worthy of these discoveries. If we are going "to see what our end will be," then we "cannot remain children forever."

I mean this with a tremendous sense of urgency. I said in the last chapter that the Kabbalistic concept of restoration (*tikkun*) has no formal parallel in contemporary science but that it has, nonetheless, a parallel in fact. In Kabbalah the concept means that how we behave has implications for the destiny of the universe. And that applies, in a different way, to the domain of science and cosmology as well. What is amazing is that we are possibly on the threshold of discoveries in the realm of the divine and on the threshold of planetary catastrophes at the same time. We are in a race between discovery and destruction. I do not mean a race metaphorically. It is as real as anything in the universe. We are close to enormous discoveries about the universe. We have been reminded of how close we are recently by several events — the defects and correction of the Hubble telescope in space, the initiation and subsequent cancellation of the supercollider project in Texas, and the success of the Cosmic Background Explorer satellite — each of which meant an advance or delay of years.

Meanwhile, in the very years that these things were happening, we have come to face the greatest threats to the existence of life on the earth since the flood: damage to our ozone protection, projections of population explosion beyond what our planet can support, destruction of rain forests that affect the atmosphere of the planet and produce drugs that are necessary for the cure of diseases, global warming, shift of nuclear weapons into ever more vulnerable locations and into the hands of more untrustworthy governments, pollution of major rivers and lakes and even the oceans, and even the skies, and even space. And so on. Both for our scientists and for the rest of us, how we think and how we behave matters, both to our survival and to our destiny. There is a role for our best scientific minds in this race, but there is also now a role for us all. We are all *necessarily* in the business of *tikkun* — repair. That is one legacy of this age. One side of this legacy is to survive. The other side more directly involves the scientific and religious quest for comprehension of the origin and meaning of our existence. We have come so far, and we are possibly so close, that it is earthshakingly mad that we are in so vulnerable a position at this very moment. It is comic, pathetic, frightening, enlightening, and, hopefully, arousing to read a remark of Hawking's that expresses the race between discovery and destruction:

> I think that there is a good chance that the study of the early universe and the requirements of mathematical consistency will lead us to a complete unified theory within the lifetime of some of us who are around today, *always presuming we don't blow ourselves up first.*[16]

It seems to me that the cosmologist Martin Rees particularly appreciated the stakes of the race when he said:

> It's quite conceivable that, even if life now exists only here on Earth, it will eventually spread through the galaxy and beyond. So life may not forever be an unimportant trace contaminant of the universe, even though it now is. In fact, I find that a rather appealing view, and I think it could be salutary if it became widely shared. Then one could properly regard the preservation of our biosphere as a matter of cosmic importance. . . . *If we snuffed ourselves out, we'd be destroying genuine cosmic potentialities.*[17]

"I SHALL FEAR NO EVIL, FOR YOU ARE WITH ME"

Part of the maturation of our species was the gradually increasing cognizance of the feeling of the disappearance of God, the feeling that we are on our own, responsible for our fate. I have referred several times to two crises that this feeling of divine eclipse has begotten. First, trust in deities served the function of mollifying essential human fears. In the face of a universe of powerful forces, belief in a supreme power that could control those forces and offer a faithful follower a measure of security helped to make life livable. "I shall fear no evil, for you are with me" (Ps 23:4; cf. Gen 26:24; Isa 41:10; 43:5; Jer 1:8; 46:28; 1 Chr 28:20). The growth and spread of the feeling of divine absence contributed to producing an age of uncertainty, insecurity, and vulnerability. Second, much of morality was based on beliefs that "God has told you what to do." Beliefs ranged from general principles ("Love your neighbor as yourself") to very specific commandments ("Don't oppress the widow and the orphan"). The feeling of divine absence undermined this basis of morality, leaving the question: on what are we to base our morality if not on the deity? This brings us back to the starting point of this chapter: the crisis in the destiny of our species, which is the legacy of the first two mysteries — and the answer to this crisis, which, hopefully, is the legacy of the third.

In an age of hiddenness of deity, how is humankind to deal with the fears that belief in deities once mollified? In pagan religion humans ascribed will, consciousness, to the things whose power we feared (storm wind, sea, sky, fire, disease, death) or on whose bounty we depended (grain, fertility, sun). We called these conscious powers gods and tried to please them so that we would prosper and not have to be afraid. Because there was a plethora of things that we feared, there was a plethora of gods. In monotheistic religion, humans sought a single God whose power could control all of these things and who told us very specifically what this God wanted us to do. Endeavoring to live according to this God's will could provide one with a degree of security. But the experience of feeling that we are on our own, which culminated in particular persons, works, and events at the threshold of this century, has left our vulnerability exposed. It has been a fearful age. Both religious and nonreligious persons, Western and Eastern, have had to come to terms with a century of life of spiritual lack: a century in which we have made wars such as never have occurred here before, and in which we have damaged the waters and the air and the land and even nearby space so badly that our continuation is in danger, in which our individual lives and our lives communally in societies are so complex that we do not understand them.

We have developed a variety of mechanisms, good and bad, to cope with these underlying fears. Looking for sources of confidence, some turn to nationalism, some to ideology, some to religious fundamentalism, some to cults. For some it is a belief in science or technology. I do not mean to belittle any of these paths of coping with our fears. Nor do I mean to suggest that people who derive such comfort from religion or ideology are not sincere in their beliefs. On the contrary. I simply mean to recognize that this comfort is one of the things that these institutions and activities provide. We also derive it from less institutional means. Many of us rely to a large extent on distraction, which is to say we think about other things. We have also known at least since Aristotle that we derive some comfort of this kind from literature, especially drama, which today includes film. Ancient audiences attended performances of tragedies, in which they released feelings of fear by concentrating them on a dramatic figure with whom they identified and then purging those feelings as that figure met his or her downfall and the play ended. Currently, too, an audience's anxiety intensifies when watching a frightening work, and then they experience a release, a wave of comfort, that occurs when the lights come up and they are safe. If it is true that such catharsis works, then a measure of the growth of the underlying fear in the world is the contemporary rise in popularity of ever more terrifying works in fiction, theater, and film. As with a painkilling drug, we need an ever higher dose, and the novels and films are becoming ever more gruesome. In a converse mechanism, we turn to humor, which disproportionately relates to things that frighten us. Think of the best ten jokes you know; nearly all will involve pain, embarrassment, or death. (There are countless jokes about war, virtually none about peace, for example.) In humor, from individual jokes to theatrical comedy, we focus on the things that frighten us, and for a moment we share a pretense that they do not bother us.

All of these (and other) mechanisms work to some extent, and all fall short of eliminating our fear. Even a pious religious believer may find a good deal about which to feel intimidated in this age; and that believer can agree that in this era of divine hiddenness the leap of faith is as difficult to make as at any epoch in human experience. In any case, even if some individuals have had the excellent fortune to have transcended their fears, the great mass of our species lives with monsters of varying kinds and varying degrees, and most do not appear to have found an antidote for their fear in a trust in a present, involved God. The phenomenon of the disappearance of God has thus brought with it this great stress, this phobic age.

It seems to me that part of the solution lies in the fact that the disappearance of God also involves the growing up of humankind. There is some security in the thought that we are coming of age and in recognizing how far we have come. In the first place, we should have some confidence because we have *made it* through about two millennia with a vague sense — and through the last century with an explicit concept — of being on our own. Further, we should derive a measure of confidence and encouragement from recognizing what we have accomplished in science, art, literature, psychology, medicine, technology, law, and a host of other areas, even when we honestly take into account our failings in all of these areas as well. We have composed works of music of such beauty, we have made discoveries in science of such profundity, we have produced books of such artistry and wisdom. It is fortifying to recognize what we have produced and what we are capable of. We all share in this legacy and this responsibility. Even those of us who cannot sing or play an instrument share in Beethoven. Even those who cannot spell share in Shakespeare. There is strength and assurance in the awareness of human heritage.

There is also strength and increased security in knowledge. A natural and substantial part of our ancestors' fear was of the unknown. Knowledge is an antidote for that sort of fear. This can mean any or all fields of knowledge, but scientific knowledge has a particularly ironic new role to play. As I discussed earlier, science contributed to the breakdown of pagan religion by de-deifying the forces of nature, thus stripping away much of the wonder associated with them. In posing new challenges to the biblical accounts, science also came to be perceived as a threat to monotheistic religion. In thus chipping away at the beliefs that had served to counter the formidable feeling of human precariousness, science left humans exposed, needing new antidotes for the old fears. But science can, in proportion to the exposure, contribute to rebuilding feelings of security. First, the extraordinary breakthroughs in cosmology can offer a new confidence: a confidence that, whatever it is that is going on in the structure of our universe, it is something that makes sense, a sense that we can discover. Popular treatments of cosmology quote, with frustrating frequency, Stephen Weinberg's remark near the end of his *The First Three Minutes* that "the more the universe seems comprehensible, the more it also seems pointless." In Lightman and Brawer's *Origins*, the editors asked some twenty-five leading cosmologists what they thought of that comment, and the most common response among them was not to disagree with Weinberg's view but to express surprise that he should even think there has to *be* a point to the universe.[18] It is revealing, if disappointing, to see individuals who are so deeply involved in this adventure and yet so little appreciate its implications. Weinberg is still looking inside the wheelbarrow, trying to find what is missing. Those others don't suspect that anything is missing. Pointless? After millennia of wondering what is going on here, we are just arriving at a threshold of understanding, from which we can begin to believe that we may actually be able to unravel our ultimate mystery. The goal, the wonder, possibly the *point*, lies on the other side of the door, and some of those with their hand on the doorknob think that it is meaningless. But the fact that we have come this close is extraordinary. It is one of the great human achievements. And the potential implication of the parallels between Big Bang and Kabbalah is that there is a spiritual, meaningful aspect of it. And this can be an enormous comfort to us following an age in which all evidence of meaning seemed lost.

Second, the revolution in scientific knowledge, and the related progress in technology, continue to bear fruits in a variety of areas. Advances in medicine, agriculture, communication, space, and other fields of endeavor, in addition to their intrinsic value, contribute to the perception that, more and more, we are not helpless in the face of the forces of nature. If science took away the reassuring belief that one could sacrifice to the god of the storm wind and thus hopefully get divine protection from storms, at least science has also made it possible to know in advance when the storm is coming and to protect ourselves better against it.

Combining the confidence that we can derive from heritage and the security that we can derive from knowledge, we can look back at the best things that humans have produced and study them — to make ourselves wiser, to appreciate what is great in us, to learn that we all participate in and share the glory of the great achievements of our individuals, as everyone in a town shares in the glory of a winning team or a hero who comes from that town. Our species is capable of such things that it is madness to be small now. Our task is to survive and to raise our knowledge and spirit to a new strength in preparation for the discoveries that lie ahead, to seek to advance ourselves because of our fear, and because of our awe in the face of something great.

Another new source of assurance may lie in the matter of consciousness as we understood it in early religion and in the context of Big Bang and Kabbalah. In pagan religion people ascribed consciousness to the forces of nature so that they could *communicate* with them. *That* is what gave people security: the belief that the forces were not silent, arbitrary, and utterly separated from them. One of the fruits of our study of Big Bang and Kabbalah is that there is a possibility of an essential, structural place for consciousness in the cosmos, a consciousness in which we participate. It may be an aspect of divinity, as in Kabbalah. It may be "the universe's way of developing a brain." It may be, we should also admit, a mistaken exercise of the anthropic principle. But the very possibility of a link between our consciousness and the universe of which we are a part, a new and more complex form of what we sought early in our religious development, offers encouragement and excitement in opposition to fears that have been with us since antiquity.

We may have to learn to get along without an immediate, visibly present, personal God. But this is bearable, and even motivating, if we understand that there lies the possibility of one day reencountering the deity. And in the interim we have the task of becoming worthy. The recognition of the dimensions of our achievement, in so many fields of human effort, deriving from so many cultures, should give us confidence. The recognition of our task, and the great rewards, should give us strength of purpose. And these are fortifications against a good deal of human fear.

"A BLESSING TO ALL THE FAMILIES
    OF THE EARTH"

On what else could we base morality if not on a God? One has to have been comatose through this century in order not to know that this is no longer just a theoretical point, not just a really good question. The problem at this stage in our species' life is not that we have different views of what is moral. We have always had those. The problem is that we need a reason to be moral. We need an underlying principle, and we need a compelling motivation. It seems to me that part of the answer lies in the same realm as the answer to the question concerning fear. It is a matter of the fate of our species, being on the brink of discovery and of destruction at the same juncture in our life. On one side there is the matter of survival; and, incredibly, at the same time that we run such enormous risks to our continuity, we are close to such monumental advancements of knowledge. The human community is close to discoveries of such magnitude that it is insane to be petty, power-hungry, spiteful, hurtful, warring — in a word, immoral — now. It was stupid before now. But now it is insane. We appear to be at a critical juncture in the development of our species (and our planet). Do we really have only Malthusian options? Is there no chance that we might act with wisdom, and recognize that in addition to family loyalty, and clan loyalty, and loyalty to a religious group or to a nation, there is species loyalty?

What might be the imperatives of a morality that is founded upon species loyalty? The "golden rule" can still provide a fundamental starting point and guideline. We have already seen that this rule functions in Christianity and in rabbinic Judaism in various formulations: "What is hateful to you, do not do to someone else." "Do unto others as you would have them do unto you." "Love your neighbor as yourself." More broadly, it means a morality based on *common* decency, *common* courtesy, and *common* sense — that is, on what all human beings can share. The underlying element of commonality bestows the practicality that classic arguments of this type lacked. The argument, "What if everybody did that?" for example, has never been a particularly persuasive argument; i.e., it was unlikely to persuade anyone to do something who was not

already predisposed to be persuaded. Why? Because it was a purely theoretical argument, and it broke down in the practical world. If Jones did
not want to vote, there was little strength in the argument "What if everybody felt like that?" because whether or not anyone or everyone else
voted did not matter at all relative to what Jones did. The outcome of the
election was the same (except in the case of when the election came down
to one vote, which happened too rarely to affect this point). So Jones was
unlikely to be persuaded by the argument. And if Jones was disposed to
rob, the question "What if everybody did that?" was not going to keep
him out of the bank. This argument received its most sophisticated formulation philosophically in Kant, but this may have quintessentially
demonstrated the problem with the theoretical argument, for Nietzsche
observed that Kant had proven the common person's morality but had
formulated it in terms that the common person could not possibly understand. He called this "Kant's joke."

A practical formulation would be more persuasive, and more likely to
work, than a theoretical one. The approach of a little book called *50
Simple Things You Can Do to Save the Earth* that was recently quite popular
captured the spirit of this formulation. Its approach was to reverse the
reasoning from "What if everyone did that?" to "Here is what we can do
if we all do this." Reformulated as an argument, it would go like this: We
tried "What-if-everyone-did-that," which was a system in which we each
still felt that just one of us would not make a difference, and that system
did not work. It is not a matter of, theoretically, what would happen if
everyone did that. It is a matter, in practical reality, of what happens
when we, as a *system*, operate with each of us thinking that as individuals
we do not matter much. The system breaks down; but it is ironic: the
system fails because it involves a mass of individuals who do not act because each knows that his or her actions alone do not make a difference;
but, if they *had* all acted, they *would* have made a difference. We must,
therefore, as individuals agree to participate in a *system* that works. That
is, we must agree to try this new system, based on the imperative of what
we can do if we all commit to act in unity, to see if it works better than
the old approach. It probably will. It would be enforced in different ways
in different places: upbringing, law, mores, public spirit, peer pressure,
teaching by example, force, curiosity, inspiration. Ideally, hopefully, it
will work in most places because a substantial number of us will be per-

suaded that (1) it will actually work and (2) we *need* to do it. We are at a crisis, a crossroads in the path of our species, at which all of our lives are really at stake. It is our numbers that have produced much of this condition, and it is in our numbers that we can remedy it.

There is also a side benefit to this system. In having an effect in solving these problems, we can each feel, more than ever before, that we are important. The old approach made us feel that we were individually weak, unimportant. The new system can make us each feel significant and strong, the way each member of a championship team feels triumphant.

In Kabbalah the notion is developed that morality is related to the very structure of the universe. Human actions participate in the universal process of movement from the primal point back to that original unity. *Tikkun* is understood to be "a path of cosmic restoration."[19] Those of us who are not Kabbalists still can appreciate that repair of the world is the necessary partner of the pursuit of cosmological discoveries. First, it is a matter of surviving to continue the pursuit; and, second, it is a matter of being worthy, being prepared for whatever it is that we are going to encounter. In the discoveries of this century in physics and astronomy, we have already had enough of a glimpse into the origin and nature of the universe that we should feel reverence for the possibilities of what awaits us. It is breathtaking that on this one planet, circling one star, in the midst of a galaxy of billions of stars, which is one of billions of galaxies, we have been able to look out, with a few instruments that we have built, across such vast distances, and we have been able to figure out so much of how this began, how long ago it began, and what holds it together. Each new discovery is potentially one that will utterly change our perception of the universe or of our place in it. A world that is preparing to face such things cannot be a world of liars, thieves, cheats, and bullies. My colleague whom I mentioned earlier could not think of a good reason why we should not kick canes out from under old ladies. I suggest that when we look our origin — and possibly our originator — in the face, we should not want to be the kind of persons who have ever kicked a cane. Call it a moral theology of reverence for the possibility. The glimpse that we have already had of the origin of the universe is a genuinely awesome thing. We have heard the echo of the origin of the universe. We have seen the expansion of the universe. We should take off our shoes on such holy ground.

The specific terms of such a moral system, its "commandments," will vary from one community to another. It is not these specifics that I mean to address here but the principle, and the motive. In the age of hidden-ness of divinity, an age which has been morally chaotic, in which we are in need of a basis of morality that will be compelling to both the theist and the atheist, that basis is staring us in the face. It is a matter of our survival and of fulfilling our destiny, seeing what our end will be. Many of us will not be able to understand this. But enough of us must under-stand and appreciate it to make it function. For those with strong beliefs in God, this is not inconsistent; it is additional. In addition to behaving morally "because God said so," they have reason to behave morally "be-cause we are all finding our way to God together." For those with no such beliefs, this is a real principle on which to base laws or rules or mores of behavior toward other human beings (and possibly toward other spe-cies as well). It is a matter of urgent, ultimate, common interest and a common goal. The principle is species loyalty, or call it loyalty to the earth. Specific implications and interpretations of the principle will vary among groups, but there are some obvious implications for all. A mo-rality based on species loyalty cannot possibly include prejudice or op-pression of one ethnic or racial or national or religious group or the poor. There will, no doubt, be some who will claim that it is in the interest of the species to oppress or restrict or eliminate some group. But they will be the equivalent of those who made such claims in the name of Chris-tianity in the past: an aberration, a perversion of real Christianity. Every morality involves being on guard against those who, instead of openly expressing their opposition to it, cynically and deviously speak as advo-cates of that morality and endeavor to twist it into its opposite. At this juncture, on such a course lies disaster. Precisely the most dangerous thing is to divide the species in the name of the good of the species. Rather the biblical picture of the promise to Abraham can be a helpful model: that a group should, in developing themselves, endeavor to be a blessing to all the families of the earth (Gen 12:3).

The matter of heritage participates in the foundations of a morality in this age as well. The great discoveries we made in this century did not self-generate. We are part of a chain of human generations, owing our debt of culture and knowledge to those who came before us. Without Newton there is no Einstein. Without Galileo there is no Hubble. Without the Bible there is no Dostoevsky. Heritage is our debt to our ancestors. We owe them something. They have left us riches. How can we pay a debt to those who are now gone? The answer, it seems to me, is that, in human relations, sometimes one repays a debt to one's benefactor by doing an act like one's benefactor's for someone else. If someone helps me and then disappears from my life, so that I can never show him or her my gratitude, what I can do to pay it back is to help someone else when I have the opportunity. We owe a debt to our ancestors; we pay it to our descendants. We can aim to achieve ever higher levels of knowledge, understanding, and sensitivity in future generations, to produce descendants who, sitting on our shoulders, will see farther than we do, who will be able to understand what we do not yet understand. How do we feel about that? Envious? Probably, but we can also feel pleased for a variety of reasons. For one, they are our children. For another, they are part of a chain that includes us; their successes are both their own and ours. For another, species loyalty. We should want to leave them a legacy of knowledge of literature, history, art, science, experience. We can be envious of their better world and at the same time do everything we can to help them have that world, a world in which they can go farther than we can. They will bring being human to a new level, possibly fulfilling Nietzsche's vision of a "superhuman." The *Übermensch* has been misunderstood — I would say it has been perverted — to mean everything from Aryans to something like the comic book superman, but Nietzsche's superhuman need not be some elite group among other humans, but our children, the child of all humans, bearing the legacy of human history and carrying it to a new level.

Recall that according to Nietzsche God died of pity for humankind and that in the Bible, as well, we found the notion of God's pity playing a central role in the process of the shift in the divine-human balance. This may be more than slightly relevant to the notion of becoming worthy of reunion with the deity. On the next meeting, humankind cannot be in a pitiful, pathetic condition. It must be a humankind of knowledge, wisdom, common self-respect, and nobility that expects to encounter its deity. For those who believe the Bible literally, take *this* literally. For those who regard it as a myth, take this as the myth's lesson. But, either way, take the point: We must be worthy of the destiny that awaits us.

A morality of species loyalty would include this imperative, to act in such a way as to advance our species. It means to act through wisdom in the way that other species act by instinct. For those who need commandments: Survive. Improve. Love others as yourself. Become worthy of reunion. That might be our goal, to improve ourselves, to learn, to develop our human spirit to a new degree in preparation for the discoveries that lie ahead; perhaps, for the first time, to seek to advance ourselves not out of pride but out of humility in the face of something great. A new reverence. That reverence and awe may — should — provide an additional motivating force for our morality. The two motives — the reality of a common danger to the species and the awe for the possibility of an impending encounter with divinity — should together be powerful enough to muster adherence to a moral code of common decency.

Basing morality on species loyalty thus merges the command of nature and the command of history, that is, the two arenas in which religions developed. The bond with nature and history that species loyalty necessarily involves can provide the quality of awe that a morality requires in order to be authoritative. The morality that I am endeavoring to picture here is one that does not depend on the presence of God for its basis, its authority, or its awe; it is based, rather, on our recognition of our common heritage and, more urgently, of our common danger. Nonetheless, through the new discoveries in cosmology, the awe for the divine may figure in this morality even in this period of divine disappearance. The universe *is* awesome. People witness the birth of a baby and frequently call it a miracle, even though it is, by definition, the opposite of what we mean by a miracle; it is nature, pure and simple. That is because we, correctly, feel the mystery and wonder of it. The parallel of Big Bang and Kabbalah is an indicator that our discovering the nature of the creation and end of the universe also means possibly discovering nothing less than the nature of God.

THE HIDDEN FACE OF GOD

Major religions seem to be born on earth every six hundred years. I do not know why this occurs. Perhaps it is coincidence. Perhaps there is some sociological explanation. My colleague David Noel Freedman and

I each noticed this independently. I do not know if others have observed it, though it seems sufficiently obvious that I assume that others have seen it as well. It is as if there is some sort of historical cycle calling for a new founder and a new doctrine in each six hundred years. Moses and the birth of Israelite religion belong to the thirteenth or early twelfth century B.C.E. Zarathustra, also called Zoroaster (the original Persian Zarathustra, on whom Nietzsche later based his hero), founder of Zoroastrianism, is traditionally located in the sixth century B.C.E. Confucius, also, lived in that century (551–479). Also Buddha (563–483). Also Lao-tse (604–531). Six hundred years later, in the first century C.E., Jesus lived. In the seventh century came Mohammed (570–632), who died almost exactly six hundred years after Jesus. By this schedule we should have expected a major religious figure and the birth of a new religion in the thirteenth century. That did not happen — though I am tempted to see the development of Kabbalah and the composition of the Zohar in that age as filling this slot in the cycle.

And by this schedule the nineteenth century was, one might say, due. It will immediately occur to some to say that what the nineteenth century got was Karl Marx and the birth of communism — instead of a religion, an anti-religion ideology. Others may see Freud and the rise of the psychoanalytic movement narrowly or the growth of psychology broadly as a development comparable to the formation of religions in the other six-hundred-year junctures. Others may see Nietzsche and the idea of the "death" of God itself as the development in religion of that historical juncture. Each of the preceding births of religions was followed by a period of growth and development, and it is only in historical perspective that we recognize them as successful. And so it may be that, at the time of this writing, it is too soon to be able to know which, if any, of these movements will come to be regarded as an event comparable to the formation of the major religions. (Developments of recent years have already raised doubt about the likelihood of communism's being so regarded.) Conceivably the nineteenth century might be, like the sixth century B.C.E., an age of ferment, in which several new movements were born. Notably, all of the three that I have mentioned here involved a rejection of the concepts of the deity that the Western religions preceding them held.

It may also be that future generations will regard the flourishing of science as such a development of this age, though really it belongs more to the twentieth century than the nineteenth. Or they may see science along with the other three as part of a broad anti-theological movement whose seeds were sown in the nineteenth century. Science has been perceived as antithetical to religion, but that opposition has changed dramatically in the last two decades of the century, as we have seen.

Whether the six-hundred-year pattern is meaningful or pure coincidence, it dramatizes the recognition that we are at a turning point in human experience, as does the obvious signpost of the approach of the year 2000, the close of the millennium, for those who reckon by the Christian year. But also for those who are not Christians (and for Christians who agree that there is no cosmic reason why great moments should only be able to come in years that are multiples of ten) the time is ripe: for a rejuvenation of our spirit, for a new reverence in the face of awesome possibilities, for restoration. Many regard the conception of God as presented in the Bible as childish. Perhaps that presentation was the level on which divinity could be understood then, and we are now approaching the point at which we may be able to come to terms with it at a more profound level. In the Bible, Yahweh's essence is unknown. Unlike the pagan deities, the God of the Bible is known only by His deeds and words while the nature of God remains a mystery. Now the possibility of learning something of the actual nature of the divine looms.

So how do the three mysteries that we have pursued in this book connect to one another? Here is one way to look at it: The first mystery is grounded in a book, the second in the lives of individual persons, the third in communities, one community being mystical and the other scientific — but all three are outer reflections of an underlying process, the search for a divine-human relationship, which can materialize through any of these mechanisms. The first mystery is focused primarily on the book rather than on the writers because the lives of those who set it down on the parchment (whether through originality, inspiration, or revelation) are so little known to us, and because the book has acquired such an exceptional status. The second is focused more on the authors because we know enough to be able to observe in their lives the sources of what came out in their books. And the third is a combination, concentrating sometimes on individual contributions but ultimately on the synthesis that each community reached. But, as in the Kabbalistic perspective, everything — persons, societies, the composition of books, the formulation of physical theories — is a shadow (a metaphor? a hypostasis?) of this process.

Here is another way to see it: All three mysteries are about communities. The Bible is a book that is quintessentially the fruit of a community. It was not written by any one or two or ten or fifty writers in a single period. It came together over centuries. Nietzsche and Dostoevsky, as we saw, are lightning rods at the tip of nineteenth-century Europe. Their work is a distillation of their singular genius and the condition of European society in their age. And the Big Bang and Kabbalistic models, as well, are not products of any one or two thinkers. Rather they are each the refined result of long sequences of contributions within two utterly different communities. All of these mysteries reflect the dynamic between individuals of genius and the forces in the communities in which they were nurtured.

Here is another way: The three mysteries mark the path of Western civilization, which begins with the biblical era and arrives at our age, in which the values of that founding era are breaking down. In this perspective, it would have been enlightening to trace all of the steps between these two epochs with the same detail that we gave to these bookends of Western civilization. But that would be a task for a whole team of scholars, and the result would be an encyclopedia, not a book. What these mysteries reveal is where we began and where we stand. The sense of diminishing divine encounter was latent in the period of our infancy and subtle in the columns of the Bible. It has become a public event and an openly discussed crisis in our era. And we are on the brink of coming of age.

No matter which of these perspectives we take, no matter whether we focus through individuals, communities, books, or civilization, no matter whether we concentrate on mysteries or on the processes for which the mysteries are metaphors, these investigations depict something that we once had, that we have lost, and that we have reason to hope that we shall someday recover in a new form. They suggest that it is our fortune, good or bad, to live at a crossroads, a particularly difficult and exciting time in this drama. And they should both frighten and inspire us to rebuild the health of our species and our planet and to proceed on to our destiny.

One of the factors participating in the disappearance of God was that people ceased saying the divine name two thousand years ago. It is ironic that, starting with Bible scholars, we have begun to use the intimate name of God again, especially since the nineteenth century, precisely in the period of acknowledged divine hiddenness. Let us hope that we are not using it in vain, but that we are moving closer to the entity that the name represents. The name Yahweh probably means "that which causes to be." And that which causes to be is what we are seeking. It is what we have been seeking all along. We may be very close to it. There is some likelihood that, as some of the conscious matter of the universe, we are created more in the divine image than we have suspected. There is some likelihood that the universe *is* the hidden face of God.

NOTES

Author's Note

1. God's name in the Bible, Yahweh, is as masculine a name as Ralph or Richard. (The feminine would have been Tahweh.) The biblical authors regularly identify God with masculine verbs and adjectives. Yahweh is pictured as a father, not a mother; as a husband, not a wife; as a king, not a queen; as a lord, not a lady. And, historically, on occasions when the ancient Israelites lapsed from monotheism, they pictured their God with a female consort. An inscription from Kuntillet 'Ajrud refers to "Yahweh . . . and His Asherah." Asherah was a goddess, also known as the queen of heaven. In the biblical text itself, as well, the prophet Jeremiah criticizes the people for worshiping the queen of heaven. The problem in Jeremiah is not that they are worshiping this goddess instead of Yahweh, but rather that they worship her *in addition* to Him (Jer 7:2, 18; 44:15–26).

Chapter 1: The Hidden Face of God

1. Richard Elliott Friedman, "Torah and Covenant," in *The Oxford Study Bible*, M. J. Suggs, K. D. Sakenfeld, and J. R. Mueller, eds. (New York: Oxford, 1992), pp. 154–163.
2. W. D. Whitt, in "The Jacob Traditions in Hosea and Their Relation to Genesis," *Zeitschrift für die Alttestamentliche Wissenschaft* 103 (1991) pp. 31–34, argues that the word *angel* (Hebrew *ml'k*) must be a "gloss" because

"ml'k is never used in poetry in parallel with either *'l* or *'lhym."* As a matter of method, when we find something singular in the text we cannot declare it a gloss because it does not occur elsewhere. Moreover, as the following discussion demonstrates, the parallel here *is* consistent with other biblical texts involving angels.

3. Cf. Josh 5:13; Judg 13:6, 9–23.

4. This paradoxical role of angels is especially striking in 2 Sam 24:16–19 and the parallel report of the same story in 1 Chr 21:15–19. In both versions, the deity speaks to the angel, so that the angel seems to be a separate being from God; but later the two versions blur the distinction between the deity's and the angel's communication to David through the prophet Gad.

5. There is a good discussion of these problems in the relationship between angels and Yahweh, with references, by Carol Newsom, "Angels," in *The Anchor Bible Dictionary*, vol. 1, pp. 248–253. My friend Professor Newsom prefers, as the explanation of the interchange between Yahweh and the angel in these stories, that they are "the expression of a tension or paradox: Yahweh's authority and presence in these encounters is to be affirmed, but yet it is not possible for humans to have an unmediated encounter with God." The idea of angels as hypostases of the deity seems to me to fit the occurrences in the narrative better, though Newsom's understanding would still be consistent with the larger development I am tracing here. See also Terence E. Fretheim, *The Suffering of God* (Philadelphia: Fortress, 1984), pp. 93–94.

6. See William H. C. Propp, *Water in the Wilderness*, Harvard Semitic Monographs 40 (Atlanta: Scholars Press, 1987).

7. Cf. Dale Patrick, *The Rendering of God in the Old Testament* (Philadelphia: Fortress, 1981), p. 93.

8. For the best treatment known to me of the mystery of Moses' face, see William H. C. Propp's "The Skin of Moses' Face — Transfigured or Disfigured?" *Catholic Biblical Quarterly* (1987).

9. Richard Elliott Friedman, "Tabernacle," *The Anchor Bible Dictionary*, vol. 6, pp. 292–300.

10. S. Dean McBride, "The Deuteronomic Name Theology" (Dissertation, Harvard University, 1969).

11. There had also been episodes of fire from the sky consuming sacrifices in the accounts of David (1 Chr 21:26) and Solomon (2 Chr 7:1, 3).

12. Grammatical explanation: The phrase in the Hebrew is *qôl d'māmâ daqqâ.* The first word, *qôl,* meaning "voice" or "sound," is a masculine noun and therefore cannot be modified by the two following words, which are feminine. The first two words, therefore, must be nouns in the construct state, and their meaning would be "a sound of hush" *(qôl d'māmâ)*. The third

word, *daqqâ*, being a feminine adjective meaning "thin" would then modify the feminine noun *dᵉmāmâ*. The line would thus be rendered "a sound of thin hush."

13. Frank Moore Cross, *Canaanite Myth and Hebrew Epic* (Cambridge, Mass.: Harvard University Press, 1973), p. 194.

14. Samuel Terrien, *The Elusive Presence* (San Francisco: Harper and Row, 1978), pp. 231f.

15. Virtually all translators and commentators have taken this story to refer to a sundial even though no such dial is mentioned anywhere in the verse. It appears to me to refer simply to the shadow of the sun on the steps of the building in which Isaiah and Hezekiah are located. A variant in the Isaiah scroll from Qumran (1QIsᵃ) supports this. See Samuel Iwry, "The Qumrân Isaiah and the End of the Dial of Ahaz," *Bulletin of the American Schools of Oriental Research* 147 (1957), pp. 27–33.

16. A recent discussion and bibliography on this verse is J. M. Wiebe, "Esther 4:14, 'Will Relief and Deliverance Arise for the Jews from Another Place?'" *Catholic Biblical Quarterly* 53 (1991), pp. 409–415. Wiebe's proposal that the verse be read as an ironic rhetorical question would render the hiddenness of the deity even more pronounced.

17. Leon Wieseltier, "Leviticus," in *Congregation*, ed. D. Rosenberg (New York: Harcourt Brace Jovanovich, 1987), p. 30.

Chapter 2: The Divine-Human Balance

1. I have tried to identify the factors that made this continuity possible in my essay, "The Hiding of the Face: An Essay on the Literary Unity of Biblical Narrative," in *Judaic Perspectives on Ancient Israel*, Jacob Neusner, Baruch Levine, and Ernest Frerichs, eds. (Philadelphia: Fortress, 1987), pp. 207–222. See also David Noel Freedman, *The Unity of the Hebrew Bible* (Ann Arbor: University of Michigan Press, 1991).

2. Earlier kings play minor roles compared to this figure; cf. Genesis 12; 14; 20; 26.

3. We might possibly take the story of Jacob's manipulating the coloring of Laban's sheep and goats as picturing Jacob in control of superhuman powers (Gen 30:27–43). Jacob makes a deal with Laban that Jacob will own all the marked sheep in the flocks, and Laban will own all the white ones. Jacob places marked sticks in front of the flocks when they mate, with the result that the offspring of these matings bear the marks, and Jacob acquires a large portion of the flocks. The problem is that we do not know what notions of

genetics (and what canons of storytelling) were operative in the formation of this story. Is Jacob to be pictured here as doing something miraculous, as performing sympathetic magic, or simply as being clever? We do not know, and therefore this story either may be taken to be a step of human participation in miraculous powers, which is then more extensively developed in the Joseph stories, or it may be taken to belong purely to the usual human realm.

4. (1) Exod 3:11; (2) 3:13; (3) 4:1; (4) 4:10; (5) 4:13.

5. Num 16:20–26 may be another case of Moses successfully persuading Yahweh to modify a decision, namely, to limit punishment to the few who are guilty of rebellion and not to be angry at the whole congregation.

6. The Hebrew is *lišmōʻa bᵉ*. The verb with the preposition *bᵉ* connotes both hearing and doing what one has heard. Cf. Deut 21:18; 1 Sam 8:7; 15:22; Jer 18:10.

7. See Baruch Halpern on the constitutional monarchy and on prophetic designation in *The Constitution of the Monarchy in Israel*, Harvard Semitic Monographs (Atlanta: Scholars Press, 1981).

8. 2 Sam 7:13–16. This appears to be a summary version of an even more powerfully worded text of the divine commitment to the Davidic dynasty in Ps 89:29–38.

9. Hebrew *nîr*, meaning a fief. The term is analyzed by Paul Hanson in "Song of Heshbon and David's NÎR," *Harvard Theological Review* 61 (1968), pp. 297–320.

Chapter 3: Historians and Poets

1. The Hebrew verb here (*ḥāzâ*) has the same root as the noun (*ḥāzôn*) in the preceding three examples. It is commonly translated "he saw," but more precisely it means "he had a vision" or "he envisioned." Cf. Ezek 12:27.

2. Often translated "The burden" (Hebrew *maśśāʾ*).

3. Daniel is counted among the narrative books in the Jewish canon and among the prophetic books in the Christian canon.

4. Other possible identifications of Tarshish are Carthage and Sardinia; see D. W. Baker, "Tarshish," in *The Anchor Bible Dictionary*, vol. 6, pp. 332–333. In any case, Jonah is sent east but goes west.

5. For an analysis of this phrase, with references to all its occurrences in the Hebrew Bible, see my article, "The Biblical Expression *mastîr pānîm*," *Hebrew Annual Review* 1 (1977), pp. 139–147; and Samuel Balentine, *The Hidden God: The Hiding of the Face of God in the Old Testament* (New York: Oxford University Press, 1983).

6. Terence E. Fretheim, *The Suffering of God*, p. 66.

7. Modern scholars generally regard this portion of the book as the work of a prophet (or prophets) who lived in the exilic and post-exilic times, a work which was attached to the book of the eighth-century prophet Isaiah. This portion is referred to as Second Isaiah (or Deutero-Isaiah). Either by this understanding in critical scholarship or by the traditional reading — i.e., that there is only one Isaiah and this portion of the book contains his prophecies about those later periods — the point remains that the exilic and post-exilic periods are understood in the prophetic texts to be an age of divine hiddenness.

8. Cf. Jer 2:6, 8. There the deity criticizes the people for *not* inquiring, "Where is Yahweh?"

9. 64:1–3 in some English translations.

10. 64:7 in some English translations.

11. See also 53:3 and my discussion of the subject of the act of hiding the face in the suffering servant passage in "The Biblical Expression *mastîr pānîm*," pp. 146–147.

12. 13:1 in some translations.

13. 44:24 in some translations. Job, too, says, "Why do you hide your face?" (13:24; cf. 34:29).

14. 88:14 in some translations.

15. 69:17 in some translations.

16. 102:2 in some translations.

17. 30:7 in some translations.

18. 22:1 in some translations.

19. 22:24 in some translations.

Chapter 4: The God of History

1. Patrick, *The Rendering of God in the Old Testament*; Erich Fromm, *You Shall Be As Gods* (Greenwich, Conn.: Fawcett, 1966).

2. Balentine, *The Hidden God: The Hiding of the Face of God in the Old Testament*, p. 115. Though Balentine was dealing only with the expression "hide the face" and not the entire development of the diminishing divine presence, he, too, criticized those who focus on the exile "in isolation from the larger framework" (p. 171).

3. Friedman, *Who Wrote the Bible?* (New York: Summit/Simon & Schuster, 1987).

4. Friedman, *Who Wrote the Bible?*, pp. 86f.

5. Friedman, *Who Wrote the Bible?*, pp. 208–214.

6. Friedman, *The Exile and Biblical Narrative*, Harvard Semitic Monographs 22 (Atlanta: Scholars Press, 1981), pp. 13–15; "From Egypt to Egypt: Dtr¹ and Dtr²," in *Traditions in Transformation: Turning-Points in Biblical Faith* (Frank Moore Cross *Festschrift*), B. Halpern and J. Levenson, eds., (Eisenbrauns, 1981), pp. 178–180; Friedman, *Who Wrote the Bible*, pp. 136–140.

7. Friedman, "The Deuteronomistic School," in *Fortunate the Eyes That See* (David Noel Freedman *Festschrift*), Astrid Beck, Andrew H. Bartelt, Paul R. Raabe, Chris Franke, eds. (Grand Rapids, Mich.: Eerdmans, 1995), note 9. My analysis of 1 Samuel is in a paper, "The First Great Writer," that I have read in colloquia but is not yet published. The reader is therefore referred to Baruch Halpern's analysis. Halpern has arrived at a division of the Samuel A and Samuel B sources which is very similar to my own in his *The Constitution of the Monarchy in Israel*, Harvard Semitic Monographs (Atlanta: Scholars Press, 1981).

8. Friedman, *The Exile and Biblical Narrative*, pp. 12–13; "From Egypt to Egypt: Dtr¹ and Dtr²," pp. 175–176.

9. D. L. Christensen, "Chronicles of the Kings (Israel/Judah)," *The Anchor Bible Dictionary*, vol. 1, pp. 991f. It is also possible that the narrative source that includes the Elijah stories is not the work that the Deuteronomist identifies as the Chronicles of the Kings of Israel but is rather some other source. I would still ascribe that source, whatever we call it, to a time close to the composition of E, so this does not affect the larger point that I am pursuing here.

10. Baruch Halpern, "Sacred History and Ideology: Chronicles' Thematic Structure — Indications of an Earlier Source," in R. E. Friedman, ed., *The Creation of Sacred Literature* (Berkeley and Los Angleles: University of California Press, 1981), pp. 35–54.

11. C. A. Moore, "Esther," *The Anchor Bible Dictionary*, vol. 2, p. 641.

12. See Jack Miles's exceptional essay on the biblical editors: "Radical Editing: *Redaktionsgeschichte* and the Aesthetic of Willed Confusion," in R. E. Friedman, ed., *The Creation of Sacred Literature*, pp. 85–99. (I use the masculine pronoun in referring to the editors here because all of the editors whose work I have analyzed thus far appear to be male.)

13. Friedman, *Who Wrote the Bible?*, pp. 225–231; "Sacred History and Theology: The Redaction of Torah," in *The Creation of Sacred Literature*, pp. 28–34. For those who are familiar with this subject, I mean specifically that one can read the P text, the D text, and the united text of JE (which were combined before reaching the redactor of the Torah) each continuously. For those who actually wish to read these texts and observe this themselves, I

have provided a chart identifying the sources of the Pentateuch in an appendix to *Who Wrote the Bible?*, pp. 246–260.

14. A classic treatment of ancient Near Eastern pagan and Israelite religion is my teacher G. Ernest Wright's *The Old Testament Against Its Environment* (London: SCM Press, 1950), which is most profitably read together with Henri Frankfort et al., *The Intellectual Adventure of Ancient Man* (Chicago: University of Chicago Press, 1946). In recent years this dichotomy has been criticized and revised so that the distinction between nature and history is not so simply drawn as in the past. The essential distinction between the deities nonetheless holds true and sheds light on the matter at hand.

15. See Baruch Halpern, *The First Historians* (San Francisco: Harper and Row, 1988).

16. I have outlined the parallels between the biblical covenants and ancient Near Eastern treaties and grants in "Torah and Covenant," in *The Oxford Study Bible* (New York: Oxford University Press, 1992), pp. 154–163. The classic works on the covenant and Near Eastern suzerainty treaties are G. E. Mendenhall, *Law and Covenant in Israel and the Ancient Near East* (Pittsburgh: The Biblical Colloquium, 1955) and Klaus Baltzer, *The Covenant Formulary* (Philadelphia: Fortress Press, 1971; German edition, 1964). The relationship between biblical covenants and Near Eastern grants was identified by Moshe Weinfeld, "The Covenant of Grant in the Old Testament and in the Ancient Near East," *Journal of the American Oriental Society* 90 (1970), pp. 184–203.

17. More precisely, the Deuteronomistic history contained seven books (Deuteronomy, Joshua, Judges, 1 and 2 Samuel, 1 and 2 Kings). Deuteronomy was included both in this collection and in the Five Books of Moses, thus providing the link between the two works. See *Who Wrote the Bible?*, pp. 101–149, 231f.

Chapter 5: The Struggle with God

1. Remarkably, this paradox, too, is the result of an editor's combination of texts from two authors. The creation in the divine image is from P, and the Adam and Eve story is from J. See *Who Wrote the Bible?*, pp. 235–236.

2. Fretheim, *The Suffering of God*, pp. 111–112.

3. "Ephraim," the name of one of the tribes of Israel, is a term that is used *pars pro toto* for the northern kingdom of Israel.

4. Deut 5:29 in some translations.

5. KJV: "O that there were such a heart in them. . . ." RSV: "Oh that they had such a mind as this. . . ." JPS: "Oh that they had such a heart as this. . . ." NJPS: "May they always be of such a mind. . . ." NEB: "Would that they

always had such a heart. . . ." REB: "Would that they may always be of a mind. . . ."

6. Or: "slow to anger."

7. Or "faithfulness"; Hebrew: *ḥesed*, a technical term in biblical covenant terminology, referring to God's fidelity to the human parties to the covenant.

8. In parallel with the term *ḥesed* here, the term "truth" (Hebrew: *ĕmet*) presumably forms a hendiadys, meaning that God is true to the human parties to the covenant.

9. See H. G. M. Williamson, "Joel," in *International Standard Bible Encyclopedia* (Grand Rapids, Mich.: Eerdmans, 1980), vol. 2, pp. 1076–1080.

10. Fretheim, *The Suffering of God*, p. 25. See also p. 41: "In the most common OT credal statement, God is said to be slow to anger (Exod 34:6, etc.)."

11. The phrases "turn the face" (Hebrew: *yāsîr pānîm*) and "hide the face" (Hebrew: *yastîr pānîm*) are similar in both sound and meaning. See Mitchell Dahood, Psalms 1–50, *The Anchor Bible* (New York: Doubleday, 1965), p. 64; Friedman, "The Biblical Expression *mastîr pānîm*," pp. 139–147; Balentine, *The Hidden God*, pp. 17, 100–103.

12. Cf. Fromm, *You Shall Be As Gods*, p. 22.

13. Cf. Fretheim, *The Suffering of God*, pp. 49–50.

14. The Hebrew is: *rab ya'ăbōd ṣā'îr*. This fascinating formulation in the text was pointed out to me by my colleague David Noel Freedman.

15. It appears that the reason why Moses is supposed to take the staff is that, in the story that precedes this in the narrative, Aaron's staff is designated as a sign to function in cases of rebellion (Num 17:25). My colleague William H. C. Propp has shown the relationship between that text and the episode of the striking of the rock in an article, "The Rod of Aaron and the Sin of Moses," *Journal of Biblical Literature* 107 (1988), pp. 19–26.

16. Fretheim, *The Suffering of God*, p. 68.

17. For this understanding of the Tree of Life I am in the debt of Nahum Glatzer. His essay, "Franz Kafka and the Tree of Knowledge," appears in his *Essays in Jewish Thought* (Tuscaloosa, Ala.: University of Alabama Press, 1978), pp. 184–191.

Chapter 6: The Legacy of the Age

1. Ber. R. XLII, 2; on the phrase "hide the face" in rabbinic literature, see Balentine, *The Hidden God*, pp. 110–113; and Friedman, "The Biblical Expression *mastîr pānîm*," pp. 144–145.

2. Leviticus 1–7; Deuteronomy 12; cf. *Who Wrote the Bible?*, pp. 114, 118, 186f.

3. Babylonian Talmud, Tractate Shabbat 31a.

4. The chain of succession from the great assembly to the rabbis is traced in Abot 1:2–18.

5. Wieseltier, "Leviticus," *Congregation*, pp. 29, 37.

6. E.g., L. Schiffman, *From Text to Tradition: A History of Second Temple and Rabbinic Judaism* (Hoboken, N.J.: Ktav, 1991), p. 179, writes that "At some point between the late first century B.C.E. and the first century C.E., the notion began to be expressed that the oral law, along with the written, had been given at Sinai." But Jacob Neusner has argued strongly that the change came later. E. P. Sanders has followed Neusner and brought additional evidence, concluding that "the rabbis of the Mishnaic period did not hold the dogma of oral law which has been attributed to them." Sanders, "Law in Judaism of the New Testament Period," in *The Anchor Bible Dictionary*, vol. 4, p. 260; see also *The Jewish Law from Jesus to the Mishnah* (London: 1989).

7. E. Urbach, *The Sages, Their Concepts and Beliefs* (Cambridge, Mass.: Harvard University Press, 1975).

8. See Urbach's discussion, with relevant texts, in *The Sages*, pp. 304–308.

9. Schiffman, *From Text to Tradition*, p. 267.

10. Jacob Neusner, ed., *Understanding Rabbinic Judaism* (New York: Ktav, 1974), p. 6.

11. Jacob Neusner, *There We Sat Down: Talmudic Judaism in the Making* (New York: Ktav, 1978), p. 102; Urbach, *The Sages*, p. 302; Frederick E. Greenspahn, "Why Prophecy Ceased," *Journal of Biblical Literature* 108 (1989), pp. 37–39.

12. Neusner, *There We Sat Down*, pp. 82–83.

13. Babylonian Talmud, Tractate Berakot 20a; cf. Julius Guttman, "The Religious Ideas of Talmudic Judaism," in Neusner, *Understanding Rabbinic Judaism*, p. 40.

14. Urbach, *The Sages*, p. 307; Neusner, *Between Time and Eternity* (Belmont, Calif.: Wadsworth, 1975), p. 37.

15. Babylonian Talmud, Tractate Bava Mesia 59b.

16. Neusner, *Understanding Rabbinic Judaism*, p. 7; and see Urbach, *The Sages*, 301f; Fromm, *You Shall Be As Gods*, pp. 62–64; C. G. Montefiore and H. Loewe, *A Rabbinic Anthology* (New York: Schocken, 1974), pp. 340f.; Nahum Glatzer, *A Jewish Reader* (New York: Schocken, 1961), pp. 131f.

17. Isadore Twersky, "Maimonides," in Neusner, *Understanding Rabbinic Judaism*, pp. 196–197.

18. Jerusalem Talmud, Tractate Hagigah 1:7. Cf. Susan A. Handelman, *The Slayers of Moses* (Albany: State University of New York, 1982), p. 171.

19. John P. Meier, "Matthew," in *The Anchor Bible Dictionary*, vol. 4, p. 638.

20. See George W. E. Nickelsburg, "Son of Man," in *The Anchor Bible Dictionary*, vol. 6, pp. 137–150.

21. Greek *logos*, which has a broader ranger of meaning than "word" in English but is nonetheless the same term used in the Greek translation of the Hebrew Bible for the words that God speaks at Sinai (Exod 24:3) and the words that Moses reports to the Israelites (Deut 1:1).

22. Luke Timothy Johnson, "Luke-Acts," in *The Anchor Bible Dictionary*, vol. 4, p. 405.

23. Paul J. Achtemeier, "Mark," in *The Anchor Bible Dictionary*, vol. 4, p. 555.

24. 22:1 in some translations.

25. He says it in a form that combines Hebrew and Aramaic, transcribed via the Greek alphabet as: "*eli eli* [or *eloi eloi*] *lama sabachthani.*"

26. "For all his high christology, Matthew keeps the element of tension between divine and human by retaining from Mark the cry of abandonment." Meier, "Matthew," in *The Anchor Bible Dictionary*, vol. 4, p. 636.

27. Fromm defends this explanation of the last words and briefly reviews related scholarship in *You Shall Be As Gods*, pp. 181–185.

28. 22:24 in some translations.

29. In recent research which I have read in colloquia (unpublished as of this date) I have argued that all references to *sheol* in the prose of the Hebrew Bible come from a single author.

30. See, e.g., Cross, *Canaanite Myth and Hebrew Epic*, p. 129; Allan Cooper, "PS 24:7–10: Mythology and Exegesis," *Journal of Biblical Literature* 102 (1983), pp. 37–60.

31. See David Noel Freedman, *Pottery, Poetry, and Prophecy* (Winona Lake, Ind.: Eisenbrauns, 1980), pp. 119–120; Cross, *Canaanite Myth and Hebrew Epic*, pp. 60–75.

32. Blaise Pascal, *Thoughts*, trans. W. F. Trotter (New York: Collier, 1910), p. 195.

Chapter 7: Nietzsche at Turin

1. Nietzsche, *The Gay Science* (also translated as *The Joyful Wisdom*, German *Die fröhliche Wissenschaft*), trans. Walter Kaufmann (New York: Vintage/Random House, 1974) Book 5, section 343: "The greatest recent

event — that 'God is dead,' that the belief in the Christian god has become unbelievable. . . ." All quotations from *The Gay Science* and *Thus Spoke Zarathustra* are from Walter Kaufmann's translations; see Works Cited for translation information on other works by Nietzsche.

2. Ernest Jones, *The Life and Work of Sigmund Freud* (1955), vol. 2, p. 344.

3. *Nietzsche: A Self-Portrait from His Letters*, Peter Fuss and Henry Shapiro, eds. and trans. (Cambridge, Mass.: Harvard University Press, 1971), p. 142.

4. Carl Pletsch, *Young Nietzsche* (New York: Free Press/Macmillan, 1991), pp. 67–68.

5. Nietzsche, *Historische-kritische Gesamtausgabe: Werke* 1 : 1 – 32; trans. in Pletsch, *Young Nietzsche*, p. 26.

6. Translated in Ronald Hayman, *Nietzsche: A Critical Life* (New York: Penguin, 1982); cf. Pletsch, p. 27.

7. Pletsch, *Young Nietzsche*, pp. 100, 206.

8. Letter to Georg Brandes, from Turin, April 10, 1888; in G. Brandes, *Friedrich Nietzsche* (London: William Heinemann, 1914), trans. from Danish, pp. 81–82.

9. Siegfried Mandel, Introduction to Lou Salomé, *Nietzsche*, p. xliv.

10. Brandes, *Friedrich Nietzsche*, p. 81.

11. Fuss and Shapiro, *Nietzche*, p. 142.

12. So Rudolph Binion argues in his *Frau Lou: Nietzsche's Wayward Disciple* (Princeton: Princeton University Press, 1968), p. 55. Hayman asserts that it was Nietzsche's idea, in *Nietzsche: A Critical Life*, in a note accompanying the photograph between pp. 220–221, as does Ben Macintyre, *Forgotten Fatherland: The Search for Elisabeth Nietzsche* (New York: HarperCollins, 1992), p. 106.

13. Because of the nature of the German article *die*, the line can also be read "Don't forget *your* whip." The ambiguity serves the effect described here.

14. It is the opening quotation of the collection *Nietzsche and the Feminine*, Peter J. Burgard, ed. (Charlottesville, Va.: University Press of Virginia, 1994), where it is identified as "Nietzsche's most famous misogynistic pronouncement" (p. 5).

15. H. F. Peters, *My Sister, My Spouse: A Biography of Lou Andreas-Salomé* (New York: Norton, 1962), pp. 103, 141. B. Macintyre briefly notes the possibility of a relationship between the photograph and the line in Nietzsche; but, translating the line "Do not forget *your* whip," he apparently does not make the connection that Peters and I have suggested; *Forgotten Fatherland*, p. 108.

16. Lou Salomé went on to a remarkable life and career. She wrote poetry, including a poem called "Hymn to Life," for which Nietzsche composed

music. It includes the line, "Have you no more joy to give me, well! you still have your suffering." (*Hast du kein Glück mehr übrig mir zu geben, wohlan! noch hast du deine Pein.*) She was Rilke's lover and a close friend of Freud. Her books include a very personal biography of Nietzsche. She died in 1937 at the age of seventy-six. Rée gave up philosophy and went into medicine, became a physician to the poor, who regarded him as a saint, and he died in a fall while hiking in the Engadine mountains of Switzerland in 1901, a year after Nietzsche's death.

17. Letters to Overbeck, from Leipzig, early September 1882, in Fuss and Shapiro, *Nietzsche*, p. 67; and from Rapallo, February 11, 1883, in Fuss and Shapiro, p. 71.

18. Salomé, *Nietzsche*, p. 12.

19. Brandes, *Friedrich Nietzsche*, p. 82.

20. *Twilight of the Idols*, Maxims and Arrows, 8.

21. Letter to Gast, from Nice, March 7, 1887, in Fuss and Shapiro, p. 97; letter to Overbeck, from Nice, February 23, 1887, in Kaufmann, *The Portable Nietzsche*, p. 454; letter to Brandes, from Turin, October 20, 1888, in Fuss and Shapiro, p. 127.

22. Letter to Brandes, from Turin, November 20, 1888, in Fuss and Shapiro, p. 132.

23. *Twilight of the Idols*, section 45.

24. There is in fact no such book by Dostoevsky. This was a French translation of *Notes from Underground* (Nietzsche read French but not Russian), but the French translators had also taken "The Landlady," and artificially combined it with *Notes from Underground* to make the two works seem like one long novel, which they titled *The Underground Spirit* (*L'Esprit Souterrain*). The two works are very different. *Notes from Underground* is a long account told in first person by a man as a sort of personal confession. "The Landlady" is a short story, told by a narrator in third person, about an episode in the life of a man, Ordynov. The French translators combined the two in such a way that one would first read the story of "The Landlady" and then assume that its hero, Ordynov, was the person speaking in *Notes from Underground*. (It is to Nietzsche's credit as a sensitive reader and literary critic that he sensed that something was wrong in this arrangement. He wrote to friends, "[It] comprises two short novels: the first a sort of strange music, the second a true stroke of psychological genius — a frightening and ferocious mockery of the Delphic 'know thyself,' but tossed off with such an effortless audacity and joy in his superior powers that I was thoroughly drunk with delight." (Letter to Franz Overbeck, from Nice, February 23, 1887, in Kaufmann, *The Portable Nietzsche*, pp. 454–455; letter to Peter Gast, from

Nice, March 7, 1887, in Fuss and Shapiro, pp. 97–98. See C. A. Miller, "Nietzsche's 'Discovery' of Dostoevsky," *Nietzsche-Studien* 2 [1973], pp. 202–257.)

25. The book is also known in English translation as *Daybreak* (German *Die Morgenröte).* Nietzsche wrote the preface sometime in the fall of 1886; his letter to his friend Overbeck describing his discovery of Dostoevsky "just a few weeks ago" is dated February 23, 1887.

26. In some translations: "subterranean."

27. "Ordynov se décida enfin à changer de chambre."

28. Miller lists a series of "striking parallels between Nietzsche's own immediate circumstances, personality and preoccupations and those of Dostoevsky's protagonist. . . ." pp. 218–225.

29. "The Landlady," in Dostoevsky, *Poor Folk and Other Stories,* trans. David McDuff (London: Penguin, 1988), p. 138.

30. "The Landlady," pp. 150–151.

31. Dostoevsky, *Notes from Underground,* in *Three Short Novels of Dostoevsky,* trans. Constance Garnett, ed. A. Yarmolinsky (New York: Anchor/Doubleday, 1960), p. 179.

32. *Notes from Underground,* p. 183.

33. *Notes from Underground,* p. 211.

34. *Notes from Underground,* p. 203. This "underground" or "subterranean" metaphor is in fact a recurring element in Nietzsche's work, both before and after his discovery of Dostoevsky. Besides the description of himself as an underground man in *Dawn,* Nietzsche uses the term in *The Genealogy of Morals* (Book 1, section 13): "born as one is to a subterranean life of struggle," and in *The Antichrist* (17), where he actually uses the French *souterrain,* the form that appears in the French title of Dostoevsky's book. And in *Thus Spoke Zarathustra* Nietzsche repeatedly plays on the words "over" and "under," from the beginning, in which Zarathustra's journey to his fellow humans is described as "Thus Zarathustra began to go under," to the famous matter of the "overman."

35. *Notes from Underground,* p. 185.

36. *Notes from Underground,* p. 217.

37. Recall the words of Salomé's poem that Nietzsche set to music, note 16 above.

38. *Notes from Underground,* p. 213.

39. *Notes from Underground,* p. 184.

40. *Notes from Underground,* p. 272.

41. *Notes from Underground,* p. 219. The underground man also uses the term resentment, French *ressentiment* (p. 296), a term that Nietzsche later

used repeatedly, in French, in his treatment of religion in *On the Genealogy of Morals* and *The Antichrist*.

42. *Thus Spoke Zarathustra*, I, Zarathustra's Prologue, section 5.

43. *Notes from Underground*, pp. 228–230, 252–253.

44. "The Landlady," p. 154.

45. "The Landlady," p. 141.

46. *Notes from Underground*, pp. 252–253.

47. Joseph Frank, *Dostoevsky: The Stir of Liberation, 1860–1865* (Princeton: Princeton University Press, 1986), p. 128n.

48. *The Insulted and Injured*, trans. Constance Garnett (Westport, Conn.: Greenwood, 1975), p. 264.

49. *The Insulted and Injured*, p. 238.

50. *The Insulted and Injured*, pp. 9, 333.

51. In the opening two pages (and again later), the narrator has a presentiment that something extraordinary is about to happen, and there are several coincidental meetings that draw key characters together. These include, notably, an inexplicable occurrence at the beginning of the book in which the narrator's chance presence when an old man dies turns out to be the intersection of what later turn out to be two halves of the story.

52. Cf. Kaufmann, *Nietzsche*, p. 340n.

53. Letter to Brandes, from Turin, October 20, 1888, in Brandes, *Friedrich Nietzsche*, p. 92.

54. Miller, "The Nihilist as Tempter-Redeemer: Dostoevsky's 'Man-God' in Nietzsche's Notebooks," *Nietzsche-Studien* 4 (1975), pp. 165–226.

55. He makes this clear in *Ecce Homo*, Book 3, section 1. "Other scholarly oxen have suspected me of Darwinism on that account." (trans. Walter Kaufmann)

56. *Thus Spoke Zarathustra*, Zarathustra's Prologue, section 3.

57. The translation is misleading with regard to gender. German *Mensch* means human, both male and female, as opposed to *Mann*, which is used for a male. Moreover, Nietzsche presumably took the term from Greek *hyperanthropos* (in Lucian, *Kataplous* 16; see Kaufmann, *Nietzsche*, p. 307), and Greek *anthropos* likewise means human, as opposed to *andros*, which is used for a male. The English word *man* merges the two, implying either human or male. *Human* and *superhuman* might be better translations of *Mensch* and *Übermensch*, but I have relied on standard translations here rather than taking on a linguistic challenge in a field in which I am not a specialist.

58. *The Devils* (*The Possessed*), trans. David Magarshack (London: Penguin, 1953), p. 126.

59. Letter to Paul Deussen, September 14, 1888, in Fuss and Shapiro, p. 124; letter to August Strindberg, December 7, 1888, in Fuss and Shapiro, p. 134.

60. *The Devils (The Possessed)*, p. 126.

61. Miller, "The Nihilist as Tempter-Redeemer: Dostoevsky's 'Man-God' in Nietzsche's Notebooks," p. 171. I should note that the preceding passages cited here are not among those that Nietzsche copied into his notebooks. Who can say if this is because he considered others more important or precisely because these points were not new to him; they would have impressed him as another marker of kinship with Dostoevsky, but he did not *learn* anything from them.

62. Letter to Gast, October 14, 1888. *Crime and Punishment* had been available in French translation since 1884. These facts plus the matter of the horse itself, which follows, leave me with little doubt that Nietzsche was very familiar with the novel. See Kaufmann's note in Nietzsche, *On the Genealogy of Morals* and *Ecce Homo*, ed. and trans. Walter Kaufmann (New York: Vintage/Random House, 1967), pp. 150–151.

63. *Thus Spoke Zarathustra*, I, section 6.

64. Walter Kaufmann points this out in *Nietzsche*, p. 340n.

65. Erich Heller, *The Importance of Nietzsche: Ten Essays* (Chicago: University of Chicago Press, 1988), p. 164.

66. I, 16; see Kaufmann, *Nietzsche*, pp. 314–316.

67. *Crime and Punishment*, trans. Constance Garnett (Cleveland: World Publishing, 1947), p. 24.

68. *Crime and Punishment*, p. 246.

69. *Crime and Punishment*, pp. 255, 446; *The Brothers Karamazov*, trans. Constance Garnett (New York: Random House, 1950), pp. 78, 312f. (Cf. 1 Cor 6:12).

70. Arthur Danto, *Nietzsche as Philosopher* (New York: Macmillan, 1965), p. 193.

71. *On the Genealogy of Morals* and *Ecce Homo*, p. 150n.; Kaufmann, *Nietzsche*, p. 340n.

72. *Crime and Punishment*, pp. 66, 68.

73. *Crime and Punishment*, pp. 71f.

74. Fuss and Shapiro, p. 133.

75. Fuss and Shapiro, p. 139.

76. Fuss and Shapiro, p. 71.

77. *Ecce Homo*, "Why I Am So Clever," section 10, and "The Case of Wagner," section 4.

78. He also used the phrase in *Nietzsche contra Wagner* and in an entry in his notebooks that year.

79. *The Gay Science*, Book 4, section 276.

80. No one known to me has observed this full chain of connections between Nietzsche and Dostoevsky, and only one writer known to me has noted the relationship to Raskolnikov's dream: Anacleto Verrecchia briefly noted the similarity of the horse portion of the dream to Nietzsche's embracing the horse in Turin in *La catastrofe di Nietzsche a Torino* (Turin: Einaudi, 1978); this work was available to me only in its German translation, *Zarathustras Ende: Die Katastrophe Nietzsches in Turin*, trans. P. Pawlowsky, (Vienna: Herrmann Böhlaus, 1986), p. 76.

Alexander Nehamas' argument that Nietzsche "looks at the world in general . . . as if it were a literary text" seems to me to add an intriguing dimension to this entire matter. *Nietzsche: Life as Literature* (Cambridge, Mass.: Harvard University Press, 1985).

81. Letter to Gast, from Turin, January 4, 1889, trans. Kaufmann, *The Portable Nietzsche*, p. 685.

82. Pss 96:1; 98:1; 149:1; 33:3; Isa 42:10.

83. Hayman, *Nietzsche: A Critical Life*, p. 344.

Chapter 8: The "Death" of God

1. Michael Platt, "Behold Nietzsche," *Nietzsche-Studien* 22 (1993), p. 69, writes of ". . . the illusions of divinity that characterized Nietzsche's madness. . . ."

2. Sections 108, 125, and 343. Nietzsche titled the book in German, *Die fröhliche Wissenschaft*, and added a subtitle in Italian "la gaya scienza." See W. Kaufmann's "Translator's Introduction" to Nietzsche, *The Gay Science*, pp. 4–7.

3. Kaufmann, *Nietzsche*, p. 97.

4. Translation by Steven Cassedy. Cf. *The Brothers Karamazov*, p. 777, for a similar analysis of dreams.

5. *The Birth of Tragedy*, section 1, p. 34.

6. Chapter 7 (B).

7. Lou Salomé, *Nietzsche*, ed. and trans. Siegfried Mandel (Redding Ridge, Conn.: Black Swan Books, 1988), p. 144; German edition: *Friedrich Nietzsche in seinen Werken* (Vienna: Carl Konegen, 1894).

8. *Daybreak*, section 312; trans. R. J. Hollingdale (Cambridge: Cambridge University Press, 1982).

9. Frank, *Dostoevsky: The Seeds of Revolt, 1821–1849* (Princeton: Princeton University Press, 1976), p. 81.

10. Sigmund Freud, "Dostoevsky and Parricide" (1928) trans. D. F. Tait, in Freud, *Character and Culture* (New York: Collier, 1963), pp. 274–293.

11. Frank, *Dostoevsky: The Seeds of Revolt*, pp. 83–87.

12. Cf. Victor Terras, *A Karamazov Companion* (Madison, Wis.: University of Wisconsin Press, 1981), p. 74.

13. Frank, *Dostoevsky: The Seeds of Revolt*, p. 83.

14. Pletsch, pp. 54, 89; Hayman, pp. 275f.

15. Letter to Brandes, from Turin, April 10, 1888; in Middleton, p. 294. See also *Ecce Homo*, Book I, section 3.

16. Sigmund Freud, *The Future of an Illusion*, James Strachey, ed. (New York: Anchor/Doubleday, 1964), p. 71; cf. pp. 23–27, 32–35, 47–48, 69, 81. (Original German edition 1927).

17. Indeed, in treating a polarity of "extremes of rejection and acceptance" in Dostoevsky, Frank ends: ". . . while the tension of this polarity may have developed out of the ambivalence of Dostoevsky's psychodynamic relation with his father, what is more important is to see how early it was transposed and projected into the religious symbolism of the eternal problem of theodicy." *Dostoevsky: The Seeds of Revolt*, p. 53.

18. Frank, *Dostoevsky: The Seeds of Revolt*, p. 70.

19. Frank, *Dostoevsky: The Seeds of Revolt*, p. 71; *Dostoevsky: The Stir of Liberation, 1860–1865*, p. 124n.

20. January 1876; Dostoevsky, *The Diary of a Writer*, trans. B. Brasol (Santa Barbara, Calif.: Peregrine Smith, 1979), p. 186.

21. F. M. Dostoevskii, *Polnoe sobranie sochinenii v tridtsati tomakh* (Leningrad: "Nauka," 1972–1990), vol. 15, p. 553; editor's note translated by Steven Cassedy. The poem by Nekrassov is "Before Dawn," from the cycle "About the Weather," 1859.

22. A. G. Dostoevskaia, *Vospominaniia* (Moscow: Khudozhestvennaia Literatura, 1971), p. 351; the translation here is by Steven Cassedy.

23. Freud, "Analysis of a Phobia in a Five-Year-Old-Boy" (1909), *The Standard Edition of the Complete Psychological Works of Sigmund Freud*, James Strachey, ed. (London: Hogarth Press) vol. 10, p. 136.

24. Letter to Gast, from Nice, March 7, 1887; in Fuss and Shapiro, pp. 97f.

25. Shestov, *Dostoevsky, Tolstoy and Nietzsche*, trans. S. Roberts (Athens, Ohio: Ohio University Press, 1969), p. 170.

26. Letter from Leipzig, c. September 16, 1882; in *Selected Letters of Friedrich Nietzsche*, ed. and trans. C. Middleton (Chicago: University of Chicago Press, 1969), p. 193.

27. Letter to Overbeck, from Sils Maria, received August 28, 1883; in Middleton, p. 218. In another letter he refers to the possibility of mental breakdown; see Hayman, *Nietzsche: A Critical Life*, p. 267.

28. *The Gay Science*, section 76.

29. *Thus Spoke Zarathustra*, II, "On Redemption."

30. *Thus Spoke Zarathustra*, I, Zarathustra's Prologue, section 5.

31. Letter from Strindberg, December 31, 1888; Middleton, pp. 344f.; in E. F. Podach, *The Madness of Nietzsche*, trans. F. A. Voigt (London: Putnam, 1931), pp. 130, 141.

32. *Thus Spoke Zarathustra*, I, section 7, "On Reading and Writing," p. 153.

33. *Dawn*, section 14. (Translation here is from *Daybreak*, trans. R. J. Hollingdale, p. 14.)

34. Podach, *The Madness of Nietzsche*, p. 214.

35. Podach, *The Madness of Nietzsche*, p. 215.

36. *Crime and Punishment*, p. 213.

37. Philip Roth, "Eli the Fanatic," in *Goodbye, Columbus and Five Stories* (Boston: Houghton Mifflin, 1959), p. 259.

38. Salomé, *Nietzsche*, pp. 88f.

39. Frank, *Dostoevsky: The Seeds of Revolt*, p. 43.

40. *Thus Spoke Zarathustra*, I, section 7, "On Reading and Writing," p. 153.

41. *The Will to Power*, trans. W. Kaufmann and R. J. Hollingdale (New York: Vintage, 1967), section 1038.

42. *Thus Spoke Zarathustra*, II, section 2, "Upon the Blessed Isles," p. 198.

43. *The Gay Science*, section 285.

44. *Ecce Homo*, Book 2, section 1.

45. *The Gay Science*, section 125.

46. Letter to Carl Fuchs, from Turin, December 18, 1888, in Middleton, p. 335; cf. R. P. Harrison, "Nietzsche in Turin," in T. Harrison, ed. *Nietzsche in Italy* (Saratoga, Calif.: ANMA Libri, 1988), p. 225; J. P. Stern, *A Study of Nietzsche* (Cambridge: Cambridge University Press, 1979), p. 31.

47. Podach, *The Madness of Nietzsche*, p. 163.

48. *The Devils*, p. 126; Miller, "The Nihilist as Tempter-Redeemer: Dostoevsky's 'Man-God' in Nietzsche's Notebooks," *Nietzsche-Studien* 4 (1975), pp. 165–226.

49. *The Brothers Karamazov*, pp. xii, 788f.

50. Gen 3:22.

51. *The Brothers Karamazov*, pp. 292–314.

52. Freud, "Dostoevsky and Parricide," p. 274.

53. *The Brothers Karamazov*, p. 294.

54. One of my students, Jesse Stirling, made this observation.
55. *Dawn*, section 14. (Translation here is from *Daybreak*, trans.R. J. Hollingdale, pp. 13f.)
56. *Thus Spoke Zarathustra*, I, section 3.
57. *The Brothers Karamazov*, pp. 771–790.
58. Nietzsche, *Selected Letters*, trans. A. N. Ludovici, ed. O. Levy (Garden City, N.Y.: Doubleday, 1921), p. 191n.

Chapter 9: The Legacy of the Age: The Twentieth Century

1. Letter to Malwida von Meysenburg, from Chur, Switzerland, May 12, 1887, in Fuss and Shapiro, p. 99. Cf. *The Gay Science*, section 371.
2. Preface to *The Antichrist*, in *The Portable Nietzsche*, p. 568.
3. Brandes, August 1900, in *Friedrich Nietzsche*, p. 103. He calls Nietzsche "the psychological life of our time," p. 104.
4. Jones, vol. 3, p. 460; Kaufmann, *Basic Writings*, p. 188.
5. Brandes, *Friedrich Nietzsche*, p. 106.
6. Peters, *My Sister, My Spouse: A Biography of Lou Andreas-Salomé*, p. 123; Kaufmann, *Nietzsche*, pp. 98f.
7. *Ecce Homo*, Book 4, section 1, p. 326.
8. *Dawn*, section 205, in Kaufmann, *The Portable Nietzsche*, p. 88.
9. *Dostoevsky: The Seeds of Revolt*, p. 379. Frank wrote these words, referring to "the past half-century," in 1975.
10. *The Gay Science*, Book 4, section 316, p. 251.
11. Barnes, *The Ruling Class* (1969), in *Collected Plays* (London: Heinemann, 1981), Act I, Scene 4, p. 26.
12. Thomas J. J. Altizer, *The Gospel of Christian Atheism* (Philadelphia: Westminster, 1966), p. 22.
13. Hamilton, "The Death of God Theologies Today," in T. J. J. Altizer and W. Hamilton, eds., *Radical Theology and the Death of God* (Indianapolis: Bobbs-Merrill, 1966), p. 47.
14. Other main figures and works associated with this movement were Gabriel Vahanian, *The Death of God*, and Paul M. van Buren, *The Secular Meaning of the Gospel*. John A. T. Robinson, *Honest to God*, and Harvey Cox, *The Secular City*, are often cited as part of the broader context relating to radical theology.
15. Richard Rubenstein, *After Auschwitz* (Indianapolis: Bobbs-Merrill, 1966), p. 245.

16. Rubenstein, *After Auschwitz*, p. 247.

17. Roger Hazelton, "The Future of God," in B. Murchland, ed., *The Meaning of the Death of God* (New York: Random House, 1967), p. 130.

18. *The Gay Science*, Book 2, section 76.

19. E.g., Hamilton: ". . . however acute the experience of the death of God may be for us, however much silence and loneliness are entailed during our time of waiting for the absent God, we are not particularly cast down or perplexed by this." "The Death of God Theologies Today," p. 50.

20. Altizer, *The Gospel of Christian Atheism*, p. 22.

21. Altizer, *The Gospel of Christian Atheism*, p. 146.

22. Rubenstein, *After Auschwitz*, p. 263.

23. Freud, *The Future of an Illusion*, p. 71.

24. *The Gay Science*, section 343.

25. Freud, *The Future of an Illusion*, p. 81.

26. Dietrich Bonhoeffer, *Letters from Prison* (New York: Macmillan, 1971). Letter of July 16, 1944; p. 360.

Chapter 10: Big Bang and Kabbalah

1. George Gamow, *One Two Three . . . Infinity* (New York: Viking, 1947).

2. Stephen W. Hawking, *A Brief History of Time* (New York: Bantam, 1988).

3. Timothy Ferris, *The Red Limit*, 2nd edition (New York: Quill, 1983); *Coming of Age in the Milky Way* (New York: Morrow, 1988).

4. Steven Weinberg, *Dreams of a Final Theory* (New York: Pantheon, 1992), pp. 241–261.

5. Dennis Overbye, *Lonely Hearts of the Cosmos* (New York: HarperCollins, 1991), p. 366.

6. Paul Davies, *The Mind of God* (New York: Simon and Schuster, 1992). Davies is also author of *God and the New Physics* (New York: Simon and Schuster, 1983).

7. Robert Jastrow, *God and the Astronomers* (New York: Norton, 1978).

8. Quoted in numerous sources, including Associated Press, August 26, 1992; *Time*, December 28, 1992.

9. Overbye, *Lonely Hearts*, pp. 185–186.

10. *The Brothers Karamazov*, p. 279.

11. William McCrea, quoted in Ferris, *The Red Limit*, p. 82.

12. John D. Barrow, *The Origin of the Universe* (New York: Basic Books, 1994), p. 3; Sandage quoted in Overbye, *Lonely Hearts*, p. 48.

13. Hawking, *A Brief History of Time*, p. 39.

14. Overbye, *Lonely Hearts*, p. 47 (italics added).

15. R. A. Alpher, R. C. Herman, "Evolution of the Universe," *Nature* 162 (1948), p. 774.

16. A. G. Doroshkevich and I. D. Novikov, "Mean Density of Radiation in the Metagalaxy and Certain Problems in Relativistic Cosmology," *Soviet Physics* — Doklady 9 (1964), pp. 111–113.

17. R. H. Dicke, P. J. E. Peebles, P. G. Roll, and D. T. Wilkinson, "Cosmic Black-Body Radiation," *Astrophysical Journal* 142 (1965), pp. 414–419; A. A. Penzias, R. W. Wilson, "A Measurement of Excess Antenna Temperature at 4080 Mc/s," *Astrophysical Journal* 142 (1965), pp. 419–421.

18. *The San Diego Union-Tribune*, April 22, 1992.

19. Joel Primack, of the University of California, Santa Cruz; *The San Diego Union-Tribune*, April 25, 1992.

20. Michael Rowan-Robinson, *Ripples in the Cosmos* (Oxford: W. H. Freeman, 1993), pp. 186–188. Rowan-Robinson offers a more measured evaluation of the discovery, rejecting its depiction as "the discovery of the century," but still calling it a "landmark."

21. For Smoot's description of the research, see George Smoot and Keay Davidson, *Wrinkles in Time* (New York: Morrow, 1993).

22. Daniel Chanan Matt, *Zohar: The Book of Enlightenment* (New York: Paulist Press, 1983), p. 22.

23. Gershom G. Scholem, *Major Trends in Jewish Mysticism* (New York: Schocken, 1961; original edition 1941), p. 217; cf. Scholem, *Kabbalah* (New York: Dorset, 1987), p. 94.

24. Scholem, *Kabbalah*, 131; Isaiah Tishby, *The Wisdom of the Zohar*, vol. 1 (New York: Oxford University Press, 1989; original Hebrew edition 1949), trans. D. Goldstein, p. 233.

25. Shim'on Labi, *Ketem Paz*, 1:124c, on Zohar 1:47a. I owe the reference and the translation to Daniel Matt, who was the first to observe the relationship between this passage and Big Bang.

26. Scholem, *Major Trends*, p. 209; cf. Scholem, *Kabbalah*, pp. 98–99, 116.

27. Moshe Idel, *Kabbalah: New Perspectives* (New Haven: Yale University Press, 1988), p. 136; Scholem, *Kabbalah*, p. 99.

28. Scholem, *Major Trends*, p. 214; Idel, *Kabbalah: New Perspectives*, pp. 137ff.

29. Scholem, *Major Trends*, p. 262, 264.

30. David S. Ariel, *The Mystic Quest* (New York: Schocken, 1988), pp. 68, 170ff.; Scholem, *Major Trends*, pp. 266–268; Scholem, *Kabbalah*, pp. 138ff.

31. Fritjof Capra, *The Tao of Physics* (New York: Fontana, 1976); Gary Zukav, *The Dancing Wu Li Masters* (New York: Bantam, 1980).

32. Leon Lederman offers a critique of Capra and Zukav, acknowledging some strengths and arguing that there are flaws, in Lederman with Dick Teresi, *The God Particle* (New York: Delta, 1993), pp. 189–191, 198.

33. Overbye, *Lonely Hearts*, p. 120.

34. Gerald L. Schroeder, *Genesis and the Big Bang* (New York: Bantam, 1990), p. 10.

35. Schroeder, *Genesis and the Big Bang*, p. 12.

36. Schroeder, *Genesis and the Big Bang*, p. 11.

37. Schroeder, *Genesis and the Big Bang*, p. 152.

38. Those who are new to textual criticism but want to understand more about its significance in the study of the Bible might begin with Emanuel Tov, *Textual Criticism of the Hebrew Bible* (Minneapolis: Fortress/Van Gorcum, 1992); Ralph W. Klein, *Textual Criticism of the Old Testament* (Philadelphia: Fortress, 1974); and Frank Moore Cross and Shemaryahu Talmon, eds., *Qumran and the History of the Biblical Text* (Cambridge: Harvard University Press, 1975).

39. See Rashi on Gen 1:6.

40. Stokes, *The Genesis Answer* (Englewood Cliffs, N.J.: Prentice-Hall, 1981).

41. At one point Schroeder seems to be aware of the Kabbalistic notion of the point that expands into the universe (pp. 64–68), but he attributes it to the medieval biblical commentator Nachmanides and never mentions Kabbalah in this context (so that it is unclear if he is even aware that Nachmanides himself was a Kabbalist), tracing this notion instead to "biblical revelation."

42. Ferris, *Coming of Age in the Milky Way*, p. 336; cf. pp. 313, 334, 348.

43. Heinz Pagels, *The Cosmic Code* (New York: Bantam, 1982), p. 305.

44. Ferris, *Coming of Age in the Milky Way*, p. 386.

45. Stephen W. Hawking and Roger Penrose, "The Singularities of Gravitational Collapse and Cosmology," *Proceedings of the Royal Society (London)* (1969), A314:529–548.

46. Roger Penrose, *The Emperor's New Mind* (New York: Penguin, 1989), p. 345.

47. Penrose, in Alan Lightman and Roberta Brawer, eds., *Origins* (Cambridge: Harvard University Press, 1990), p. 420.

48. Scholem, *Kabbalah*, p. 101; cf. p. 94.

49. Tishby, *The Wisdom of the Zohar*, p. 233.

50. Matt, *Zohar*, p. 22.

51. Trans. Matt, *Zohar*, p. 49.

52. Davies, *The Mind of God*, p. 226. Cf. Rudy Rucker, *Infinity and the Mind* (New York: Bantam, 1983), pp. 225ff.

Chapter 11: Religion and Science

1. James B. Hartle and Stephen W. Hawking, "Wave Function for the Universe," *Physical Review* (1983) D28:2960.

2. Hawking, *A Brief History of Time*, p. 138; Davies, *The Mind of God*, pp. 63–69; Ferris, *Coming of Age in the Milky Way*, pp. 363f.; Overbye, *Lonely Hearts of the Cosmos*, pp. 369–371.

3. The traditional rendering of Gen 1:1 is "In the beginning, God created the heavens and the earth." A more grammatically accurate rendering according to some modern scholars (and Rashi) would be, literally: "In the beginning of God's creating the heavens and the earth, the earth was unformed and void." This sounds a bit clumsy in English and has generally been recast as "When God began to create the heavens and the earth, the earth was unformed and void."

4. Hawking, *A Brief History of Time*, pp. 140f.

5. See Daniel Matt, *"Ayin:* The Concept of Nothingness in Jewish Mysticism," in Robert K. C. Forman, ed., *The Problem of Pure Consciousness: Mysticism and Philosophy* (New York: Oxford University Press, 1990), p. 143.

6. Scholem, *Kabbalah*, p. 148; see pp. 144–152.

7. Scholem, *Kabbalah*, p. 150.

8. Quoted in Ferris, *The Red Limit*, p. 114.

9. Robert Wright, "Science, God and Man," *Time* (December 28, 1992), p. 40.

10. Albert Einstein, "Religion and Science," in Einstein, *Ideas and Opinions* (New York: Bonanza, 1954), p. 38; originally written for the *New York Times Magazine* (November 9, 1930), pp. 1–4.

11. Einstein, *Ideas and Opinions*, pp. 38, 39.

12. Lederman and Teresi, *The God Particle*, p. 190.

13. Ferris, *Coming of Age in the Milky Way*, pp. 367–368.

14. Ferris, *Coming of Age in the Milky Way*, p. 387.

15. Davies, *The Mind of God*, p. 20.

16. Davies, *The Mind of God*, p. 232.

17. Letter to Gast, August 1881, quoted in J. P. Stern, *A Study of Nietzsche*, p. 15; see also Fuss and Shapiro, p. 58.

18. *The Mind of God*, pp. 228–229.

19. Roger Penrose, *The Emperor's New Mind: Concerning Computers, Minds, and the Laws of Physics* (New York: Penguin, 1991).

20. Penrose, *The Emperor's New Mind*, p. 448.

21. In Lightman and Brawer, *Origins*, p. 434.

22. Quoted in Wright, "Science, God and Man," p. 43.

23. Ferris, *Coming of Age in the Milky Way*, p. 379.

24. Penrose, *The Emperor's New Mind*, p. 295; Ferris, *Coming of Age in the Milky Way*, pp. 364f.

25. Scholem, *Kabbalah*, p. 152 (emphasis added). See also Moshe Idel's explication of "the human or psychological understanding of the Sefirot" in *Kabbalah: New Perspectives*, pp. 137, 146ff.

26. Scholem, *Major Trends*, pp. 233, 275.

27. Scholem, *On the Mystical Shape of the Godhead* (New York: Schocken, 1991), p. 242; *Major Trends*, p. 265; Idel, *Kabbalah: New Perspectives*, p. 57.

28. Lawrence Fine, *Safed Spirituality* (New York: Paulist Press, 1984), pp. 62f.

29. Liebes, *Studies in the Zohar* (Albany, N.Y.: State University of New York Press, 1993), pp. 55, 57.

30. Scholem, *Major Trends*, p. 274.

31. Liebes, *Studies in the Zohar*, p. 54.

32. Scholem, *Kabbalah*, p. 143; *Major Trends*, p. 275.

33. Scholem, *Major Trends*, p. 247.

Chapter 12: Divine-Human Reunion

1. Cf. *Who Wrote the Bible?*, pp. 236–238.

2. *Beyond Good and Evil*, trans. Walter Kaufmann (New York: Vintage, 1966), section 52.

3. *Beyond Good and Evil*, section 52. Nietzsche's feelings toward the New Testament are more complex, combining harsh criticism with a special affection for the person of Jesus and a powerful fascination with the crucifixion.

4. Pletsch, *Young Nietzsche*, p. 91.

5. *Ecce Homo*, "Why I Write Such Good Books"; *The Birth of Tragedy*, section 3.

6. *Ecce Homo*, "Why I Write Such Good Books"; *Thus Spoke Zarathustra*, section 1.

7. *The Brothers Karamazov*, p. 783.

8. Salome, *Nietzsche*, p. 133.

9. *Thus Spoke Zarathustra*, III.

10. Scholem, *Kabbalah*, pp. 116–122.

11. Salomé, *Nietzsche*, pp. 128f.

12. Robert Jastrow, *God and the Astronomers*, p. 114, has written of those who are guilty of "trivializing the origin of the world by calling it the Big Bang, as if it were a firecracker."

13. Rubenstein, *After Auschwitz*, p. 241.

14. Scholem, *Kabbalah*, p.154.

15. Arthur C. Clarke, *2001: A Space Odyssey* (New York: Signet, 1968); "The Sentinel," in Clarke, *Across the Sea of Stars* (New York: Harcourt, Brace, 1953).

16. Hawking, *A Brief History of Time*, p. 167 (emphasis added).

17. In Lightman and Brawer, eds., *Origins*, p. 169 (emphasis added).

18. Others take exception, notably Roger Penrose and Martin Rees.

19. Scholem, *Kabbalah*, pp. 111, 143.

WORKS CITED

Achtemeier, Paul J. "Mark." *The Anchor Bible Dictionary*. Vol. 4, pp. 541–557.

Alpher, R. A., and Herman, R. C. "Evolution of the Universe." *Nature* 162 (1948).

Altizer, Thomas J. J. *The Gospel of Christian Atheism*. Philadelphia: Westminster, 1966.

——, and Hamilton, William. *Radical Theology and the Death of God*. Indianapolis: Bobbs-Merrill, 1966.

Ariel, David S. *The Mystic Quest*. New York: Schocken, 1988.

Baker, D. W. "Tarshish." *The Anchor Bible Dictionary*. Vol. 6, pp. 332–333.

Balentine, Samuel. *The Hidden God: The Hiding of the Face of God in the Old Testament*. New York: Oxford University Press, 1983.

Baltzer, Klaus. *The Covenant Formulary*. Philadelphia: Fortresss Press, 1971; German edition, 1964.

Barnes, Peter. *The Ruling Class* (1969). In *Collected Plays*. London: Heinemann, 1981.

Barrow, John D. *The Origin of the Universe*. New York: Basic Books, 1994.

Beckett, Samuel. *Waiting for Godot*. New York: Grove Weidenfeld, 1954.

Binion, Rudolph. *Frau Lou: Nietzsche's Wayward Disciple*. Princeton: Princeton University Press, 1968.

Bonhoeffer, Dietrich. *Letters from Prison*. New York: Macmillan, 1971.

Brandes, Georg. *Friedrich Nietzsche*. Trans. by A. Chater. London: William Heinemann, 1914.

Burgard, Peter J., ed. *Nietzsche and the Feminine*. Charlottesville, Va.: University Press of Virginia, 1994.

Capra, Fritjof. *The Tao of Physics*. New York: Fontana, 1976.

Christensen, Duane L. "Chronicles of the Kings (Israel/Judah)." *The Anchor Bible Dictionary*. Vol. 1, pp. 991f.

Clarke, Arthur C. *2001: A Space Odyssey*. New York: Signet, 1968.

———. "The Sentinel." In Arthur C. Clarke, *Across the Sea of Stars*. New York: Harcourt, Brace, 1953.

Cooper, Allan. "PS 24:7–10: Mythology and Exegesis." *Journal of Biblical Literature* 102 (1983), pp. 37–60.

Cross, Frank Moore. *Canaanite Myth and Hebrew Epic*. Cambridge: Harvard University Press, 1973.

———, and Talmon, Shemaryahu, eds. *Qumran and the History of the Biblical Text*. Cambridge: Harvard University Press, 1975.

Dahood, Mitchell. Psalms 1–50. *The Anchor Bible*. New York: Doubleday, 1965.

Danto, Arthur. *Nietzsche as Philosopher*. New York: Macmillan, 1965.

Davies, Paul. *The Mind of God*. New York: Simon and Schuster, 1992.

———. *God and the New Physics*. New York: Simon and Schuster, 1983.

Dicke, R. H., Peebles, P. J. E., Roll, P. G., and Wilkinson, D. T. "Cosmic Black-Body Radiation." *Astrophysical Journal* 142 (1965), pp. 414–419.

Doroshkevich, A. G., and Novikov, I. D. "Mean Density of Radiation in the Metagalaxy and Certain Problems in Relativistic Cosmology." *Soviet Physics — Doklady* 9 (1964), pp. 111–113.

Dostoevskaia, A. G. *Vospominaniia*. Moscow: Khudozhestvennaia Literatura, 1971.

Dostoevsky, Feodor. *The Brothers Karamazov*. Trans. by Constance Garnett. New York: Random House, 1950.

———. *Crime and Punishment*. Trans. by Constance Garnett. Cleveland: World Publishing, 1947.

———. *The Devils (The Possessed)*. Trans. by David Magarshack. London: Penguin, 1953.

———. *The Diary of a Writer*. Trans. by B. Brasol. Santa Barbara, Calif.: Peregrine Smith, 1979.

———. *The Insulted and Injured*. Trans. by Constance Garnett. Westport, Conn.: Greenwood, 1975.

———. *Notes from Underground*. In *Three Short Novels of Dostoevsky*. Trans. by Constance Garnett and ed. by A. Yarmolinsky. New York: Anchor/Doubleday, 1960.

————. *Poor Folk and Other Stories*. Trans. by David McDuff. London: Penguin, 1988.

The Earthworks Group. *50 Simple Things You Can Do to Save the Earth*. Berkeley, Calif.: Earthworks Press, 1989.

Einstein, Albert. *Ideas and Opinions*. New York: Bonanza, 1954.

Ferris, Timothy. *Coming of Age in the Milky Way*. New York: Morrow, 1988.

————. *The Red Limit*. 2nd ed. New York: Quill, 1983.

Fine, Lawrence. *Safed Spirituality*. New York: Paulist Press, 1984.

Frank, Joseph. *Dostoevsky: The Seeds of Revolt, 1821–1849*. Princeton: Princeton University Press, 1976.

————. *Dostoevsky: The Stir of Liberation, 1860–1865*. Princeton: Princeton University Press, 1986.

Frankfort, Henri, et al. *The Intellectual Adventure of Ancient Man*. Chicago: University of Chicago Press, 1946.

Freedman, David Noel. *Pottery, Poetry, and Prophecy*. Winona Lake, Ind.: Eisenbrauns, 1980.

————. *The Unity of the Hebrew Bible*. Ann Arbor, Mich.: University of Michigan Press, 1991.

Fretheim, Terence E. *The Suffering of God*. Philadelphia: Fortress, 1984.

Freud, Sigmund. "Analysis of a Phobia in a Five-Year-Old Boy" (1909). In *The Standard Edition of the Complete Psychological Works of Sigmund Freud*. Vol. 10. Ed. by James Strachey. London: Hogarth Press.

————. "Dostoevsky and Parricide" (1928). Trans. by D. F. Tait. In Freud, *Character and Culture*. New York: Collier, 1963, pp. 274–293.

————. *The Future of an Illusion*. Ed. by James Strachey. New York: Anchor/ Doubleday, 1964.

Friedman, Richard Elliott. "The Biblical Expression *mastîr pānîm*." *Hebrew Annual Review* 1 (1977), pp. 139–147.

————, ed. *The Creation of Sacred Literature*. Berkeley, Calif.: University of California Press, 1981.

————. "The Deuteronomistic School." In *Fortunate the Eyes That See* (David Noel Freedman *Festschrift*). Ed. by Astrid Beck, Andrew H. Bartelt, Paul R. Raabe, and Chris Franke. Grand Rapids, Mich.: Eerdmans, 1995.

————. *The Exile and Biblical Narrative*. Harvard Semitic Monographs 22. Atlanta: Scholars Press, 1981.

————. "From Egypt to Egypt: Dtr[1] and Dtr[2]." In *Traditions in Transformation: Turning-Points in Biblical Faith* (Frank Moore Cross *Festschrift*). Ed. by B. Halpern and J. Levenson. Winona Lake, Ind.: Eisenbrauns, 1981, pp. 167–192.

———. "The Hiding of the Face: An Essay on the Literary Unity of Biblical Narrative." In *Judaic Perspectives on Ancient Israel*, ed. by Jacob Neusner, Baruch Levine, and Ernest Frerichs. Philadelphia: Fortress, 1987, pp. 207–222.

———. "Torah and Covenant." In *The Oxford Study Bible*, ed. by M. J. Suggs, K. D. Sakenfeld, and J. R. Mueller. New York: Oxford University Press, 1992, pp.154–163.

———. *Who Wrote the Bible?* New York: Summit/Simon and Schuster, 1987.

Fromm, Erich. *You Shall Be as Gods*. Greenwich, Conn.: Fawcett, 1966.

Fuss, Peter, and Shapiro, Henry, eds. and trans. *Nietzsche: A Self-Portrait from His Letters*. Cambridge: Harvard University Press, 1971.

Gamow, George. *One Two Three . . . Infinity*. New York: Viking, 1947.

Glatzer, Nahum. *Essays in Jewish Thought*. Tuscaloosa, Ala.: University of Alabama Press, 1978, pp. 184–191.

———. *A Jewish Reader*. New York: Schocken, 1961.

Greenspahn, Frederick E. "Why Prophecy Ceased." *Journal of Biblical Literature* 108 (1989), pp. 37–39.

Halpern, Baruch. *The Constitution of the Monarchy in Israel*. Harvard Semitic Monographs. Atlanta: Scholars Press, 1981.

———. *The First Historians*. San Francisco: Harper and Row, 1988.

———. "Sacred History and Ideology: Chronicles' Thematic Structure–Indications of an Earlier Source." In *The Creation of Sacred Literature*, ed. by R. E. Friedman. Berkeley, Calif.: University of California Press, 1981, pp. 35–54.

Handelman, Susan A. *The Slayers of Moses*. Albany: State University of New York, 1982.

Hanson, Paul. "Song of Heshbon and David's NÎR." *Harvard Theological Review* 61 (1968), pp. 297–320.

Harrison, Thomas, ed. *Nietzsche in Italy*. Saratoga, Calif.: ANMA LIBRI, 1988.

Hartle, James B., and Hawking, Stephen W. "Wave Function for the Universe." *Physical Review* (1983), D28:2960.

Hawking, Stephen W. *A Brief History of Time*. New York: Bantam, 1988.

———, and Penrose, Roger. "The Singularities of Gravitational Collapse and Cosmology." *Proceedings of the Royal Society (London)* (1969), A314: 529–548.

Hayman, Ronald. *Nietzsche: A Critical Life*. New York: Penguin, 1982.

Hazelton, Roger. "The Future of God." In *The Meaning of the Death of God*, ed. by B. Murchland. New York: Random House, 1967, pp. 128–137.

Heller, Erich. *The Importance of Nietzsche: Ten Essays.* Chicago: University of Chicago Press, 1988.

Hemmings, F. W. J. *The Russian Novel in France, 1884–1914.* New York: Oxford University Press, 1950.

Idel, Moshe. *Kabbalah: New Perspectives.* New Haven: Yale University Press, 1988.

Iwry, Samuel. "The Qumrân Isaiah and the End of the Dial of Ahaz." *Bulletin of the American Schools of Oriental Research* 147 (1957), pp. 27–33.

Jastrow, Robert. *God and the Astronomers.* New York: Norton, 1978.

Johnson, Luke Timothy. "Luke-Acts." *The Anchor Bible Dictionary.* Vol. 4, pp. 404–420.

Jones, Ernest. *The Life and Work of Sigmund Freud.* Vol. 2. 1955.

Kaufmann, Walter, ed. *Basic Writings of Nietzsche.* New York: Modern Library, 1992.

———. *Nietzsche: Philosopher, Psychologist, Antichrist.* Princeton: Princeton University Press, 1974.

Klein, Ralph W. *Textual Criticism of the Old Testament.* Philadelphia: Fortress, 1974.

Lederman, Leon, with Teresi, Dick. *The God Particle.* New York: Delta, 1993.

Liebes, Yehuda. *Studies in the Zohar.* Albany, N.Y.: State University of New York Press, 1993.

Lightman, Alan, and Brawer, Roberta. *Origins.* Cambridge: Harvard University Press, 1990.

Macintyre, Ben. *Forgotten Fatherland: The Search for Elisabeth Nietzsche.* New York: HarperCollins, 1992.

Matt, Daniel Chanan. "*Ayin:* The Concept of Nothingness in Jewish Mysticism." In *The Problem of Pure Consciousness: Mysticism and Philosophy.* ed. by Robert K. C. Forman. New York: Oxford University Press, 1990.

———. *Zohar: The Book of Enlightenment.* New York: Paulist Press, 1983.

McBride, S. Dean. "The Deuteronomic Name Theology." Dissertation, Harvard University, 1969.

Meier, John P. "Matthew." *The Anchor Bible Dictionary.* Vol. 4, pp. 622–641.

Mendenhall, G. E. *Law and Covenant in Israel and the Ancient Near East.* Pittsburgh: The Biblical Colloquium, 1955.

Middleton, Christopher, ed. and trans. *Selected Letters of Friedrich Nietzsche.* Chicago: University of Chicago Press, 1969.

Miles, John. "Radical Editing: *Redaktionsgeschichte* and the Aesthetic of Willed Confusion." In *The Creation of Sacred Literature,* ed. by R. E. Friedman. Berkeley, Calif.: University of California Press, 1981, pp. 85–99.

Miller, C. A. "The Nihilist as Tempter-Redeemer: Dostoevsky's 'Man-God' in Nietzsche's Notebooks." *Nietzsche-Studien* 4 (1975), pp. 165–226.

———. "Nietzsche's 'Discovery' of Dostoevsky." *Nietzsche-Studien* 2 (1973), pp. 202–257.

Montefiore, C. G., and Loewe, H. *A Rabbinic Anthology*. New York: Schocken, 1974.

Moore, Carey A. "Esther." *The Anchor Bible Dictionary*. Vol. 2, pp. 633–643.

Nehamas, Alexander. *Nietzsche: Life as Literature*. Cambridge: Harvard University Press, 1985.

Neusner, Jacob. *Between Time and Eternity*. Belmont, Calif.: Wadsworth, 1975.

———. *There We Sat Down: Talmudic Judaism in the Making*. New York: Ktav, 1978.

———, ed. *Understanding Rabbinic Judaism*. New York: Ktav, 1974.

Newsom, Carol. "Angels." *The Anchor Bible Dictionary*. Vol. 1, pp. 248–253.

Nickelsburg, George W. E. "Son of Man." *The Anchor Bible Dictionary*. Vol. 6, pp. 137–150.

Nietzsche, Friedrich W. *The Antichrist*. In *The Portable Nietzsche*, trans, and ed. by Walter Kaufmann. New York: Viking, 1954, pp. 565–656.

———. *Beyond Good and Evil*. Trans. by Walter Kaufmann. New York: Random House/Vintage, 1966.

———. *Daybreak* (or *Dawn*, German: *Die Morgenröte*). Trans. by R. J. Hollingdale. Cambridge: Cambridge University Press, 1982.

———. *The Gay Science* (or *The Joyful Wisdom*, German: *Die fröhliche Wissenschaft*). Trans. by Walter Kaufmann. New York: Vintage/Random House, 1974.

———. *On the Genealogy of Morals* and *Ecce Homo*. Ed. and trans. by Walter Kaufmann. New York: Vintage/Random House, 1967.

———. *Selected Letters*. Trans. by A. N. Ludovici. Ed. by O. Levy. Garden City, N.Y.: Doubleday, 1921.

———. *Thus Spoke Zarathustra*. In *The Portable Nietzsche*, trans. and ed. by Walter Kaufmann. New York: Viking, 1954, pp. 103–439.

———. *Twilight of the Idols*. In *The Portable Nietzsche*, trans, and ed. by Walter Kaufmann. New York: Viking, 1954, pp. 463–563.

———. *The Will to Power*. Trans. by W. Kaufmann and R. J. Hollingdale. New York: Vintage, 1967.

Overbye, Dennis. *Lonely Hearts of the Cosmos*. New York: HarperCollins, 1991.

Pagels, Heinz. *The Cosmic Code*. New York: Bantam, 1982.

Pais, Abraham. *Subtle Is the Lord*. New York: Oxford University Press, 1982.

Pascal, Blaise. *Thoughts.* Trans. by W. F. Trotter. New York: Collier, 1910.

Patrick, Dale. *The Rendering of God in the Old Testament.* Philadelphia: Fortress, 1981.

Penrose, Roger. *The Emperor's New Mind: Concerning Computers, Minds, and the Laws of Physics.* New York: Penguin, 1989.

Penzias, A. A., and Wilson, R. W. "A Measurement of Excess Antenna Temperature at 4080 Mc/s." *Astrophysical Journal* 142 (1965), pp. 419–421.

Peters, H. F. *My Sister, My Spouse: A Biography of Lou Andreas-Salomé.* New York: Norton, 1962.

Platt, Michael. "Behold Nietzsche." *Nietzsche-Studien* 22 (1993).

Pletsch, Carl. *Young Nietzsche.* New York: Free Press, 1991.

Podach, Erich F. *The Madness of Nietzsche.* Trans. by F. A. Voigt. London: Putnam, 1931.

Propp, William H. C. "The Rod of Aaron and the Sin of Moses." *Journal of Biblical Literature* 107 (1988), pp. 19–26.

———. "The Skin of Moses' Face — Transfigured or Disfigured?" *Catholic Biblical Quarterly* 49 (1987), pp. 375–386.

———. *Water in the Wilderness.* Harvard Semitic Monographs 40. Atlanta: Scholars Press, 1987.

Roth, Philip. *Goodbye, Columbus.* Boston: Houghton Mifflin, 1959.

Rowan-Robinson, Michael. *Ripples in the Cosmos.* Oxford: W. H. Freeman, 1993.

Rubenstein, Richard. *After Auschwitz.* Indianapolis: Bobbs-Merrill, 1966.

Rucker, Rudy. *Infinity and the Mind.* New York: Bantam, 1983.

Salomé, Lou. *Nietzsche.* Ed. and trans. by Siegfried Mandel. Redding Ridge, Conn.: Black Swan Books, 1988; German edition: *Friedrich Nietzsche in seinen Werken.* Vienna: Carl Konegen, 1894.

Sanders, E. P. *Jesus and Judaism.* Philadelphia: Fortress, 1985.

———. *The Jewish Law from Jesus to the Mishnah.* London: SCM, 1989.

———. *Judaism: Practice and Belief, 63 BCE–66CE.* London: SCM, 1992.

———. "Law in Judaism of the New Testament Period." *The Anchor Bible Dictionary.* Vol. 4, pp. 254–265.

Schiffman, Lawrence. *From Text to Tradition: A History of Second Temple and Rabbinic Judaism.* Hoboken, N.J.: Ktav, 1991.

Scholem, Gershom. *Kabbalah.* New York: Dorset, 1987.

———. *Major Trends in Jewish Mysticism.* New York: Schocken, 1961. First edition 1941.

———. *On the Mystical Shape of the Godhead.* New York: Schocken, 1991.

Schroeder, Gerald L. *Genesis and the Big Bang.* New York: Bantam, 1990.

Shaffer, Peter. *Amadeus.* New York: New American Library, 1984.

————. *Equus*. New York: Avon, 1974.

Shestov, Lev. *Dostoevsky, Tolstoy and Nietzsche*. Trans. by S. Roberts. Athens, Oh.: Ohio University Press, 1969.

Smoot, George, and Davidson, Keay. *Wrinkles in Time*. New York: Morrow, 1993.

Stern, J. P. *A Study of Nietzsche*. New York: Cambridge University Press, 1979.

Stokes, William Lee. *The Genesis Answer*. Englewood Cliffs, N.J.: Prentice-Hall, 1981.

Terras, Victor. *A Karamazov Companion*. Madison, Wis.: University of Wisconsin, 1981.

Terrien, Samuel. *The Elusive Presence*. San Francisco: Harper and Row, 1978.

Tishby, Isaiah. *The Wisdom of the Zohar*. Trans. by D. Goldstein. Vol. 1. New York: Oxford University Press, 1989. First Hebrew edition 1949.

Tov, Emanuel. *Textual Criticism of the Hebrew Bible*. Minneapolis, Minn.: Fortress/Van Gorcum, 1992.

Urbach, Ephraim. *The Sages, Their Concepts and Beliefs*. Cambridge: Harvard University Press, 1975.

Verrecchia, Anacleto. *La catastrofe di Nietzsche a Torino*. Turin: Einaudi, 1978. Cited here in German trans. *Zarathustras Ende: Die Katastrophe Nietzsches in Turin*. Trans. by P. Pawlowsky. Vienna: Herrmann Böhlaus, 1986.

Weinberg, Steven. *Dreams of a Final Theory*. New York: Pantheon, 1992.

Weinfeld, Moshe. "The Covenant of Grant in the Old Testament and in the Ancient Near East." *Journal of the American Oriental Society* 90 (1970), pp. 184–203.

Wheeler, John Archibald. *A Journey into Gravity and Spacetime*. New York: Scientific American Library, 1990.

Whitt, W. D. "The Jacob Traditions in Hosea and Their Relation to Genesis." *Zeitschrift für die Alttestamentliche Wissenschaft* 103 (1991), pp. 31–34.

Wiebe, J. M. "Esther 4:14: 'Will Relief and Deliverance Arise for the Jews from Another Place?'" *Catholic Biblical Quarterly* 53 (1991), pp. 409–415.

Wieseltier, Leon. "Leviticus." In *Congregation*, ed. by D. Rosenberg. New York: Harcourt Brace Jovanovich, 1987.

Williamson, H. G. M. "Joel." *International Standard Bible Encyclopedia*. Vol. 2. Grand Rapids, Mich.: Eerdmans, 1980, pp. 1076–80.

Wright, G. Ernest. *The Old Testament Against Its Environment*. London: SCM, 1950.

Wright, Robert. "Science, God and Man." *Time* (December 28, 1992).

Zukav, Gary. *The Dancing Wu Li Masters*. New York: Bantam, 1980.

ACKNOWLEDGMENTS

I pursued a portion of the research for this book while a visiting fellow at Clare Hall at the University of Cambridge, England. I am grateful to Clare Hall, its president Anthony Low, and Professor H. G. M. Williamson for kind hospitality during that splendid stay.

I also wrote portions of the book while working with my colleague Thomas Levy in Jerusalem on a joint archaeological project of the University of California, San Diego, and Hebrew Union College. Thanks to Professor Levy and to Hebrew Union College and its dean, Michael Klein, for their hospitality and support.

While working on this book I learned through the academic grapevine that the Kabbalah scholar Daniel C. Matt had observed the parallels of Big Bang and Kabbalah as well and was working on a book of his own on this subject. I made his acquaintance and now think of him as a friend. There is a stereotype of scholars as being absurdly protective of their work and threatened by the idea of being beaten to an idea by anyone else. The stereotype is not without basis. But our acquaintance has been an exception. Matt was gracious with his time and thoughts. We exchanged ideas and showed our manuscripts to each other before publication. I gratefully acknowledge his help and beneficial criticism. In particular I am in his debt for making known the passage from Shim'on Labi, *Ketem Paz*, concerning the expansion of the universe. I urge readers who are interested in pursuing this further to turn to his forthcoming book *God and the Big Bang*, which is both learned and exciting.

The manuscript was also read and very helpfully criticized by my colleagues at the University of California, San Diego, Professors David Noel Freedman and David Goodblatt, and by my friends Paul Meyer and Robert Price. I am also grateful to my colleagues in the Biblical Colloquium for admitting me into their distinguished society and for offering valuable criticism to portions of this material that I presented at the 1993 meeting.

Thanks are due to my colleague Professor William H. C. Propp and our program coordinator Laurel Mannen, who produced the art that appears in Chapters 10 and 11.

The translation of the excerpt from Dostoevsky's *Crime and Punishment* presented a unique problem. I needed an English rendering of a Russian work that a German reader, Nietzsche, read in French translation. I turned to another colleague at UCSD, Professor Steven Cassedy, whose impressive skills in each of these languages made it possible to translate from the French edition that Nietzsche read with sensitivity to its Russian origin and its German understanding. I thank him for this and for helpful advice in my research.

I am thus blessed with exceptional colleagues, especially the four with whom I work the most and closest: David Noel Freedman, David Goodblatt, Thomas Levy, and William H. C. Propp, who show by their example that the phrase "a gentleman and a scholar" still has a referent.

I am also grateful to my students at the University of California, with whom I have worked on the contents of this book over the years, and from whom I continue to learn.

Through my studies of the work of the authors and editors of the Bible over many years, I think that I have an especially strong appreciation of the importance of editors in producing worthwhile books. Mark Chimsky and Jim Silberman at Little, Brown each contributed in a different way to formulating and refining this book. My gratitude to them is of biblical proportions.

My biblical studies did not teach me anything about literary agents. Moses never had an agent. But I still know how much I owe my agent, Elaine Markson, whose confidence and tenacity and warmth and good humor I admire and appreciate.

One other person read the manuscript and enhanced it on many points, my wife, Randy Linda. Also, our conversations helped me to crystallize thoughts and solve problems. It has been argued that the biblical phrase that is used in the account of the creation of woman in Genesis, *'ēzer k^enegdô*, should not be understood as "help meet" or "fit helper" as it is usually understood. Rather, the noun *'ēzer* also means "strength" in some biblical passages, and the Genesis phrase thus understood would mean "a corresponding strength." This strikes me as a more attractive and accurate conception of woman. And it captures the quality of my wife, whose strengths advance our respective work and enrich both of our lives.

Richard Elliott Friedman
San Diego, California
January 1995

INDEX

Also by Richard Elliott Friedman:
WHO WROTE THE BIBLE?

This highly acclaimed best-seller brings the world of the Bible and the people who wrote it vividly to life in a fascinating work by one of our foremost Bible scholars. In an analysis that reads as compellingly as a detective story, Richard Elliott Friedman focuses on the central books of the Old Testament—Genesis, Exodus, Leviticus, Numbers, and Deuteronomy—and makes a persuasive argument for the identities of their four different authors. Drawing upon the most recent archaeological discoveries, and challenging many conventional theories of biblical scholarship, Friedman sheds light on both the world in which these writers lived and the marvel of the Bible's synthesis, on how the various documents were brought together to form a single text. *Who Wrote the Bible?* enriches our understanding of the Bible as literature, as history, and as a sacred text and is indispensable for anyone who loves and reads the Good Book.

"Provocative . . . Friedman has gone much further than other scholars in analyzing the identity of the biblical authors . . . promises to rekindle heated debate about the Good Book's origins."—*U.S. News & World Report*

"Thought-provoking. . . . Of interest to anyone who, aware of the unevenness and problems in the biblical text, seeks a sympathetic and perceptive guide."—Robert Davidson, *New York Times Book Review*

"One can see brilliantly presented some of the questions a truly honest reading of biblical texts engenders and can also see intriguingly presented one possible set of answers to them."—James A. Sanders, *Los Angeles Times Book Review*

"*Who Wrote the Bible?* is a fascinating and brilliant book. It is more than a record of past discoveries. It is full of new insights and fresh discoveries. I read it at one sitting. I have spent much of my lifetime reading books about the Bible and must confess that I do not remember another that I could not lay aside unfinished."—Frank Moore Cross, Hancock Professor of Hebrew and Other Oriental Languages, Harvard University